PRIVATE LIVES/PUBLIC CONSEQUENCES

WILLIAM H. CHAFE

PRIVATE LIVES/

PUBLIC CONSEQUENCES

Personality and Politics

in Modern America

HARVARD UNIVERSITY PRESS
Cambridge, Massachusetts
London, England
2005

Publication of this book has been supported through the generous
provisions of the Maurice and Lula Bradley Smith Memorial Fund.

Library of Congress Cataloging-in-Publication Data

Chafe, William Henry
Private lives/public consequences : personality and politics in modern
America / William H. Chafe.
p. cm.
Includes bibliographical references and index.
ISBN 0-674-01877-X (alk. paper)
1. United States—Politics and government—20th century—Psychological aspects.
2. Political leadership—United States—Psychological aspects. 3. Politicians—United
States—Psychology. 4. Presidents—United States—Psychology. I. Title.

E743.C425 2005   2005050771
973'.099—dc22

*For Lila and Jordan, the next generation
in the hope that the leaders of our future may
inspire faith, not dismay*

CONTENTS

PRIVATE LIVES/PUBLIC CONSEQUENCES

INTRODUCTION

In August 1921, after a vigorous day of sailing and swimming, Franklin Delano Roosevelt discovered he had no feeling in his legs. Within days he understood he was a "polio," a victim of the epidemic of infantile paralysis that was sweeping the nation and that for most victims meant a lifetime of helplessness. Roosevelt faced a choice: to accept the role of aristocratic invalid, or to engage the new realities of his life and create his own future.

The night in 1943 when a Japanese destroyer sheared his PT boat in two, John F. Kennedy desperately tried to rescue a dying comrade in the dark waters of the Solomon Sea, then rallied the remaining members of his crew to swim, with the stronger men towing the injured, to a distant island. Some time later, after he and his men had reached safety, Kennedy wrote to the young woman who was his closest confidante at the time. In the letter he ruminated on the futility of war and concluded that the suffering of innocent people could never be justified and that the generals who sent young men to war should always be listened to with skepticism.

Two moments, two individuals, two people making decisions that helped shape the history of our time.

In this book I seek to understand how such moments have molded the direction, the personality, and the life choices of those who have become our national leaders. I begin with an old-fashioned conviction—that individual leaders make a difference in a society. Up to now, much of my scholarly life has been devoted to the opposite premise: in my research and writing I have focused on the way social movements, not individuals, have transformed our recent past. I do believe that people who have come together collectively to generate new visions of social justice have altered the contours of recent history—witness the civil rights struggle in America and the women's revolution around the world. These movements have changed, in fundamental ways, our thinking about both individual rights and community well-being. Yet these movements involved a dialectical process: by dint of their will and tenacity, individuals like Martin Luther King Jr. participated in movements for change that in turn inspired average citizens to seize power over their own lives and make change happen. King himself did not kindle, but rather responded to, the grassroots energies that started the civil rights movement before he himself became involved. And then there is the larger dialectic: between those who possess power and those who do not; between crusaders for social change and representatives of the established social order.

At the heart of these historical dialectics stand individual human beings. These are people who, for complicated reasons of talent, upbringing, wealth, and personal resources, find themselves in a position to make decisive choices—whether to go toward peace or war, whether to support equal rights for oppressed minorities or defend a caste system of inherited privilege, whether to broaden access to high-quality health care or retain a system in which many do not benefit from medical expertise. At such moments a decision has to be made, and that decision is in the hands of an individual political leader.

The leader's choice can determine the fate of a nation. Had Abraham Lincoln not decided to issue an emancipation proclamation, the abolitionists' struggle to end slavery and redefine freedom might have failed, and America would have been delayed even further in its long overdue effort to confront the sin of racism. If George Washington had chosen to continue as president after two terms in office, establishing a model for continuous rule rather than regular and prescribed changes of regime, America might well have become a monarchy rather than a republic, and perhaps would not have developed a party system, an orderly succession of rulers, and a vibrant, if imperfect, electoral process.

But even if we recognize the degree to which individual actors may shape an era, how do we explain their choices? Why do particular leaders act as they do at any given moment? What causes some to take the path of least resistance, siding with the majority of their advisors and public opinion polls, while others embrace the most difficult choices? What patterns of experience explain the way different leaders approach difficult decisions?

To answer these questions requires an assessment of the lives of the leaders being discussed. Although some political scientists view "rational choice" as the driving force behind individual decisions, and although economists see choices as shaped by market forces, many observers are more impressed by the mysteries of the decisionmaking process, curious about what specific factors may determine a given leader's response to events. These are the irresolvable riddles of the human condition. How much is genes, how much is education, how much is family, how much is faith and inspiration? What is there in the personal profile of a leader that predisposes him or her to make a decision in a certain direction?

In the eight biographical essays that follow, which focus on American leaders of the second half of the twentieth century, I address the relationship between personal experience and politics, exploring the background factors behind a given leader's choice of a particular path or pattern of behavior. These essays do not reflect new research or immersion in primary sources. Nor are they informed by any theoretical model of the life cycle, such as those put forward by Gail Sheehy and Daniel Levinson. Rather, these essays are interpretive historical and biographical assessments rooted in three decades of reflection on change and power in modern America. But the essays do begin with a set of assumptions about the human condition. The first is that family and the circumstances of one's upbringing are critical for the shape of one's subsequent life. The second is that a series of choices, usually in adolescence, form a pattern as to how an individual approaches a challenging situation. The third is that in many instances a profound personal crisis, such as the contraction of polio or the sinking of *PT 109*, creates a departure point that informs future actions, calling one back repeatedly to a moment in time that profoundly altered one's life. The fourth is that most people's lives play out of all these themes, not in a preordained way, as in a Greek tragedy, but as a process in which we make our own choices and shape our own history. Each of the lives discussed here speaks to the importance of the personal in determining how and why pivotal decisions were made.

1

THE ROOSEVELTS
A Partnership Unprecedented

Looking back on her teen years, Anna Roosevelt, the daughter of Franklin and Eleanor Roosevelt, recalled watching her father grapple with the reality of polio. "It [was] traumatic," she said, "[to] see your father, whom you've regarded as a wonderful playmate, who took long walks with you, [who] could out-jump you, . . . [then] suddenly you look up and you see him walking on crutches—trying, struggling in heavy steel braces. And you see the sweat pouring down his face, and you hear him saying, 'I must get down the driveway today—all the way down the driveway.'" Poignantly, Anna Roosevelt encapsulated in her recollection the tenacity, the strength, and the spiritual courage that stood at the core of her father's life.

◆ ◆ ◆

Rarely in politics do a husband and wife act in tandem to shape the agenda of an era. Franklin and Eleanor Roosevelt did so—not through premeditated design, but as a consequence of two strong and independent personalities seeking to work their wills on each other as well as on their society.

In contemporary America it has become conventional to say that the personal is political and the political personal. Scholars have focused new attention on the private struggles of the public actors they study, realizing that a person's emotional and family history may have a significant impact on the way that person engages the world of public policy. The evolution of political personalities is the product not only of school, church, and political socialization, but also of at least two other ingredients: the private crises that inevitably accompany maturation, and significant personal relationships that provide a touchstone for choices that are made.

Eleanor and Franklin Roosevelt exemplify in a powerful way the intersection of the personal and the political. They grew up in separate branches of the same distinguished aristocratic family. Each thus started life with advantages available to very few of their generation. Yet both experienced personal traumas that profoundly shaped their approach to the world. Those traumas helped determine the way they engaged those around them, as well as the issues they confronted. And their interaction with each other, in turn, drove the politics of the years from the Progressive era through the end of World War II. The Roosevelts' political choices were inextricably connected to their personal histories.

◆　◆　◆

Franklin Delano Roosevelt was the only child of Sara Delano and James Roosevelt, both scions of aristocratic Hudson River Valley families. The Roosevelts doted on their son, creating a world of security and comfort that conveyed a sense that he could have whatever he wanted, and that nothing should stand in the way of his wishes. The family's estate in Hyde Park, New York, brimmed with fresh flowers from the gardens, strawberries and cream from the farm, and the aura, as Sara often said, of "living life as it should be lived." "All that is within me goes back to the Hudson," FDR once observed. The estate was a place synonymous with Sara, who, especially in the years after her husband suffered a heart attack, reigned like a queen over her kingdom, granting no one else influence or authority over what transpired there. "Hers was a loving and adoring autocracy," her son's biographer Geoffrey Ward has written, "but an autocracy nonetheless."

The relationship between Franklin and Sara was so close that it gave some people pause. Relatives on one side of the family talked about Franklin's being a "mama's boy," almost too refined and delicate, sort of a "miss Nancy" because of the way "he pranced around and fluttered." Sara's generosity to her son went hand in hand with domination. She was a central presence. After her husband's death during their son's freshman year at Harvard—a stage of life when most young men are setting out to chart their own identity—Sara moved to an apartment in Boston to be closer to Franklin. She may have been "an indulgent mother," one friend said, "but [she] would not let her son call his soul his own."

This suffocating quality of Sara's parenting has caused biographers to wonder about the long-term impact of the mother-son relationship on Franklin's personality. The strong pressure to appreciate Hyde Park and conform to the expectation that everything in life was fine left little room for any expression of negative emotions. Complaining was not allowed. A child had to hide discontent or anger because the mandate was to be happy and charming. This prohibition, Doris Kearns Goodwin has suggested, may "explain Franklin Roosevelt's lifelong tendency to guard his weaknesses and shortcomings as if they were scars, making it difficult to share his true feelings with anyone."

For self-protection, Franklin learned early to dissemble and to use superficial charm and chattiness to obscure conflict. He never told his parents of his unhappy experiences at Groton, where he came late as a student and suffered repeated social rejection; nor did he confide in his mother his similar failures at Harvard, including being denied admission to the elite Porcellian Club. Sara's desire for her son to be serene and content meant that he could not reveal any of his conflicts or disappointments. In Geoffrey Ward's words, "The effort to become his own man without wounding his mother fostered in him much of the guile and easy charm, love of secrecy and skill at maneuver [that] he brought to the White House."

The other side of the equation was what FDR's grandson John Boettiger Jr. later described as a lifelong "insensitivity towards and discomfort with profound and vividly expressed feeling." In large part, Boettiger said, this was the result of "his early sheltering from ugliness and jealousy and conflicting interests."

◆ ◆ ◆

Whatever one might say of Anna Eleanor Roosevelt's childhood, being sheltered from ugliness and conflict was not part of it. Like her distant cousin Franklin, Eleanor—born in 1884 as the first child and only daughter of Elliott and Anna (Hall) Roosevelt—grew up in upper-class circumstances, surrounded by privilege. Yet by the time she was ten years old, both of her parents had died, as had her brother Elliott; she and her brother Hall were the only survivors.

From the beginning Eleanor appears to have struggled for emotional acceptance and warmth. "I was a solemn child," she recalled, "without beauty. I seemed like a little old woman entirely lacking in the spontaneous joy and mirth of youth." Her mother called her "Granny" and, in Eleanor's memory at least, treated her quite differently from her son, warmly embracing the boy while being only "kindly and indifferent" to her little girl. From most of her family, young Eleanor received the message that she was "very plain," almost ugly, and certainly "old-fashioned." After her parents died she went to live with her grandmother, who was also without warmth. As Eleanor's cousin Corinne later remarked: "It was the grimmest childhood I had ever known. Who did she have? Nobody."

In fact, Eleanor did have one person—her father. "He was the one great love of my life as a child," she later wrote, "and . . . like many children, I have lived a dream life with him." Described by his friends as "charming, impetuous, high-spirited, big-hearted, generous, [and] friendly," Elliott exhibited ease and grace in all his social interactions. With Eleanor he developed an intimacy that seemed almost magical. "As soon as I could talk," she recalled, "I went into his dressing room every morning and chattered to him . . . I even danced with him, intoxicated by the pure joy of motion . . . until he would pick me up and throw me into the air." She dreamed of the time when they would go off together: "Always he and I . . . and someday [we] would have a life of our own together."

But Elliott's capacity for ebullient play and warm love coexisted with the seeds of self-destruction—alcoholism, irresponsibility, cruelty. He never found an anchor, either in public life or in business, to provide stability for himself and his family. Elliott's emotional imbalance quickly produced problems in his marriage and banishment from the household. The last four years of his life were tumultuous. Elliott nourished his relationship with Eleanor through letters to "father's own little Nell," writing of the "wonderful long rides . . . through the grand snow-clad forests, over the white hills" that he wanted them to enjoy together. But his long-awaited visits often ended in disaster, as when he left Eleanor with the doorman at New York's Knickerbocker Club, promising to return, but went off on a drunken spree instead. The pain of betrayal was exceeded only by Eleanor's love for the man she believed was "the only person who really cared." Looking back later in life for an explanation of her inability to express emotions spontaneously, she concluded that the trauma of her childhood was the main cause. "Something locked me up," she wrote.

In all likelihood this self-diagnosis was on target. Eleanor's subsequent inability to let herself go fits a pattern frequently found among children of alcoholics. "I looked at everything from the point of view of what I ought to do," she remembered, "rarely from the point of view of what I wanted to do . . . I was never carefree." The children of alcoholics, according to experts, often find it difficult to develop self-esteem or to trust anyone, undervalue their own worth, and become preoccupied with using service to others as a means of winning acceptance. Through the rest of her life, Eleanor was both unable to let herself go and have fun and determined to find satisfaction and validation through iron-disciplined service. It was not an easy combination.

The pattern she would subsequently follow was nurtured by the three years Eleanor spent as a student at Allenswood, a girls' school outside London presided over by Marie Souvestre, daughter of a well-known French philosopher and radical. At

Allenswood Eleanor found for the first time a circle of warmth and support. According to her cousin, "She was beloved by everybody. Eleanor's room every Saturday would be full of flowers because she was so admired." Souvestre, who passionately embraced unpopular crusades such as the defense of Dreyfus in France and the cause of the Boers in South Africa, was especially important. Eleanor would recall "the three years which I spent with her as the beginning of an entirely new outlook on life." Marie Souvestre toured the continent with her student, confiding in her and expressing the affection that made it possible for Eleanor to flower. Describing her stay at Allenswood as the "happiest years of my life," Eleanor noted: "Whatever I have become since had its seeds in those three years of contact with a liberal mind and strong personality." The love and admiration were mutual. "I miss you every day of my life," Souvestre wrote to Eleanor in 1902.

The influence of Marie Souvestre did not end when Eleanor returned to the United States at the age of seventeen to make her debut in New York society. Notwithstanding the rush of parties and dances, she kept her eye on the more serious world of ideas and social service. Souvestre had written to her in 1901: "Even when success comes, as I'm sure it will, bear in mind that there are more quiet and enviable joys than to be among the most sought-after women at the ball." Heeding the injunction, Eleanor plunged into settlement-house work and social activism.

Much of Eleanor Roosevelt's subsequent political life can be traced to this early involvement with social reform. At age eighteen she joined the National Consumers League, headed by Florence Kelley. The League was committed to securing health and safety for workers—especially women—in clothing factories and sweatshops. On visits to these workplaces, Eleanor learned firsthand the misery of the working poor and developed a lifelong commitment to their needs. At the same time she joined the Junior League and commenced work at the Rivington Street Settlement House, where she taught calisthenics and dancing and witnessed both the deprivation of the poor and the courage of slum dwellers who sought to improve their lot. Although she retained many of the ethnic and class biases of her background, Eleanor discovered that she preferred social work to debutante parties. Gradually she came to be recognized as a key member of a network of social reformers in New York City. She had begun to find a mission and fulfillment through service.

At this same time, Eleanor found herself beckoned by the prospect of renewed personal happiness. Her cousin Franklin focused his considerable charm on winning her hand in marriage. By all accounts, Franklin saw in Eleanor a seriousness of character and purpose that provided a welcome counterweight to his own tendency to be superficial. Like his mother, Eleanor seemed to know her own mind. Franklin delighted in their intellectual exchanges, as well as in the excitement of discovering romantic love. Eleanor, in turn, saw in Franklin the same spontaneity, warmth, and generosity that she had worshiped in her father—a spark and ebullience—but minus her father's recklessness. The link seemed evident when she sent Franklin a letter signed "little Nell." But this time Eleanor hoped to build in reality the life she had only imagined with her father. "I am hungry for you every moment, you are never out of my thoughts," she wrote to her fiancé in an atypical display of feeling. "I feel as though we would have such a long arrears of kisses and cuddly time to make up when we get home."

Almost immediately, however, the sunshine of the courtship had to confront the shadow of Sara's abiding presence in Franklin's life. He had not told his mother of his interest in Eleanor, and when finally he announced his plans to marry her, he assured Sara that marriage would "never change what we have been and always will be to each other—only now you have two children to love and to love you." Sara tried to delay and obstruct the engagement, but failing that, determined to show her command of the new circumstances, asserting her authority and treating Eleanor like a child. The young couple spent their first week of marriage at Hyde Park and almost every weekend thereafter returned to visit. Sara lectured Eleanor on her appearance—she once told her "if you'd just run your comb through your hair, dear, you'd look so much nicer"—and continued to control the family estate and all that happened there. At dinner in Hyde Park, Franklin sat at one end of the table, Sara at the other, with Eleanor in between. By the fireplace there were two wing chairs, one for the mother, the other for the son. Eleanor was like an uninvited guest.

Sara's interference became more painful after the young couple had children. After their marriage on March 17, 1905, the young Roosevelts settled in New York City while Franklin finished his studies at Columbia Law School. For most of this time they lived in a brownstone, their part of the house accessible by connecting doors to Sara's side of the same brownstone. Within a year Anna was born (1906), then the next year James (1907), and two years later Franklin. (This first Franklin died in infancy; a second son named Franklin was born later.) Frightened by her inexperience in dealing with children and lacking confidence in herself, Eleanor allowed her mother-in-law and the prevailing "experts" of the time to dictate her approach to the children. Her daughter Anna recalled her as unpredictable, sweet one moment, critical and demanding the next: "Mother was always stiff, never relaxed enough to romp . . . Mother loved all mankind, but she did not know how to let her children love her."

Eleanor herself recognized the problem. "It did not come naturally to me to understand little children or to enjoy them," she later said. "Playing with children was difficult for me because play had not been an important part of my own childhood." Instead of comforting her daughter and sons when they were in pain, she urged upon them an attitude of stoicism and endurance, as if to say that emotion was a sign of bad character. By contrast, Sara gave the children everything they wanted, going behind Eleanor's back to grant wishes that Eleanor had denied, providing warmth and love and receiving the same in return. "As it turned out," Eleanor would recall, "Franklin's children were more my mother-in-law's children . . . than they were mine." Sara agreed, referring to the younger Roosevelts as "my children" and asserting: "Your mother only bore you." It was not a happy time, and for decades thereafter Eleanor attributed part of the emotional pain of her children's divorces and personal problems to her own insecurity in the role of mother.

◆ ◆ ◆

In these years Franklin was becoming increasingly involved in politics. Neither skilled nor deeply interested in practicing law, he spent the period after law school carrying on workaday legal tasks with a notable lack of excitement. The suggestion that he run for a seat in the New York state assembly kindled his interest. Without displaying any deeply held political beliefs, Roosevelt cultivated local constituents, showing a strong interest in people's lives before trying to persuade them to vote for the new

Democrat in town. His election to the assembly gave him new energy. Vaguely reformist in his politics, he soon gained a reputation for being flexible, even slippery in his approach to political disputes. He joined the anti-Tammany crusade, causing some old-line Irish politicians to call him a "bigot . . . [who] didn't like poor people . . . [and] was a patronizing sonofabitch." But he was also able to make a deal. As Geoffrey Ward has observed: "The creative uses of indirection . . . were built into him from infancy. Raised alone by loving but anxious parents, he had learned early that the best technique for getting one's way was often to do one thing while chattering pleasantly about something else."

Roosevelt's ability to combine smooth charm with a reputation for reformist instincts made him a logical candidate for a position in President Woodrow Wilson's administration. Now aided by the political advice and acumen of Louis Howe—a brilliant but unsuccessful businessman and journalist—Roosevelt secured the position of assistant secretary of the navy, the same post held in the late 1890s by his distant cousin Theodore Roosevelt. Franklin was now intent on following his cousin's career line. As he and Howe schemed to advance his name, he frequently garnered more attention than his superior, Navy Secretary Josephus Daniels, on issues of preparedness and public advocacy of a strong navy. By the end of his eight years in the Wilson administration, Roosevelt had maneuvered successfully enough to win the nod as Democratic presidential candidate James Cox's running mate in 1920.

Franklin's turn to politics compounded the strains already evident in his relationship with Eleanor. Even as a young lawyer with newborns at home, he had taken to spending more and more time at his club or out with friends, leaving Eleanor to tend to family matters. Although Eleanor did not formally object to what she called her husband's "sprees," she kept detailed records of his comings and goings, and her quietly suffering stance conveyed its own signal that she saw herself as a martyr. Ever busy, she maintained three households—one in Albany or Washington, another in Hyde Park, and a third at Campobello, the Roosevelt summer home on an island off the coast of Maine —and was constantly busy supervising both the moves and the social life in all three settings. But she communicated her own bleak sense of her marital relationship when she described a young wife, on Campobello, "who wept many tears because after an absence of some weeks, her husband on his return talked to her more about his business than about his love for her with the result that she thought the romance and glamour of marriage were gone forever."

Whatever the quality of their earlier intimacy, Eleanor and Franklin's marital ties had deteriorated. After the birth of their last child, John, in 1916, Eleanor later told Anna, she ended sexual relations with Franklin, tired from having given birth to six children in eleven years. According to Anna, Eleanor had never enjoyed sex, always considering it an "ordeal to be borne." As time passed, the couple's social life took on a bifurcated quality, Franklin the carefree bon vivant, Eleanor the quietly suffering sober companion.

Thus Eleanor and Franklin were increasingly at odds with each other. Whenever one triggered the anger or hurt of the other, they moved even further apart. Franklin's party-loving nature blossomed ever more when faced with Eleanor's strictures, her self-pity, and her dour disposition. Franklin's irresponsibility, meanwhile, reinforced Eleanor's determination to be honorable, self-sacrificing, and noble. Only if they could bring their opposite inclinations into some kind of constructive interaction would the centrifugal forces in their relationship be harnessed to a positive end. Otherwise, disaster loomed ahead.

As it turned out, disaster came first, only later to be followed by accommodation. Franklin had never learned to express his emotions honestly, either with Sara or with Eleanor. Hence he dealt with his conflicts with Eleanor by disguising them, laughing away her concerns, not communicating his own unhappiness. Instead, he searched for a different kind of companionship and gratification in a hidden way, dissembling all the while and even relishing his ability to get away with living two lives simultaneously. His chosen companion was Lucy Mercer, a descendant of an aristocratic family that had fallen on hard times, who now worked as Eleanor's social secretary. She was "beautiful, charming, and absolutely delightful," Teddy Roosevelt's daughter Alice Longworth said of Lucy. Tall, graceful, and intelligent, she offered Franklin some of the qualities Eleanor could not provide—social ease, gracious small talk, a willing and nonjudgmental audience for his stories. Especially when Eleanor was away at Campobello, Franklin included "Miss Mercer" in his social entourage, usually describing her, to Eleanor at least, as accompanying their friend Nigel Law. In reality, many of those who saw Franklin and Lucy together immediately recognized the romance. Josephus Daniels even removed Lucy Mercer from the navy department after she took a job there during the First World War—in all likelihood because he and Mrs. Daniels had heard the rumors about her affair with Franklin. Others took a different view: "He deserved a good time," Alice Longworth opined; "he was married to Eleanor."

Eleanor remained unaware of her husband's deceit until 1918, when Franklin contracted pneumonia while returning from Europe. Unpacking his suitcase while he convalesced, she discovered a cache of love letters from Lucy. "The bottom dropped out of my own particular world," Eleanor later told a friend, "and I faced myself, my surroundings, my world, honestly for the first time." It was a devastating moment that confirmed her worst fears about betrayal and her deepest anxieties about her own self-worth. Whatever else she did or attempted, this moment would leave a wound that could not be healed. "I can forgive, but I cannot forget," she said.

The disaster did not end the marriage. Eleanor offered Franklin a divorce, but Louis Howe argued that the scandal would end Franklin's political career, and Sara would not hear of it, engineering an agreement for the couple to stay together if Franklin would stop seeing Lucy. Franklin consented. A rapprochement of sorts commenced, and certainly over the years a strong sense of caring reappeared. But never again would Franklin and Eleanor achieve the magical sense of being together "for life, for death," in which a word or look would communicate everything. Instead, as James Roosevelt has written, after his father's affair with Lucy Mercer, his parents "agreed to go on for the sake of appearances, the children and the future, but as business partners, not as husband and wife."

It was America's entry into World War I that allowed Eleanor to reassert the public side of her personality, which for the previous twelve years had been subordinated to her roles as child-bearer, mother, and wife. As Eleanor's biographer Joseph Lash has noted, "The war gave her a reason acceptable to her conscience to free herself of the social duties that she hated, to concentrate less on her household, and to plunge into work that fitted her aptitude." She rose at five A.M. to coordinate activities at the Union Station canteen for soldiers on their way to training camp, took charge of Red Cross activities, supervised the knitting rooms at the navy department, where volunteers made mittens and scarves for soldiers, and spoke at patriotic rallies. Her interest in social welfare led to her drive to improve conditions at St. Elizabeths mental hospital, while her sensitivity to suffering came forth in her visits to wounded soldiers. "[My son] always loved to see you come in," one mother wrote. "You always brought a ray of sunshine."

The war thus gave Eleanor the opportunity to express talents and energies that could be traced back to Rivington Street Settlement House, the Junior League, and Marie Souvestre. While the discovery of her husband's affair was both traumatic and transformative, in the case of Eleanor's reemergence as a public personality, it was a reinforcing event, not a causal one. In fact, Eleanor and Franklin had embarked on separate (though related) public roles well before Eleanor found Lucy Mercer's love letters.

After the electoral defeat of the Democrats' Cox-Roosevelt ticket by Warren G. Harding and Calvin Coolidge in 1920, Eleanor took on an increasingly political role. Moving back to New York, she became active in the League of Women Voters, newly formed by leaders of the National American Woman Suffrage Association after the Nineteenth Amendment gave women the vote in 1919. At the time of her marriage in 1905, Eleanor had opposed suffrage, thinking it inconsistent with women's proper role; now, as coordinator of the league's legislative program, she kept track of bills that came before the Albany legislature, drafted laws providing for equal representation of women and men, and worked with Esther Lape and Elizabeth Read on the league's lobbying activities. In 1921 she also joined the Women's Trade Union League—then viewed as "left-leaning"—and found friends there as well as political allies. In addition to working for the regulation of maximum hours and minimum wages for women workers, Eleanor helped raise funds for the WTUL headquarters in New York City. She formed close friendships with first- and second-generation immigrants such as Rose Schneiderman and Maud Swartz, an indication of just how far she had moved from the upper-class provincialism of her early years.

When Franklin returned to New York after his electoral loss, he was already planning with Louis Howe the next steps he should take in his political career. Now both husband and wife were more absorbed in their public roles than in family matters. Ruminating on their full schedules, Eleanor once remarked: "I wish we did not lead such a hectic life . . . a little prolonged quiet might bring us together." But then came a natural second thought: "It [also] might do just the opposite! I really don't know what I want or think about anything anymore." Pursuing their separate tracks of public involvement, the two seemed likely to travel further and further apart.

But then in 1921, at the age of thirty-nine, Franklin contracted polio. The disease would propel his life and his partnership with Eleanor into a new trajectory.

Infantile paralysis—polio or "I.P."—was among the most feared and least understood diseases in America until a vaccine for its prevention was developed in the early 1950s. It swept through geographical areas in epidemics. Contracted in a variety of ways, it was often associated with public places, including beaches, and with summer heat. The incubation period varied, but Franklin probably contracted the virus just before traveling to Campobello in 1921. The disease started to take its toll shortly after he arrived on the island. Thinking himself just overtired and stiff, he set out on a ferocious agenda of physical activities, sailing, foot-racing across the island with his children, swimming in the ice-cold waters of the Bay of Fundy. That evening he suffered chills and a fever. The next morning, unable to walk normally and feeling no strength in his legs, he went to bed—but still with no idea that these might be symptoms of a dreaded disease. Only after days of deterioration and the calling in of a specialist from Boston was Franklin's condition diagnosed as infantile paralysis. Even then, so little was known of the appropriate treatment that for weeks nurses, Eleanor, and family friends massaged the patient's legs—later viewed as a questionable course of action for a polio victim.

Becoming a "polio," as victims of the disease called themselves, proved to be the most searing, life-shaping, and character-forming event in Franklin's experience—at least as critical for him as his affair with Lucy Mercer had been for Eleanor—and decisive as well for his relationship with Eleanor and others in his intimate circle. Helpless, out of control, and fearful of losing his life, he was forced to fall back on the lessons of his childhood. Having once learned to fool the world and his parents by being cheerful and chatty when in fact he was deeply troubled, he now used a similar facade of self-confidence as a screen behind which he could rally his inner reserves and chart a course of action that would allow him to retain as much control as possible over his life. He learned to propel himself personally and politically when he could no longer do so physically. In public he would hide or minimize his infirmity so that no one would guess his powerlessness. While plumbing the depths of his security as the scion of an aristocratic family to find the strength to pursue his objectives, he would convey to others the image of a light-hearted, convivial raconteur. All this he started to do as he lay in his bed at Campobello, determined never to let the world know how helpless he felt.

Her husband's affliction further expanded Eleanor's public role. She now became Franklin's personal representative in the political arena. With the aid of Louis Howe—now her own close friend as well as Franklin's—she mobilized women in Dutchess County, where Hyde Park was located, then moved on to the state Democratic party, organizing all but five counties by 1924. "Organization," she noted, "is something to which [the men] are always ready to take off their hats." No one did the job better. Leading a delegation to the Democratic convention in 1924, Eleanor fought (unsuccessfully) for equal pay legislation, a constitutional amendment allowing Congress to regulate child labor, and other planks endorsed by women reformers—all the while fuming at being forced to wait while the men on the platform committee decided whether to hear her or not. By 1928 Eleanor Roosevelt was clearly a political leader in her own right. Once just a "political wife," she had gradually extended that role, using it to advance her own confidence and agenda. She had become a champion of women's issues.

Eleanor allied herself with Franklin and against his mother in his struggle to reject the life of an invalid and remain a respected and vigorous public presence. Sara now hoped her son would resume his place as a Dutchess County aristocrat, presiding over his estate as men of his station were expected to do, and not incidentally providing her with devoted companionship. Eleanor and Louis Howe conspired with Franklin to sabotage that plan, keeping Franklin's name in the news, devising ways for him to appear more active than he was. In this critical moment Franklin, perhaps for the first time, chose the strength of Eleanor over the strength of his mother.

Eleanor also gave Franklin critical private support during these first months. She nursed him, sat up with him, encouraged him—even did her part in the practice of massaging his legs. Geoffrey Ward depicts this point in Eleanor's life as one of considerable ambivalence. Eleanor, he points out, "had few remaining illusions about her husband: he had not proven serious or honorable enough for her . . .; she had found him too sinuous, too cautious, too willing to abandon principled positions and sacrifice personal friends in the interest of personal advancement." Yet, Ward concludes, Franklin's polio allowed her to play a fulfilling new private role in his life: "She could again find solace . . . in being useful."

Although much has been made of this period of private service and nursing, it would be a mistake to see Franklin's polio as having significantly altered Eleanor's own emotional life. Ever since her discovery of his unfaithfulness, Eleanor had found new interests and new outlets for personal affection. In the network of women reformers she found intimate friendship as well as political camaraderie. During the 1920s she spent one night each week with Elizabeth Read and Esther Lape, reading books together and talking about common interests. She also became close with fellow members of the Women's Trade Union League such as Rose Schneiderman, inviting them to Hyde Park for picnics. Molly Dewson, both a reformer and a politico, became an especially close friend, to whom Eleanor wrote in 1932: "The nicest thing about politics is lunching with you on Mondays."

Many of Eleanor's friendships during the 1920s and 1930s were with women who lived with other women. She had become particularly close to Nancy Cook and Marion Dickerman, activists who lived together in New York City. In 1926 she moved with them into Val-Kill, a newly constructed cottage at Hyde Park, an event that accurately symbolized her growing detachment from

Franklin and his mother, and her desire to carve out a life of her own. (Franklin approved of the project.) Although she returned to the "Big House" at Hyde Park whenever Franklin was present, it was never without resentment and anger. She and Dickerman purchased Todhunter, a private school in New York, where Eleanor taught three days a week, even after Franklin was elected governor of New York. The three women also managed a furniture crafts factory at Val-Kill. The linen and towels at Val-Kill were monogrammed "EMN," and the women constituted as much a "family" for Eleanor during these years as Franklin and her children did.

Parallel to her developing independence as a political figure, therefore, was Eleanor's autonomous emotional world, populated largely by independent women, many of them in relationships that today would be called lesbian partnerships, who gave Eleanor support and recognition she did not or could not find with Franklin. Franklin and some others referred to these friends as "she-males." Nevertheless, these women provided an emotional anchor for Eleanor as she increased her public role as a representative for the agenda that she and Franklin shared. His polio broadened their political partnership—but for Eleanor, it did not restore their private emotional bond.

Franklin, too, developed in these years a series of intimate relationships that almost entirely replaced the private ties he once had shared with Eleanor and later with Lucy Mercer. Being a "polio" exacted a huge emotional as well as physical toll. On the one hand, he needed desperately to retain some hope that he could regain partial use of his legs—a need that caused him to explore myriad possibilities for therapy, from swimming in the Florida Keys to purchasing a health resort at Warm Springs, Georgia, where he and other polios could try the curative power of the hot mineral waters. On the other hand, he had to come to grips with the permanent effects of his illness, accepting his limits and working within those limits to achieve what he could. Geoffrey Ward, a fellow victim of polio, portrays the personal dimensions of the struggle in his description of FDR's first day back at his office: "Hanging from his crutches, watching the ground before him carefully, and trying not to see the people staring at him, he heaved himself across the sidewalk, his chauffeur at his side. Despite the chill October air, sweat ran off his face, drenched his shirt, patterned the shoulders of his jacket. He would always sweat heavily when attempting to walk in public—a sign of both the real exertion required to move and the added stress a proud man felt at having to display his helplessness before strangers."

At this difficult stage of rehabilitation, Eleanor did not always provide the understanding and warmth that her husband craved. She had been a pivotal force in encouraging his decision to remain active, and she had certainly done her part in nursing him. But she was not able to respond in the playful, flirtatious, reinforcing way that he needed. Sometimes she was didactic, lecturing him on what to do; at other times she appeared insensitive to his feelings, once asking him for two pairs of golf socks for their son "as you don't use them now." When Eleanor protested the plan to purchase Warm Springs because of the expense, Franklin mockingly responded: "I suppose I'd better do all I can to learn to move about as much as possible. I don't want to be a useless burden to the rest of my family."

To meet his emotional needs, Franklin turned to others, the most important of whom was Missy LeHand, his secretary. Alert, sensitive to his every mood, fun-loving, and politically shrewd, Missy offered the companionship and support that Franklin found nowhere else. "If only Mother could have learned to ease up," the Roosevelts' son Elliott said, "things would have been so different with Father, for he needed relaxation more than anything in the world. But since she simply could not bring herself to unwind, he turned instead to Missy, building with her an exuberant, laughing relationship, full of jokes, silliness and gossip." The difference was reflected in a simple statistic. During the critical rehabilitation period of 1925 through 1928, FDR spent 116 of 208 weeks away from Hyde Park. Missy was with him for 110 of those weeks, Eleanor for only 4.

Staff members loved Missy because she was such fun, so smart, and so attractive as she played hostess for Franklin. Others saw the relationship as more romantic. Laura Delano, Franklin's cousin, declared: "Missy was the only woman F ever loved, everybody knows that." Elliott agreed that his father and Missy were lovers: "Everyone in the closely knit inner circle of father's friends accepted it as a matter of course. I remember being only mildly stirred to see him with Missy on his lap as he sat in a wicker chair . . . holding her in his sun-browned arms . . . He made no attempt to conceal his feelings about Missy."

Whatever the nature of Franklin's physical relationship with Missy, there can be little question that she was in love with him, and that for nearly two decades she offered him the humor, understanding, and reinforcement that Eleanor could not provide—just as Eleanor found in women friends like Molly Dewson, Nancy Cook, and Marian Dickerman the emotional support she no longer received from Franklin. It was an arrangement of special—some would say bizarre—complementarity; and it would make possible another kind of partnership that possessed a momentum and strength all its own.

That partnership centered on politics. Having begun as a

stand-in for her husband at political events in the months after he contracted polio, Eleanor had steadily expanded her role, combining her position at the center of a network of women reformers with her growing ability to fuse feminist reform with political party activism. Eleanor walked on picket lines with Rose Schneiderman, edited the *Women's Democratic News*, and advised the League of Women Voters on political tactics, lowering, if not eliminating entirely, the barriers between politics and reform. "To many women," she noted, "and I am one of them, it is difficult to care enough [about an issue] to cause disagreement or unpleasant feelings, but I have come to the conclusion that this must be done for a time so we can prove our strength and demand respect for our wishes." By standing up for women in politics, Eleanor Roosevelt became a model for others to follow. She also earned the admiring if grudging respect of men—including her husband—who recognized a talented organizer when they saw one.

Franklin, meanwhile, persisted in his determination to use politics as the forum for his own redemption and rehabilitation, pursuing his lifelong ambition to follow his cousin Teddy to the White House. With Louis Howe as an ever-present tutor and guide, Franklin kept informed about both local and national political machinations. The political moves he made revealed his understanding of the importance of timing and symbolism. Nowhere was this sensibility better displayed than in his decision to place New York governor Al Smith's name in nomination for the presidency at the 1924 Democratic convention. Smith might have little chance of winning, given the split in the party over religion, prohibition, and the Ku Klux Klan. But the convention stage provided a dramatic setting for his return to political life.

The scene in Madison Square Garden brimmed with emotion.

A supreme crescendo for the governor—and even more for the courageous victim of infantile paralysis who would now show that despite the disease he was once again a political force. "Outwardly," the Roosevelts' son James said, "[Father] was beaming, seemingly confident and unconcerned, but his . . . fingers dug into my arms like pincers—I doubt that he knew how hard he was gripping me. His face was covered by perspiration." Geoffrey Ward describes the moment:

> He began moving slowly toward the podium alone, sweat beading his brow, jaw grimly set, eyes on the floor—left crutch forward and weight shifted to it, right leg hitched forward, right crutch forward, left leg hitched forward, again and again—following in full view of twelve thousand delegates, alternates and spectators the lurching fifteen foot path he had laboriously traced in his library . . . It seemed to take an age, but when he finally stood at the podium, unable even to wave for fear of falling, but grinning broadly, head thrown back and shoulders high, in the exaggerated gesture that would now become his trademark, the delegates rose to their feet and cheered for three minutes, and as they did so the sun broke through the clouds above the Garden skylight and poured down upon him.

Whatever pain and struggle his rehabilitation had entailed, this moment helped to justify it all. Franklin Delano Roosevelt was back, with a drama and power that magnified tenfold his previous political appeal. Now there was substance beneath the genial exterior—a strength that came from something other than the security of having been raised in the upper class. Using the nomination speech as his launching pad, Roosevelt reentered the political arena with gusto. When Al Smith ran for president in 1929 against Herbert Hoover, Roosevelt was elected to succeed Smith as governor of New York. In that office he put together an effective team of managers and reformers, did as well as any governor in the country in combating the Depression, and prepared to be a candidate for the presidency of the United States.

◆ ◆ ◆

Franklin's battle with polio had reinforced certain of his personality traits, such as his tendency to conceal his emotions. As a polio himself, the biographer Geoffrey Ward has special insight into the experience Franklin confronted. It is characteristic of polios, Ward writes, to have "massive feelings of guilt and alienation," to feel that "by falling ill they [have] failed to live up to the expectations of others to whom they [have] then become a burden." Fighting such feelings required developing a steely new inner strength. Hence the importance of Franklin's stubborn attempts to walk again and his willingness to endure years of painful therapy and exercise. The goal was to be able to present himself as he wanted people to see him. Once, when asked why he persisted with his regimen of rehabilitation, he answered that he wished to be able to stand in front of people and have them not be aware that he was crippled—in short, to be a whole man in the eyes of those others who would validate or reject his identity as a person and politician.

That goal required that he become even more skilled at hiding his true feelings—not only obscuring how physically impaired he was, or how painfully he had to struggle to walk, but also concealing his feelings of vulnerability and conflict. When one is that close to total helplessness, it requires total trust in another to risk exposing the little emotional self that is left—hence the need, drawing on years of earlier experience with his mother and with friends and with Eleanor, to disguise his deepest feelings. It was part of his nature, Eleanor told her friend and biographer Joe Lash, "not to talk to anyone of intimate matters."

What he did instead was to talk all the time about other subjects. Always a gregarious and charming raconteur, he now honed his talent for dominating conversation and controlling his environment. Many polios, Geoffrey Ward has noted, need "to entertain as well as converse." Given Franklin's dependence on others for even the simplest human needs, and his fear that people were with him only out of kindness, "it became important for him to be able simultaneously to talk people into doing his bidding and to relieve himself of the burden of asking for their help by putting on a nonstop show—'walking on your tongue,' as one polio has called it." This was what Franklin called his "Exhibit A" persona, according to his friend Margaret Suckley. But the other side of that persona was the fear of rejection and isolation. "I'm either exhibit A," he told Suckley, "or left completely alone."

With a few selected friends and relatives—including his daughter Anna, Missy, Margaret Suckley, Harry Hopkins, and Louis Howe—Franklin felt a security that enabled him to relax and be natural. But never would he display the full measure of his emotions. "Through all his talkativeness," commented the labor reformer and future cabinet member Frances Perkins, "there ran a kind of reserve . . . He dropped the curtain over himself. He never told you, or anyone else, just what was going on inside his mind—inside his emotions . . . I think he never intended to reveal himself."

While polio reinforced Franklin's need to hide behind a cheerful façade, it also gave him an inner strength, a steadiness and conviction that enabled him to deal with crises. With his fellow polios at Warm Springs, he developed an empathy with people struggling and suffering that informed much of his approach to politics. "Anyone who has gone through [that]," Eleanor observed, "is bound to have a greater sympathy and understanding of the problems of mankind." Confronted by his own helplessness, Franklin could have chosen either a path of surrender or one of resistance. Choosing the latter meant both acquiring new strengths and digging deep to find a resilience he had never needed before. "There had been a plowing up of his nature," Frances Perkins said. "The man emerged completely warmhearted with new humility of spirit and a firmer understanding of profound philosophical concepts."

In part, this core of strength built on Franklin's childhood, his security in the Hyde Park setting, the religious traditions that became part of his character. But having to cope with polio had also called on resources that armed him in a new way to deal with disaster. Having faced a catastrophic crisis within himself, he could deal with crises in the world. When he heard the full diagnosis of his condition, Eleanor recalled, "he was completely calm. His reaction to any event was always to be calm. If it was something that was bad, he just became almost like an iceberg, and there was never the slightest emotion that was allowed to show." The calm reflected one side of the ordeal he had endured, the refusal to show emotion the other side. Both existed in a new form after his struggle with polio.

Because of these changes, Eleanor and Franklin developed a new pattern of partnership and collaboration—a pattern that was both distant and intimate. The partners now looked outside their relationship for emotional sustenance, and yet they depended on each other for the achievement of their shared objectives. Theirs was a political marriage that gave new meaning to the idea of men and women acting together in the public realm. It could only have taken the shape it did because of the private tragedies that prevented them from responding to each other's deepest needs.

◆ ◆ ◆

Eleanor Roosevelt approached the idea of being first lady of the nation with trepidation. In her years as the wife of the governor of New York (1929–1932), she had still been able to teach school three days a week, maintain contact with her friends, and largely fashion her own schedule. If her husband was elected president, she feared, the constraints of the White House would rob her of all those freedoms, putting her in a social straitjacket that offered no room to do anything but host White House teas and supervise servants. She faced the prospect with dread.

Yet Eleanor's role in the campaign belied her fears. She coordinated the activities of the women's division of the Democratic National Committee, continuing an executive role she had played in Al Smith's campaign in 1928. Working closely with her good friend Molly Dewson, she mobilized thousands of women as precinct workers to carry the party's program to local voters. As part of this effort, the women distributed reams of "rainbow fliers," brightly colored sheets featuring extensive factual discussion of issues relevant to women such as child care, education, and nutrition. When the election was over, Molly Dewson took over the women's division. Naturally, the two women continued their close association, corresponding daily about appointing women to office and securing action on issues that would appeal to women, minorities, and professionals such as social workers and educators.

As it turned out, Eleanor Roosevelt was able to use her new position to recruit most of her former friends to come to Washington. Instead of being shut off from her network of women reformers by being in the White House, she could rally them to the capital, where their role in the federal government offered them an unprecedented opportunity to achieve their reform ends on a national stage. Ellen Woodward, Hilda Worthington Smith, and Florence Kerr, reformers with whom Eleanor had worked in the 1920s, all held executive offices in the Works Progress Administration, while the journalist Lorena Hickok acted as the eyes and ears for WPA director Harry Hopkins as she traveled across the country to observe the impact of the New Deal's relief programs. Mary Anderson, director of the Women's Bureau—an agency established during World War I to oversee working conditions among women in the labor force—recalled that women government officials had formerly dined together in a small university club. "Now," she said, "there are so many of them that we need a hall."

As first lady, Eleanor created a forum for transmitting these women's views and concerns across the country. She began a series of press conferences to which only women reporters were admitted, and where the first lady insisted on making hard news as well as providing the expected social tidbits for the women's page. For example, she introduced the black educator Mary McLeod Bethune to the press corps to talk about her work with minority youth in the National Youth Administration. Such sessions conferred new status and prestige on the female press corps, and underlined the importance of women's issues to the first lady. Her efforts helped form a community of women in journalism and government. When the all-male Gridiron Club held its annual dinner to spoof the president and his male colleagues, the first lady initiated a Gridiron Widow's Club where the women in Washington could engage in their own social satire.

Largely as a result of Eleanor Roosevelt's activities, women achieved a strong voice in the New Deal. The Roosevelt administration's social welfare policies reflected a reform perspective grounded in women's experience in the social settlement movement and in organizations such as the National Consumers League. When a particularly difficult issue came up, the first lady would invite Molly Dewson to the White House and seat her next to the president, to give her a chance to win him over to her point of view. Eleanor's own political role appears most clearly in her work in the reelection campaign of 1936, when she coordinated the efforts of both women and men and again used the educational approach developed by the women's division in 1932. More than sixty thousand women canvassed the electorate, handing out "rainbow fliers" as the party's principal literature. For the first time women received equal representation on the Democratic Platform Committee, in what the *New York Times* called "the biggest coup for women in years."

Eleanor Roosevelt's fear that she would have no active role as a president's wife had been unfounded. She toured the country repeatedly, surveying conditions in the coal mines, visiting relief projects, and speaking out on behalf of the disadvantaged. When she returned from such trips, her husband interrogated her closely about the conditions people faced—their diets, the crops they were planting, their attitudes toward the government. So frequent and expected were her trips that at one point the *Washington Times* ran the following headline: "MRS. ROOSEVELT

Spends Night at White House." The first lady entered the homes of millions of people through her newspaper column, "My Day." Her radio programs, her lectures, and her writings communicated to the country her deep compassion for those who suffered. At the White House, in turn, she acted as advocate for the poor and disenfranchised. "No one who ever saw Eleanor Roosevelt sit down facing her husband," wrote the president's advisor Rexford Tugwell, "and holding his eyes firmly, [and saying] to him, 'Franklin, I think you should' . . . or 'Franklin, surely you will not' . . . will ever forget the experience . . . It would be impossible to say how often and to what extent American governmental processes have turned in a new direction because of her determination." She had become, in the words of the columnist Raymond Clapper, a "Cabinet Minister without portfolio—the most influential woman of our times."

Mrs. Roosevelt had continued the pattern she had established in the years after World War I of seeking fulfillment through her own public career as a political figure and reformer. By virtue of her skill, her persistence, and her capacity for building coalitions, she neatly complemented her husband's political activities, while also giving him a set of perspectives and a body of information that proved indispensable to his presidency.

◆　◆　◆

Franklin Roosevelt, meanwhile, thrived in his new responsibilities by refining the patterns of calm, dissembling, and control by indirection that he had perfected during his years of convalescence from polio. Few presidents had faced a worse set of circumstances. More than one-quarter of the U.S. population was unemployed. Millions had lost their homes because they could not make their mortgage payments, and now so many banks themselves were closing that people feared the entire financial system would collapse. Stock prices were still very low, families doubled and tripled up with relatives to stay alive, and relief agencies received far more requests for help than they could possibly meet. Yet the president greeted these crises with an ebullient self-confidence. His head cocked, his chin raised, cigarette holder pointed to the sky, he gave the impression that everything was going to be fine. If it was a lie, it was a lie that the nation needed desperately to hear.

Others marveled at the effect. "There's something that he's got," Harry Hopkins told Frances Perkins. "It seems unreasonable at times, but he falls back on something that gives him complete assurance that everything is going to be all right that I can't even grasp." Franklin Roosevelt knew everything would be all right because at the worst time of his life, when nothing was all right, when everything was falling apart, he had nevertheless found the strength and calm to endure. He knew what it was to come back from devastation, Isaiah Berlin noted: "So passionate a faith in the future implies an exceptionally sensitive awareness . . . of the desires, hopes, fears, loves and hatreds, of the human beings who compose [one's society]." Part of this awareness he had learned as a child; early on he knew how to please people. But this was more—perhaps only explainable in one who had struggled with other polios around a pool at Warm Springs to get to the water and use it for strength.

Franklin's approach to the Depression was both temperamental and a reflection of his experience with trial and error when he was seeking a way to learn to walk again. Whatever might work was worth a try. There was neither ideology nor consistency in the legislation of his administration's first hundred days—or its first thousand days. An Economy Act went hand in hand with billions of dollars of spending for relief; a bill (the National Industrial Recovery Act) sanctioning collusion among giant monopolies to fix prices with a measure empowering labor unions to organize; an adventure in state-owned utilities that some would call socialism (the Tennessee Valley Authority) with a measure to save the entire banking system and keep it in private hands. Each program was offered up as a trial in the hope that eventually something would work. The key was to keep trying—as it had been with seeking treatment for polio—with the underlying conviction that if you explored enough paths you would find one that led to recovery.

This approach was less a plan than an attitude based on faith, on confidence in oneself and one's ability to win people's support. More critical than anything else was convincing the American people that something could be done, that something would be done, and that the president was able to respond effectively. And Franklin Roosevelt was skilled at convincing those he spoke with. "He could make a casual visitor believe that nothing was so important to him that day as this particular visit," his aide Samuel Rosenman said, "and that he had been waiting all day for this hour to arrive. Only a person who really loved human beings could give that impression." And a person whose experience with helplessness had taught him to be sensitive to others and whose use of empathy and identification with others could win them over while also deflecting attention from his own weakness.

Such sensitivity contributed to Roosevelt's capacity to relate to the American people almost as neighbors, as though he could see and hear them. In the extraordinarily successful radio broadcasts he called "fireside chats," he talked in homely but vivid detail about the everyday problems all Americans faced. "He was conscious of their faces and hands," Frances Perkins said, "their clothes and homes . . . As he talked, his head would nod and his hands would move in simple, natural, comfortable gestures. His face would smile and light up as though he were actually sitting on the front porch or in the parlor with them. People felt this, and it bound them to him in affection." That ability went hand in hand with the personal, temperamental attitude that underlay all of his approaches to ending the Depression.

❖ ❖ ❖

Eleanor Roosevelt provided political intelligence and shrewd advice to reinforce Franklin's impulse toward activism. Her own issues and concerns automatically received a hearing, if not always an affirmative response. What she could not provide was the easy banter or emotional reinforcement that her husband also needed.

The social highlight of each day for the president was the evening cocktail hour, when he could preside with conviviality, light conversation, and good humor over a gathering of friends and guests. Sitting in his study, surrounded by prints of ships, and mixing martinis and more exotic drinks, Franklin used this time to relax, to rejuvenate, to pick up the latest gossip and mischievously convey some of his own. Missy LeHand was always there, Harry Hopkins frequently, and assorted others, most chosen for their charm and ability to entertain their host. Eleanor, who disliked alcohol and disapproved of drinking, rarely appeared, even when she was in Washington, until the gathering was nearly over. She would come in only long enough to have a quick talk with a guest—or her husband—about an issue that concerned her. There was no light touch, no playful banter. As her niece El-eanor Wotkyns noted, "Work had become for Eleanor almost as addictive as alcohol." Even on an evening supposedly devoted solely to celebration such as New Year's Eve, the first lady would work until a few minutes before midnight, dutifully appear for a few toasts, then return to her correspondence until two or three o'clock.

Franklin continued to turn to others for his recreational and emotional fulfillment. Missy lived at the White House, occupied a third-floor room, and constantly made herself available to the man she loved—to go over his stamps late at night, to serve as hostess for his dinner parties when Eleanor was away, to round up surprise guests who could be counted on to entertain him and distract him temporarily from the burdens of office.

Eleanor, too, continued to find her emotional fulfillment from others. She turned primarily to friends, mostly women, who shared her concerns and commitments, and whom she could trust with her deepest feelings. One of these special people was her daughter, Anna. After a difficult period during Anna's adolescence, the mother and daughter achieved a breakthrough in which Eleanor told Anna of Franklin's infidelity, and the two became much closer. When Anna started a romantic relation-ship with John Boettiger before their divorces were final, Eleanor offered total support, seeming to relive her own early romance with Franklin through their daughter's experience. A poignant letter to Anna written on Christmas Eve 1935 reveals the emo-tional ties that had developed between mother and daughter. "The dogs and I have felt sad every time we passed your door," Eleanor wrote. "It was hard to decorate the tree or get things dis-tributed without you . . . and if anyone says much I shall weep for I have had a queer feeling in my throat when I thought of you." One cannot imagine Eleanor writing a similar letter to her husband at this stage of her life.

Eleanor Roosevelt's most intense relationship in the early 1930s was with Lorena Hickok. The two became close during the 1932 campaign when Hickok was covering the prospective first lady as a reporter for the Associated Press. "That woman is unhappy about something," Hickok noted. As the women began to talk about their lives, they developed an affection so strong that Hickok felt compelled to resign her position as a reporter because she could no longer write objectively about the Roosevelts.

Within a short time the women were exchanging daily letters and phone calls, the contents of which suggested that they were in love. "Hick darling," Eleanor wrote on March 6, "how good it was to hear your voice. It was so inadequate to try to tell you what it meant. Jimmy was near and I could not say, je t'aime et je t'adore as I long to do, but always remember I am saying it and I go to sleep thinking of you and repeating our little saying." The next night Eleanor wrote again: "All day, I thought of you, and another birthday I will be with you and yet tonight you sounded so far away and formal. Oh! I want to put my arms around you. I ache to hold you close. Your ring is a great comfort. I look at it and think she does love me or I wouldn't be wearing it."

Hickok returned Roosevelt's devotion. "I've been trying today to bring back your face . . .," she wrote. "Most clearly I remember your eyes, with the kind of teasing smile in them, and the feeling of that soft spot, just northeast of the corner of your mouth against my lips. I wonder what we will do when we meet—what we will say . . . Well, I'm rather proud of us, aren't you? I think we have done rather well."

Over time the relationship cooled somewhat, largely because of Eleanor's inability to give herself unreservedly to Hickok. "I know you often have a feeling for me," Eleanor wrote, "which for one reason or another I may not return in kind." Responding to Hick's jealousy of her children and other friends, Eleanor asked her to understand "that I love other people the same way or differently, but each one has their place and one cannot compare them." Yet the explanation did not suffice. "I never meant to hurt you, . . . but that is no excuse for having done it. It won't help you in any way, but I'll never do to anyone else what I did to you." She just could not let herself go emotionally, Eleanor said, and so, "I am pulling myself back in all my contacts now."

Many have speculated about whether Roosevelt and Hickok had a sexual relationship. Hickok had other lesbian partners, and certainly the tone of the women's correspondence suggests at a minimum that they had erotic feelings for each other. Roosevelt, however, often expressed negative attitudes toward sex, expressed repugnance toward homosexuality in conversations during the 1920s, and repeatedly mentioned her own inability to "let herself go." Her statement about Hickok "having a feeling for me which for one reason or another I may not return in kind" could easily be an allusion to sexual desire. Whatever the case, this relationship illustrates the emotional closeness that Eleanor sought with people other than her husband. As Joseph Lash noted: "She had a compelling need to have people who were close, who were hers, and upon whom she could lavish help, attention, tenderness. Without such friends, she feared she would dry up and die."

❖   ❖   ❖

But Franklin was not one of those to whom she turned. Instead, the political and personal relationship between the Roosevelts during the 1930s continued the pattern that had emerged in the years after World War I. Each brought political and personal strengths to their partnership. Franklin was the less ideological of the two. Unconcerned with consistency, he was willing to move from support of trusts and monopolies in the National Industrial Recovery Act in 1933 to a more skeptical stance in the Public Utilities Holding Company Act of 1935 and the Temporary National Economic Committee in the late 1930s. Alternately friendly to national planners and to those who wanted to return government to the people, President Roosevelt was above all concerned with finding something that would work.

Eleanor Roosevelt, in contrast, sought out the oppressed and became their advocate. Over and over again, she answered pleas for help with a sensitive letter, an admonition to a federal agency to take action, or even a personal check. Poor textile workers in the South and garment workers in the North found her willing to advance their cause in White House councils. Largely because of her efforts, the issue of civil rights for black Americans received a hearing at the White House. Although she had been raised in an environment suffused by racism (she called her servants in Washington in the 1910s "pickaninnies"), as first lady she was one of the few voices in the administration insisting that racial discrimination had no place in American life.

As always, Eleanor led by example. At a 1939 meeting in Birmingham inaugurating the Southern Conference on Human Welfare, she came face to face with segregation ordinances that required complete separation of blacks from whites in all public forums. (The person charged with enforcing the statute was "Bull" Connor, who would become infamous in the 1960s for using fire hoses and police dogs against civil rights demonstrators.) Faced with an order reprehensible to her moral values,

Mrs. Roosevelt insisted on placing her chair so that it straddled the black and white sides of the aisle, thereby locating herself half on the black side, half on the white side, imaginatively confounding—and dramatizing the absurdity of—the Jim Crow system.

Eleanor urged her husband to support federal anti-lynching legislation, and began a sustained alliance with Walter White of the National Association for the Advancement of Colored People (NAACP). When the president's press secretary Steve Early complained that White was obsessed with lynching, the first lady responded: "If I were colored, I think I should have the same obsession that he has." Nor would she let Franklin evade the issue. "I'm deeply troubled by the whole situation," she wrote, "as it seems to me a terrible thing to stand by and let it continue and feel that one cannot speak out as to his feelings." Although in the end the president refused to support anti-lynching legislation, and even failed to use the power of the White House to condemn racism, the few steps he did take—most notably creating a "Negro" cabinet to advise him on racial matters and supporting social welfare policies responsive to black needs—could be traced to his wife's influence.

In all these ways, if imperfectly, the two protagonists complemented each other. Eleanor returned from her travels full of fervor about the injustices she had seen and the importance of taking action immediately. Franklin listened and weighed the political consequences, acting selectively and pragmatically, providing a larger context within which Eleanor could propose her own strategies for action. The days when she came back from trips were the only occasions when the two Roosevelts devoted time exclusively to each other. As Doris Kearns Goodwin points out, "these long relaxing talks had become the bond between

husband and wife, a source of continued enjoyment in one another." Using the one facet of their relationship that remained
healthy and valued, they built what they could from the juncture
of their personal and political interests. What they built was
enough to make a difference in the leadership their country received in a time of crisis.

◆　◆　◆

Franklin Roosevelt's serenity, strength, and calm were more
needed than ever when the threat of world war intensified at the
end of the 1930s. For nearly a decade his administration had
struggled with the persistent and intractable dilemmas of an
economy gone awry. But the Depression crisis paled beside the
emergence of fascist imperialism in Germany and nationalistic
expansionism in Japan. President Roosevelt knew it was incumbent on the United States to fight fascism—in spite of the political strength of neutralists and isolationists. By focusing on Nazism's threats to Americans' fundamental beliefs in freedom of
religion, freedom of political expression, and freedom of labor,
he steadily altered American public opinion. Simultaneously, he
used covert and indirect means to provide practical support for
opponents of fascism. In all of this, he showed a steadiness and
consistency significantly greater than he demonstrated on domestic issues.

It was when the crisis came to a head, first with Germany's invasion of Poland and the Low Countries and later with Japan's
bombing of Pearl Harbor, that Roosevelt rose most courageously
to the challenge. Instinctively, he understood the importance of
doing everything necessary to help Britain and France—and then
Russia—even though his generals urged him to focus on build-

ing up the U.S. armed forces. His course of action entailed a tremendous risk of losing weapons to Germany that America might well need to defend itself. Moreover, one instrument of his policy—the exchange of American destroyers for access to British naval bases—risked provoking a German declaration of war. Still, Roosevelt proceeded with that policy and again with the lend-lease plan of shipping armaments (under convoy) to the Allies, accepting the risks and acting with steely determination.

Roosevelt was at his best in the way he presented his plans to the American people. To justify sending unlimited military aid to the Allies, he talked of the way a person responds when his neighbor's house is burning down. A good neighbor, he said, lends his friend the hose necessary to put out the fire, and only later worries about getting it back. In terms everyone could understand, the president argued persuasively not only that America should help its friends but also that doing so was the best way Americans themselves might avoid war. This was the fundamental person-to-person communication that Franklin had always excelled at, a skill he had honed when trying to communicate with fellow polios at Warm Springs. He had learned to relate to other people at a basic level and speak to them from a common reservoir of understanding.

When the Japanese attacked Pearl Harbor, America suddenly had no choice but to go to war. "I think the boss must have a great load off his mind," Secretary of the Navy Frank Knox told Frances Perkins. "At least we know what to do now." With total calm, the president processed the news, conveyed confidence to his aides, and then set out to reassure the country, combining moral outrage with firm conviction that democracy would triumph. In a superb demonstration of his own resilience and character, he made contact with the deepest layers of faith in the American people. People heard the president, Samuel Rosenman said, and began to return "tenfold" the confidence they sensed from him.

Besides drawing upon his own hard-won inner strength, Roosevelt tapped a collective reservoir of religious strength in this perilous time. Never an ardent believer, he nevertheless had grown up participating in the everyday rituals of his local Episcopal church in Hyde Park, and in the "civic religion" that Americans were accustomed to practicing. Now these religious bonds became part of the arsenal he could deploy to rally the American people. The president invoked these ties in speeches to the Congress and nation, and in his meetings with Allied leaders. When he met with Britain's prime minister, Winston Churchill, at sea off the Newfoundland coast, the session ended with a common religious service, with the crews of the ships from both nations participating. Churchill noted that the shared worship service strengthened everyone—"the same language, the same hymns, and more or less the same ideals . . . Every word seemed to stir the heart and none who took part in it will forget the spectacle presented." Roosevelt agreed. "If nothing else happened while we were here," he commented, "[the joint service] would have cemented us." His ability to call on these deep springs of common conviction helped the president rally the nation for the long fight ahead, with precisely the combination of calm, vision, and determination needed to stay the course.

Eleanor confronted her own moment of crisis as the war began, not knowing quite how to adjust her role to the new challenges. In some ways her new uncertainty resembled her initial feelings about moving to the White House. "Living here is very oppressive," she wrote to Anna soon after the United States entered the war, "because Pa visualizes all the possibilities, as of course he must, and you feel very impotent to help. What you think or feel seems of no use or value, so I'd rather be away and let the important people make their plans and someday I suppose they will get around to telling us plain citizens if they want us to do anything." This self-pitying letter reflected Eleanor's momentary disequilibrium. As Doris Kearns Goodwin points out, Franklin had less time now for conversations exclusively with Eleanor. Moreover, Franklin had turned to Harry Hopkins —once Eleanor's confidant and friend—as his chief companion. "He is staying here [at the White House]," Eleanor's secretary wrote to Anna, "and has gone completely over to the other side of the house." Eleanor needed to feel she was doing something worthwhile for the war effort, and for a time she had difficulty finding her niche.

Yet the uncertainty quickly faded, as it had when she adjusted to being first lady in the early 1930s. Although Goodwin hypothesizes that the war brought a major break in the Roosevelt's relationship—"The husband who had been her close friend would now be more remote . . . The man who loved nothing more than the detailed stories of her travels now had little time and less inclination to listen to her"—such a perspective perhaps romanticizes the earlier bonds between the two. Continuity, rather than discontinuity, seems to have characterized their ties. Since before Franklin's election to the presidency, Eleanor had been an independent actor as well as a partner, an agitator as well as a supporter. Now the familiar roles resumed, perhaps attenuated somewhat by the diminution in time the two spent alone together, but consistent in pattern with what had gone before.

The first lady was concerned that the social issues she most cared about might take second place to the war effort. Naturally, the president focused primarily on mobilizing a victorious war machine, but his wife made it clear very quickly that social issues were an integral part of that mobilization. Continuing her role as the administration's leading advocate of black civil rights, Eleanor pressed Franklin hard to make sure that the new jobs that were opening up in defense industries should be available to blacks as well as whites. When A. Philip Randolph of the Brotherhood of Sleeping Car Porters threatened a massive March on Washington in 1941 unless the president acted to protect Negro economic rights, Eleanor intervened aggressively to persuade her husband and other reluctant officials to listen to the Negro case and to respond. Her influence is surely visible in Franklin's 1941 executive order on Fair Employment Practices, which banned discrimination "because of race, creed, color, or national origin" in government jobs and in defense industries receiving federal contracts. Similarly, Eleanor pressured the secretary of war to improve conditions for blacks in the armed forces.

Eleanor also continued her activism on other issues to which she had devoted her public life. She insisted that administration officials consult women activists and incorporate roles for women as a major part of their planning and staffing for wartime operations. Always the recipient of copies of letters between women's groups and government officials, she was ever ready to add her voice to those seeking to preserve and advance women's interests. When it seemed that many New Deal social welfare programs would be threatened by war, she acted to protect government initiatives directed at the young, at tenant farmers, and at others at the bottom of the social ladder. Increasingly as well, she devoted herself to the dream of international cooperation, perceiving more than most the revolutions arising in Africa and Asia and the threat of postwar conflict.

Eleanor Roosevelt proved especially tenacious in her defense of the rights of European Jews seeking to escape Nazi oppression. When Jewish refugees repeatedly received less than an enthusiastic response from state department officials, she energetically intervened, beseeching her husband as well as the secretary of state to aid those being excluded by bureaucratic rules and racially biased officials from finding a safe haven. Parents, wives, or children separated from loved ones always found an ally when they sought help from the first lady.

In spite of the war, Eleanor traveled as much or even more than she had at the height of the New Deal. Her concern for people was poignantly expressed in visits to wounded veterans in army hospitals overseas. When the world of hot dogs and baseball seemed millions of miles away, suddenly Eleanor Roosevelt would appear, spending time at each bedside, taking names and addresses to write letters at home, bringing the message that America cared.

Perhaps inevitably, the worlds of Franklin and Eleanor became more separate in these years. He was less able to tolerate her advocacy of unpopular causes, or her insistence on calling attention to conflicts within the administration. "She was invariably frank in her criticism of him," one of his speechwriters recalled, "[and] sometimes I thought she picked inappropriate times . . . perhaps a social and entertaining dinner." Anna described one occasion when her mother, entering the cocktail hour as usual at the very end, approached the president with a sheaf of papers insisting that she talk to him about an issue.

> I just remember, like lightning, that I thought, "Oh God, he's going to blow." And sure enough, he blew his top. He took every single speck of that whole pile of papers, threw

them across the table at me and said, "Sis, you handle these tomorrow morning." I almost went through the floor. She got up. She was the most controlled person in the world. And she just stood there a half second and said, "I'm sorry." Then she took her glass and walked toward somebody and started talking. And he picked up his glass and started a story. And that was the end of it. Intuitively, I understood that here was a man plagued with God knows how many problems and right now he had twenty minutes [before dinner] . . . He wanted to tell stories and relax and enjoy himself—period. I don't think that Mother had the slightest realization.

Franklin drew more into himself in these days of crisis. "I saw him often," Frances Perkins said. "He dropped a curtain over himself. He never told you, or anyone else, just what was going on inside his mind." When America was not yet in the war but the military buildup was increasing with lend-lease and other programs, Franklin still depended heavily on Missy LeHand. But some thought he began to find Missy too demanding emotionally. "He didn't like weepy women," his grandson said. "He was turned off by people who couldn't fit into his game." Then, in June 1941, Missy suffered a stroke and a complete emotional collapse. Her plight was explained by the White House maid Lillian Parks as coming from "the strain of loving and knowing nothing would come of it." Missy could no longer meet Franklin's needs, and he seemed callous in his response to her illness. "It seemed only that he resented her for getting sick and leaving him in the lurch," Eliot Janeway remarked. "This was proof that he had ceased to be a person; he was simply the president. If something was good for him as president, it was good; if it had no function for him as president, it didn't exist." (And yet, to give Franklin his due, although he rarely visited Missy in her sickroom, he paid for around-the-clock care for her, communicated directly with her doctors, and changed his will to leave half of his estate to her.)

For a brief period, Harry Hopkins was a partial substitute. He moved into the White House, spent most of his evenings with the president, and offered conviviality as well as friendship. There were evenings, Hopkins told a friend, when in the middle of the war Franklin was left entirely alone except for the company that he, Hopkins, provided. But then Hopkins fell in love, and although his wife moved into the White House with him, his relationship with Franklin was never the same. The Hopkinses' decision to move out, Doris Kearns Goodwin notes, "seemed to suggest an ebbing of affection, a form of abandonment." Franklin was no longer the centerpiece of Hopkins's life.

The person who came closest to taking Missy's place was probably Princess Martha, wife of Prince Olav, the exiled leader of Norway. Beautiful, charming, flirtatious, and bright, the princess appeared to do for Franklin what Lucy had done so many years before. "Martha would sit and simper and tell him how wonderful and beautiful he was," one observer noted. The Roosevelts' son Jimmy speculated that a real romance may have blossomed between his father and Princess Martha. White House diaries showed that Franklin spent more time with Martha than with virtually any other friend during these years—at Hyde Park, the White House, and elsewhere. He even used Harry Hopkins's wife Louise as a chaperone to contain the gossip. Eleanor later commented: "There always was a Martha for relaxation, for the non ending pleasure of having an admiring audience for every breath."

Eleanor's friendships with women continued to be an important part of her life, although some figures such as Molly Dewson had now left Washington. Lorena Hickok had moved into the White House, and while the relationship between the two of them never rekindled to the intensity it had reached in 1932–1933, they remained close and in frequent contact. Eleanor's attitude toward Franklin, in turn, remained distant. She could not fathom his indifference to Missy's situation. "She could never get accustomed to his lack of real attachment to people," Joseph Lash said. Ironically, Eleanor seemed to most observers far more solicitous of Missy in her illness than did Franklin.

Eleanor's major emotional focus during these years was the same Joseph Lash to whom she confided her observation about Franklin's lack of attachment to people. She had met Lash in the 1930s when, as a leader of the American Student Union, he arranged for her to speak at meetings of student activists. Thereafter, an intense bond developed between the two. "[It was] as close a relationship as I ever knew Mother to have," Anna said. Eleanor seemed attracted to Lash's youth and a quality one observer called his "romantic melancholy." Lash speculated about Mrs. Roosevelt's attachment to him: "Perhaps my miseries . . . reminded her of her own when she was young. Insecurity, shyness, lack of social grace, she had to conquer them all, and helping someone she cared about do the same filled a deep unquenchable longing to feel needed and useful . . . She had a compelling need to have people who were close, who in a sense were here and upon whom she could lavish help, tenderness." She gave him presents, corresponded with him almost daily, and looked forward eagerly to when they could be together. "Do come up whenever you are free," she wrote to Lash. "I'll be at the house soon after six waiting to both kiss and spank you and I would love it if you have nothing else that calls, to have you stay the night. It will be nice to tuck you in and say good night on your birthday!"

Eleanor's involvement with Lash led to a bizarre and disgraceful episode, with the government spying on its own first lady. Because of Lash's leadership of the American Student Union, he was suspected of being pro-communist and was placed under counterintelligence surveillance during the war. His letters to and from Eleanor were opened by government agents, and the first lady's hotel room was bugged when she visited Lash. Government spies made the unfounded allegation that Mrs. Roosevelt and Lash were having an affair. As a result, Lash—a soldier at the time—was sent to the Far East. Even there, however, Eleanor managed to see him. "It was wonderful to be with you," she wrote after meeting him on Guadalcanal; "the whole trip now seems to me worthwhile. It is bad to be so personal but I care first for those people I love deeply and then for the rest of the world I fear." It appears that Eleanor's relationship with Lash provided as much or more fulfillment than any relationship that Franklin found in these years.

At least twice during the final years of the war, Franklin tried to reestablish a husband-and-wife relationship with Eleanor— the kind of closeness they had enjoyed in the early years of their marriage. The setting for the potential rapprochement may have been established by the deaths of Franklin's mother and Eleanor's brother Hall. Eleanor, alarmed by Sara's appearance when she returned to Hyde Park from a trip, called Franklin in Washington and urged him to come quickly. He arrived just in time to see his mother before she died. The loss rocked him, and Eleanor's sensitivity to his feelings made a powerful impact. "She showed him more affection during those days than at any other time I can recall," Jimmy Roosevelt remembered.

Franklin did the same for Eleanor a few days later, when her alcoholic brother succumbed to cirrhosis of the liver. After he died, Eleanor left the hospital and went to Franklin's study to tell him what had happened. "Father struggled to her side," Jimmy recalled, "and put his arms around her. 'Sit down,' he said, so tenderly I can still hear it. And he sank down beside her and kissed her and held her head on his chest . . . She spent her hurt in Father's embrace . . . For all they were apart, both physically and spiritually much of their married life, there remained between them a bond that others could not break."

Soon after these two deaths, Franklin asked Eleanor to join him on a train trip to inspect various military facilities. On the train, he asked her to think about patching up their personal relationship, with Eleanor spending more time at home, helping him at the White House, traveling with him on the weekends. "I think he was really asking her to be his wife again, in all aspects," Jimmy said. "He had always said she was the most remarkable woman he had ever known, the smartest, the most intuitive, the most interesting, but because she was always going somewhere he never got to spend time with her. Now that Missy was gone and his mother was dead and Harry [Hopkins] had Louise, he was lonely and he needed her." Once more, on a later train trip, Franklin tried to talk to Eleanor about the life they might live together after the White House, going on cruises, visiting distant continents. And at Christmas 1944 he confided in his son Elliott that he hoped he and Eleanor might get together again.

But Eleanor said no. She had been hurt too many times. She now observed Franklin as much with distant detachment as with the warm sympathy she showed at the time of his mother's death. As she had told Lorena Hickok in 1936, Franklin was a nice person, and a great man, but a "stranger" to her. Other causes and other people had taken his place, and she was unwilling to be hurt again. As Anna explained it, Franklin had "too much security and too much love" from others, while Eleanor had not enough. For Eleanor, the chance that they might once again find emotional closeness with each other did not seem worth the risk.

And so Franklin took other measures to fulfill his emotional needs. Like Eleanor, he had a strong relationship with their daughter, and when Anna visited her parents in 1943 while her husband was serving overseas, Franklin proposed that she move back to the White House and be his companion—hosting dinners as Missy had done, presiding with him over the beloved cocktail hour, working on his stamp collection, cheering him up. Anna accepted, thus becoming the third or fourth person to take her mother's place as co-head of the president's household.

During these final years, Lucy Mercer Rutherford, now a widow, also reappeared as a pivotal part of Franklin's life. They had stayed in touch, and he had arranged, discreetly, for her to attend each of his inaugurations. They wrote to each other, and starting in 1940 they often spoke by phone. Soon they started to see each other again as well. His train stopped near her home so they could spend time together; she visited the White House when Eleanor was away. Now, at Franklin's request, Anna included Lucy in White House dinner parties when her mother was on trips. Lucy spent Thanksgiving of 1944 at Warm Springs with Franklin, listening to his tales of different places and events as he drove her about the countryside in a car custom-fitted with hand controls. When Lucy told Anna of their drives, Anna noted: "Mother was not capable of giving him this—just listening. And of course, this is why I was able to fill in for a year and a half, because I could listen." Others who performed the same function were Franklin's cousin Laura Delano and an even more distant relation, Margaret Suckley, both of whom spent hours with Franklin in the final years of his life, offering the companionship he craved as release from the stresses of war.

Appropriately perhaps, these women were with Franklin in Warm Springs in the spring of 1945 when he journeyed there to recover from the strain of his trip to the Crimean town of Yalta, where he had conferred with Churchill and the Soviet premier, Joseph Stalin. When the president reported to Congress about the Yalta conference, he spoke for the first time in public from his wheelchair. His eyes were hollow, his voice sometimes blurred. Arriving in Warm Springs, he seemed to one secret service man "the worst looking man I ever saw who was still alive." But Lucy was there, and so were other women friends, and slowly he regained his spirits. Then on April 12, while having his portrait painted by a friend of Lucy's, he slumped forward, complained of a terrible pain in the back of his head, and collapsed. As soon as it became clear that the president would not recover, Lucy left Warm Springs. Franklin died later that afternoon. Eleanor arrived the next day to begin the final stage of their forty-year partnership.

◆ ◆ ◆

In revisiting such a tale, one is struck by many features: the way the cultural norms of an era constrain and shape what it is permissible to do and to say, even to feel; the capacity of patterns of behavior, once established, to resist all efforts at change; the creative ability of human beings to adapt, reach out, and find new sources of fulfillment. But perhaps above all, revisiting the story of the Roosevelts accentuates one's awareness of the complicated ways in which individual narratives help to shape and define the public narratives with which they intersect. This is not to say that personality controls politics. But it does mean that the texture and substance of public life cannot be fully understood without an appreciation of individual personalities as they deal with personal as well as public history.

In the case of Eleanor and Franklin Roosevelt, there were many things the two principals could not do for each other. Trained from childhood to be guileful and dissembling, Franklin rarely expressed himself openly about his emotional life. Especially when conflict or negative emotions were involved, he found it difficult, perhaps impossible, to reveal his feelings. This tendency became traumatically entrenched when he contracted polio. Having faced the vulnerability of helplessness, he found it even harder to display or express weakness and need, or to risk rejection by entering into open conflict with a friend or family member. For these reasons, he could never state clearly his emotional needs or express directly his dependence on Eleanor. He may have longed for her to be a jovial companion and helpmate, but he could not risk rejection by exposing his vulnerability to her.

Eleanor suffered the problem in reverse, at least initially. She wore her heart on her sleeve. With her father, and then later with Franklin, she did risk herself, placing unconditional trust in those she loved. Because the trust was so total, however, its disappointment became an unbearable betrayal. If Franklin's self-esteem in childhood was boundless, Eleanor's was almost nonexistent—until Marie Souvestre and the girls at Allenswood nurtured and cultivated it. Even then, however, Eleanor retained a sternness, a seriousness, and a tendency to equate self-worth with a life of service. Once she suffered betrayal a second time in Franklin's affair with Lucy Mercer, Eleanor could find safety and self-esteem only by creating her own world of causes and service. This world brought with it new loved ones and friends, but it distanced her from her husband.

It may be that Franklin and Eleanor's investment in what remained of their relationship gave their political partnership a prominence it might otherwise not have had. Their inability after a certain number of years to negotiate the terrain of emotional affection and conflict only reinforced the degree to which their remaining interaction would draw its energy and endurance from discourse about public questions. Hence the critical importance of Eleanor's trips and the precious time—the only time they had alone—when she returned and they could focus upon the lessons she had learned. In such instances, Franklin's inability to walk the fields or enter the mines was complemented by Eleanor's peripatetic quest to make herself useful. The degree to which Eleanor could influence and shape Franklin's stance on public issues—from relief to civil rights to refugee policies—reflected precisely the narrowness to which their relationship was confined.

There was a sadness to their story as it unfolded. Eleanor adopted the stance of an observer, remarking on Franklin's charm but not letting herself succumb to it. She described herself as viewing him almost as a "stranger"—as the president, but not as a husband, friend, or lover. And yet, in the opinion of many who knew her, Eleanor had defined as out of bounds for herself a role that in fact she deeply desired. Margaret Suckley observed: "I think [Eleanor] is a very great person, and that her greatness springs in large measure from the depth of her love for him. As far as I can see, she is lacking in only one thing, and that is the ability to relax and play with him." And Suckley wrote in her diary right after Franklin's death: "I believe [Eleanor] loved him more deeply than she knows herself, and his feeling for her was deep and lasting. The fact that they could not relax together, or play together, is the tragedy of their joint lives, for I believe from everything that I have seen of them, that they had everything else in common. It was probably a matter of personalities."

Yet in the end what came from those personalities was the most remarkable political partnership of a century. She was his moral anchor, helping to moor him when otherwise he might have drifted off course on issues such as race relations, women's rights, Jewish refugees, and social reform. He, in turn, gave her a touchstone of political reality that helped frame her objectives. Their dialogue defined the leadership provided by the Roosevelts—his based on the steadfastness and inner strength he had found in confronting polio, hers based on the determination to serve humankind that had sustained her in the face of rejection by both her father and her husband.

The result was two leaders of immense and lasting impact. "It was his hand, more than that of any other single man," the *New York Times* editorialized after Franklin's death, "that built the great coalition of the United Nations . . . It was his leadership which inspired free men in every part of the world to fight with greater hope and courage. Gone, now, is this talent and skill . . . Gone is the fresh and spontaneous interest which this man took, as naturally as he breathed air, in the troubles and the hardships and the disappointments and the hopes of little men and humble people."

Eleanor provided much of the substance of his concern with average citizens. From her earliest work in the Rivington Street Settlement House to her activism on behalf of the Women's Trade Union League and the National Consumers League in the 1920s, she spoke for the disenfranchised and oppressed. In the

1930s and 1940s she insisted on advancing racial equality. After Franklin's death her hand and vision shaped the United Nations Declaration of Human Rights. And in the 1950s and early 1960s she continued her devotion to women's rights and civil rights. Upon her death in 1962, Adlai Stevenson declared: "What other single human being has touched and transformed the existence of so many? . . . She walked in the slums and ghettos of the world, not on a tour of inspection . . . but as one who could not feel contentment when others were hungry."

The eulogies were deserved. Transcending the tragedies of their personal lives, Eleanor and Franklin Roosevelt had helped forge much of the best there was in America in the history of the twentieth century.

2

MARTIN LUTHER KING JR.
Toward the Promised Land

Just hours before preaching what was to be his last sermon, Martin Luther King Jr. engaged in an intense confrontation with his closest colleagues in the civil rights movement. Fed up with turning the other cheek, many of them were moving toward renouncing nonviolence except as a temporary tactic; they demanded a tougher, more militant, more physical confrontation with whites who were striving to suppress the sanitation workers' strike in Memphis, Tennessee. In response, King bared his soul, pleading with his colleagues to remain committed to nonviolent love, not as a political gambit, but as a religious credo, an article of faith. In the peroration of his sermon at Memphis's leading black church that night he declared: "I don't know what will happen now . . . We've got some difficult times ahead . . . [but] I'm not worried, . . . I'm not fearing any man [because] mine eyes have seen the glory of the coming of the Lord." Whatever others might do, he would persist in living the faith that sustained him and gave his life meaning.

Most political leaders guard their inner feelings, reveal little of their motivation or anguish, and disguise any reference to the relationship between their private and public lives. That was true of Franklin Roosevelt, and would be true of individuals as diverse as John F. Kennedy, Richard M. Nixon, and Ronald Reagan. It was not true of Martin Luther King Jr. From the day in 1955 when he assumed direction of the Montgomery Improvement Association and commenced his twelve-year sojourn as chief spokesman for the most important social movement in American history, King shared with his parishioners, his friends, and his colleagues the internal tensions, agonies, and reflections that shaped his personal as well as political life. These revelations, though occasionally maudlin and self-serving, offered lucid insights into the torment and the transcendence that gave King his significance. In effect, King provides an example of the personal traits and concerns that more traditional political leaders seek to hide.

King described his early years in Atlanta as almost idyllic: "[It was as though] life had been wrapped up for me in a Christmas package. I didn't have to worry about anything. I [had] a marvelous mother and father . . . [who] went out of their way to provide everything for their children." At home, King's biggest problem was a strong-willed father who wished to dictate what his children would do. As pastor of a large congregation, Martin Luther King Sr. could provide material security for his family, but he also expected to make the decisions on their religious faith, what schools they would attend, whom they would marry, and what careers they would pursue. The son named after him posed a challenge on all four counts.

Although King clearly valued the church as a presence in his life, he also developed an early skepticism about the literalism of his father's faith. Especially when his grandmother died, King started to question the reality of physical immortality, and to push his father on the intellectual underpinnings of his faith. When King went to Morehouse to pursue his college studies, his skepticism continued. There, he later said, "the shackles of fundamentalism were removed from my body." Nevertheless, King had to come to grips with overbearing pressure from his father to join his ministry. Not for the first time, King compromised with his father, simultaneously announcing his willingness to become a preacher *and* his determination to go to Crozer Seminary, a rather unorthodox institution near Philadelphia, to continue exploring the intellectual challenges of Christianity.

Flowering academically in this new environment, King grappled with questions of how Christians should engage with the world around them. Initially King was enamored of the Social Gospel, embodied in the writings and teachings of Walter Rauschenbusch. According to Rauschenbusch, it was the task of the church to carry Jesus' message into society and transform the world into the kind of just society that Christ's teachings demanded. But then King read Reinhold Niebuhr, whose principal thesis—best articulated in his classic *Moral Man and Immoral Society*—was that sin and evil permeated society, so that it was naive and hypocritical for Christians to presume that they could alter institutions and social structures according to the doctrines of the Social Gospel. King wrote in a paper at Crozer in 1951: "Only the superficial optimist who refuses to face the realities of life fails to see this patent fact."

Soon the tension between these two intellectual traditions were complicated further by King's exposure to the work of other theologians, including Paul Tillich, about whom King wrote his doctoral dissertation at Boston University. King was especially taken by Tillich's distinction between different forms of love—erotic love, brotherly love, and unconditional love—and the implications of these for how human beings conducted themselves. In many ways, the rest of King's life would be shaped by his attempts to chart a course between the optimistic engagement of Rauschenbusch and the tempering realism of Niebuhr, with Tillich's sense of love as an intervening force serving as the critical mediator. While he would never cease to acknowledge Niebuhr's insistence on recognizing man's inhumanity to man, neither would he forswear the redemptive power of *agape*—unconditional Christian love—to engage and eventually overcome the sinfulness of all humans.

Through all these early years, King could not escape the central reality of race. Although his family's relative affluence and security protected him from some of the savagery of racist oppression, the awareness of stigma and difference regularly appeared, perhaps even reinforced by King's otherwise comfortable existence. W. E. B. Du Bois wrote of the trauma he experienced as a third grader in Great Barrington, Massachusetts, when a classmate refused to exchange calling cards with him, setting off in Du Bois's head the startling realization that he was different— forever the "other"—in a world where color meant everything. King endured a similar moment of discovery when a white childhood friend, with whom he had played regularly, suddenly broke off contact. "I will never forget what a great shock this was to me," he later wrote; "here, for the first time, I was made aware of the existence of a race problem."

Later there were equally searing experiences—being told by a bus driver, returning from a high school debate, to give up his seat for whites; seeing his father called "boy" by a policeman. "From that moment on," King recalled, "I was determined to hate every white person . . . [and] as I grew older, this feeling continued to grow." As a teenager King wrote a letter of protest to the *Atlanta Constitution* after the 1946 firing-squad lynchings of two African-American married couples in Monroe, Georgia. Such experiences gave Niebuhr's reflections on the sinfulness of humankind a resonance. "Some of the experiences that I encountered," King said, "made it very difficult for me to believe in the essential goodness of man."

Still, all these influences remained relatively inchoate until given focus and definition by King's experience in Montgomery, Alabama. Once again resisting his father's impulse to control, King had married Coretta Scott, a New England Conservatory of Music student whom he met in Boston (not an appropriate minister's wife, the senior King said, and certainly not a representative of Atlanta's black elite families). Furthermore, he defied his father's entreaties to return to the fold as assistant minister of Ebenezer Baptist Church in Atlanta, instead taking a pastorate miles away in Montgomery, at the Dexter Avenue Baptist Church—also a church with a distinguished history and considerable affluence, but one far less given to emotionalism and evangelicalism than Ebenezer or many other black Baptist churches in the South. It was through his role as Dexter's new minister that King found himself chosen as the leader of the Montgomery bus boycott in December 1955, forced to confront and discover the meaning of his faith.

The boycott itself crystallizes virtually all the lessons of the civil rights movement. Although perceived by many whites as a sudden and new expression of black discontent, in fact it had long been in the planning, reflecting the determination of many African Americans to act in ways that would force change. E. D. Nixon of the Brotherhood of Sleeping Car Porters (whose head, A. Philip Randolph, had gained concessions from President Roosevelt by threatening a March on Washington in 1941) led one group seeking a case around which to launch a protest. Jo Ann Robinson, chair of the Women's Political Council—a group of women seeking reform through education and voting—led another group. Since World War II African-American women had organized vigorously to protest sexual assaults by white men on black women, and these networks were now ready for action. Twice in the past year, arrests of black women for resisting Jim Crow bus regulations had almost resulted in boycotts. But E. D. Nixon had felt those two cases were not "clean" or "pure" enough to garner support for a mass movement. Then, in late 1955, Mrs. Rosa Parks, a dignified, universally respected and loved member of the community, was arrested for refusing to give up her seat to a white person, and the multiple networks of civil rights activists went into action. King himself was not involved initially, but in many ways he was an ideal compromise choice to become the spokesperson for the movement. New to town, he had few of the scars or enemies of prior battles; well educated and well spoken, he would be an excellent public representative. Almost by accident, therefore, Martin Luther King Jr. became the consensus choice of a movement already in progress.

Immediately he provided the movement with a signature theme, and he learned from its struggles the personal meaning of his faith. Within hours of accepting his new role as head of the boycott, King had to address a mass rally at the Holt Avenue Baptist Church. How, he asked himself, could he distinguish this boycott from the illegal and immoral boycotts used by segregationists? And on what grounds could he ask people to risk arrest and break the law in a society where for years African Americans had been emphasizing the need for whites to *obey* the law? King found the answer in his appeal to the higher law of morality, and in what would become the ever more refined message that civil disobedience in the spirit of nonviolence and love could be the means for redeeming America. "We are not wrong in what we are doing," he preached. "If we are wrong—the Supreme Court of this nation is wrong . . . If we are wrong—God almighty is wrong . . . If we are wrong—justice is a lie."

In the crucible of this new struggle, with his faith tested as it had never been before, King experienced a decisive and life-altering conversion to the personal meaning of Christ's presence in his life. A month after the boycott began, King received another of what had become nightly harassing telephone calls. This time the call found him exhausted and depressed. "Listen nigger," the midnight caller said, "we've taken all we want from you. Before next week, you'll be sorry you ever came to Montgomery." After the call King was unable to sleep, tormented by visions of his little daughter, innocent and smiling yet threatened by this madness. That dark night, pacing in the kitchen of his house, he broke down, acknowledging his fear and crying out for God's help. As David Garrow narrates the story in his biography of King, the young minister prayed: "Lord, I must confess that I'm weak now. I'm faltering. I'm losing my courage." And then, in that moment of helplessness, King heard an inner voice saying: "Stand up for justice, stand up for truth . . . the voice of Jesus saying still to fight on. He promised never to leave me, never to leave me alone. No never alone. No never alone. He promised never to leave me, never to leave me alone . . . [And] almost at once, my fears began to go. My uncertainty disappeared." Until then, King's faith had been that of "an inherited religion," with no personal experience of God "in the way you must [have] . . . if you're going to walk the lonely paths of life." That night he found a personal bond with God, which provided the anchor that would sustain him through trials sufficient in intensity and pain to break almost any other mortal. The faith of intellectual knowledge had now become deep, overpowering, and personal.

◆ ◆ ◆

As he approached each crisis of the civil rights movement, Martin Luther King Jr. drew upon the intellectual underpinnings of his faith, grounded in his study of Niebuhr, Rauschenbusch, and Tillich. "Love" remained central to his approach. Over and over again, King inserted into traditionally emotional sermons brief intellectual digressions in which he discoursed about the different varieties of love. Even when he was addressing the twenty-five thousand people who made a "Prayer Pilgrimage" to Washington in 1957 about the importance of voting rights— "Give us the ballot," he exhorted, and "all else will follow"—King managed to slip in a discussion of *eros, filios,* and *agape,* the three Greek words describing different forms of love. *Eros,* he pointed out, was the erotic quest for union with the other, exemplified by the great passionate relationships of literature. *Filios* described the love of brothers and sisters for each other—the abiding attachments and obligations within family settings. But it was *agape* that King wished his audiences to understand. This was a love that knew no conditions or limits. It was the love embodied in God's decision to sacrifice his only son, in order that through the gift of that life, the separation between man and God could be ended, all divisions healed, and humanity once again restored to wholeness and health. This was the love of redemptive suffering, accepting death on the cross as the means of saving humankind.

Agape was at the core of what King believed should be the civil rights movement's gift to America. As African Americans endured suffering, accepted violence, and turned the other cheek when their oppressors brutalized them, they enacted the same kind of unconditional, pure love that Jesus expressed in his willingness to die to redeem humanity. Nonviolence, combined with love, thus provided a way to engage one's oppressors and turn their hearts from hatred toward acceptance and reconciliation. It was the powerful message that could simultaneously galvanize a people suffused by religious faith and reach out to "enemies" who, at least in theory, shared a faith in the same God and the same Christian values.

Yet love—*agape*—did not stand by itself. Rather, in King's formulation, it remained always yoked with and informed by a commitment to justice. If the love of nonviolent redemptive suffering was the New Testament's contribution to King's strategic vision, his commitment to justice, with its insistence on confronting evil and raging against it, was the Old Testament's contribution. If the love of appealing to humanity's better side instead of attacking the oppressor exemplified King's faith in the Social Gospel of Walter Rauschenbusch, justice, with its determination to confront evil at every turn, embodied King's understanding of Niebuhr's sense of humanity's sinfulness.

King first set forth the combination in his message to the Holt Avenue congregation on the eve of the boycott. "We are not here advocating violence," he told the churchgoers; "we have over-come that." Rather, the movement in Montgomery would em-body the Christian message of love and transformation. But, King went on, "I want to tell you this evening that it is not enough for us to talk about love . . . Love is one of the pinnacle parts of the Christian faith. [But] there is another side called jus-tice. And justice is really love in calculation. Justice is love cor-recting that which would work against love . . . Standing beside love is always justice . . . Not only are we using the tools of per-suasion—but we've got to use the tools of coercion." Hence King's repeated insistence on recognizing the God of judgment that says "be still and know that I am God," calling all of his creatures to the tribunal of justice.

From the very beginning, then, King yoked in dynamic ten-sion the forces of redemption and those of prophecy. It was not enough simply to *plead* for enemies to renounce hatred; rather, one had to *demand* that evil be confronted, and to *force* the crisis that would compel action and reform. If the one side of King's approach offered to white Americans the positive message that through racial change they could atone for three centuries of racism and move forward as a single nation with no more retri-bution, the other side conveyed the coldly realistic assessment that evil had to be named and condemned, with no restraint or equivocation, and that judgment was near if change did not occur.

This dynamic tension persisted through King's twelve years of civil rights leadership. It was most pointedly and powerfully ex-pressed in the "Letter from a Birmingham Jail," which King wrote in his jail cell in 1963 as a response to "moderate" white clergymen who attacked the Birmingham protests for being un-timely and too radical. Angered by the clergymen's accusation that he was an "outsider" interfering in local matters, King retorted: "I am in Birmingham because injustice is here . . . Injustice anywhere is a threat to justice everywhere. We are caught in an inescapable network of mutuality, tied in a single garment of destiny." To the ministers' plea for patience and their wish to avoid tension, King was equally assertive: far from seeking to avoid conflict, he wrote, "nonviolent direct action seeks to create . . . a crisis and foster such tension that a community which has constantly refused to negotiate is forced to confront the issue . . . I must confess that I am not afraid of the word 'tension' . . . Constructive, nonviolent tension . . . is necessary for growth."

With a prophetic power that unfortunately may have eluded his audience, King reminded the ministers, as Frederick Douglass had a hundred years earlier, that "freedom is never voluntarily given by the oppressor." Hence to wait for such a gift, or simply to petition that it be offered, amounted to a denial of Niebuhr's basic instinct—that society and its institutions harbored evil. What, King asked, should he say to his six-year-old daughter when she asked "why she can't go to the public amusement park that has just been advertised on television, and [when I] see tears welling up in her eyes when she is told that Funtown is closed to colored children." The only just and loving response, he declared, was to break a law that is unjust, accept the consequences, and use the emotion of love *(agape)* to heal and redeem divisions.

King's prophetic voice achieved its most majestic clarity when he expressed his "regrettable conclusion that the Negro's great stumbling block in his stride toward freedom is not the White Citizen's Councilor or the Ku Klux Klanner, but the white moderate, who is more devoted to 'order' than to justice; who prefers a negative peace which is the absence of tension to a positive peace which is the presence of justice." To those who contended that progress was being made and patience rewarded, King responded: "Human progress never rolls in on wheels of inevitability; it comes through the tireless efforts of men willing to be co-workers with God, and without this hard work, time itself becomes an ally of the forces of stagnation."

King's linking of prophecy and love reached a crescendo a few paragraphs later when he wrote of having been called an extremist. Had not Jesus, he mused, been an extremist for love when he urged his disciples to "do good to them that hate you, and pray for them which despitefully use you"? So perhaps the issue was whether one wished to be an extremist "for hate or for love, . . . for the preservation of injustice or the extension of justice . . . Perhaps the South, the nation, and the world are in dire need of creative extremists." In his direct denunciation of the politics of moderation, King carried to its logical conclusion his belief that love and justice were inextricably united, and at the same time he served notice that if America wanted the healing balm of love it also had to live with the scorching intensity of militant protest. Never again would King articulate this core of his faith in so incisive or dramatic a form; yet the reliance on the dynamic tension between love and justice would persist, through constant testing, even to the last meeting he had with his movement colleagues in Memphis.

◆　◆　◆

If the dialectic between justice and love represented one reference point for King's life, the tension between King's own personal wishes and the power of a divine calling constituted another of equal or even greater importance. King had the strength and will to chart his own path in the face of determined resistance from his father—witness his journey north to Crozer and Boston University, his decision to marry Coretta Scott, and his choice of Montgomery for his first pastorate. The same strength carried him through the stresses of the most critical days of the civil rights movement. But by that time, and increasingly, his strength was grounded in a sense of being part of a larger process, destined by divine will—a cosmic force sufficiently strong to overwhelm even his strongest desire to pursue his individual agenda.

Clearly King had an exalted view of his own authority and prerogatives. When he arrived at the Dexter Avenue Baptist Church, he wasted no time in letting the congregation know who was in charge. "The pastor's authority is not merely humanly conferred but divinely sanctioned," he told his parishioners in an early declaration of purpose. "Leadership never ascends from the pew to the pulpit, but it invariably descends from the pulpit to the pew." Although partly informed by his awareness of problems previous pastors had experienced with a mercurial congregation, King's statement also reflected an almost baronial presumptiveness that grew out of his early life as a child of privilege. He would have his own way, pursue his own desires, regardless of the forces arrayed against him.

But then came the movement, and the experience of powerlessness when he had to acknowledge the exhaustion of his resources and plead for help. It was at this moment that King became personally as well as intellectually aware of larger forces in his life over which he exercised no control—forces that he must surrender to no matter what his personal wishes, and that would show him the way even when he felt most confused and lost. He now saw that he was simply a part of a larger process, not its creator or definer. "If Martin Luther King had never been born," he said of the bus boycott, "this movement would have taken place. I just happened to be here. You know there comes a time when time itself is ready for a change. That time has come in Montgomery and I had nothing to do with it."

Not only did such a statement acknowledge the truth of the broader base from which the movement for freedom had sprung in Montgomery, it also informed the people that the struggle was ultimately their own, and that they need not—and should not—depend upon him. "I did not start this boycott," he told a crowd gathered at his house after it had been bombed; "I want it to be known the length and breadth of this land that if I am stopped, this movement will not stop." "Whether we want to be or not," he told another audience in Montgomery, "we are caught in a great moment of history, . . . bigger than Montgomery, . . . part of that great movement for freedom [throughout the world]."

By articulating the sense of being called by a higher power to persist in the struggle for freedom, King also invoked a sense of destiny that justified and exalted decisions that otherwise ran totally counter to his self-interest or personal desire. It was as if the revelation in his kitchen of God's solace and protection raised his engagement to a different plane. "If anybody had asked me a year ago to head this movement," he said to his congregation in 1957, "I tell you honestly that I would have run a mile to get away from it. I had no intention of being involved in this way . . . [But] as I became involved, and as people began to derive inspiration from their involvement, I realized that the choice leaves your own hands . . . then you know that you no longer have a choice, you can't decide *whether* to stay in or get out, you *must* stay in it." If King himself no longer had a choice because he had been called, neither did those who made up the body and soul of the movement.

King found this belief that he was part of a divinely ordained mission indispensable to making decisions in the face of conflicting advice. After their house was bombed in January 1956, King and Coretta went to Atlanta, where they came under intense pressure from "Daddy" King to remain in safety and not return to their damaged home. All of the elder King's allies rallied to help him make the case, and his son felt isolated and helpless. But he found the resolve to declare that he must go back—immediately. He felt the same sense of intervention by an outside force as he debated with his movement colleagues whether to seek to be arrested in the ever more volatile demonstrations in Birmingham in the spring of 1963. King left the room to pray over his decision, and when he returned he wore the movement uniform of blue denim overalls, signaling his intention to join the imprisoned. A year later, faced with a similar choice of whether to go to Mississippi, where he would be an easy target for assassination, King wavered. "I want to live a normal life," he said. But living a normal life was not part of being called, and so he went.

Belief in divine guidance proved most crucial when King confronted threats of violence and death. At times the prospect of imminent death at the hands of the movement's enemies overwhelmed him, inducing a martyr-like response. "If anyone should be killed," he told one congregation during an exhausting week full of travel and bombings right after the bus boycott had ended, "let it be me." But then he went back to the moment when God became more than an abstraction to him:

There were moments when I wanted to give up and I was afraid, but You gave me a vision in the kitchen of my house . . . [and] since that morning I can stand up without fear. So . . . tell Montgomery they can keep shooting and I'm going to stand up to them; tell Montgomery they can keep bombing and I'm going to stand up to them. If I had to die tomorrow, I would die happy because I've been to the mountaintop and I've seen the promised land, and it's going to be here in Montgomery.

To a remarkable extent, King shared his existential dilemmas with those around him, talking out the conflict between his personal desires and his higher calling. Repeatedly he spoke of the "temptation of wanting to retreat to a more quiet and serene life," and of the desire to escape. "I'm tired of marching . . . for something that should have been mine at first," he told a church rally in 1966. "I'm tired of living every day under the threat of death. I have no martyr complex. I want to live as long as anybody in this building tonight, and sometimes I begin to doubt whether I'm going to make it through. I must confess I'm tired." But then he would declare: "I don't march because I like it, I march because I *must*." Fear was something he had learned to live with. "I have always felt that ultimately along the way of life, an individual must stand up and be counted and be willing to face the consequences, whatever they are," he told a reporter. "If he is filled with fear, he cannot do it. And my great prayer is always that God will save me from the paralysis of crippling fear."

King's faith made it possible for him to fuse his personal commitment with his sense of having been called. Because there was a higher mission to which he *must* respond, he could say: "I *choose* to identify with the poor. I *choose* to give my life for the hungry . . . I *choose* to live for and with those who find themselves seeing life as a long and desolate corridor with no exit sign. This is the way I'm going. If it means suffering a little bit, I'm going that way. If it means sacrificing, I'm going that way. If it means dying for them, I'm going that way, because I heard a voice saying, 'Do something for others'." At such moments free will, personal decision, and obligation to fulfill God's purpose became as one, enhancing the strength not only of King but of all those who heard him testify about his torment.

This was also the strength that enabled King to listen to those who challenged him. He understood that he was a product of the movement, not its creator, and that it nourished and sustained him, as he did those who worked with him. Nowhere did this knowledge serve him better than when his colleagues in the Student Nonviolent Coordinating Committee (SNCC) accused him of being subservient to the liberal "establishment," derided him as "de Lawd," and demanded that he pursue more militant tactics. In the midst of the Albany (Georgia) movement, when King was under attack for not violating a federal injunction and going to jail, he sat down for hours with those younger SNCC members who had denounced him most fiercely. Absorbing their verbal assaults, he heard the truth of their accusations, but refused to make the encounter a battle, somehow informed and sustained by the larger cause that united them all. "King and the students had created their own charged space," Taylor Branch has written. In that space they could listen to and learn from one another; they could acknowledge that no one was beyond the challenge to "grow a little bit more" in the struggle.

King's conviction that he had been called by God was part of his strength. In an interview with David Frost he spoke of "an inner sense of assurance," attributing it to "a sense of cosmic companionship." "We have a responsibility to set out to discover what we are made for," he told one audience, "to discover what we are called to do. And after we discover that, we should set out to do it with all the strength and all the power we can muster ... [assured that] there is something in the very structure of the cosmos that will ultimately bring about fulfillment and the triumph of that which is right." Yet in the darkest moments, when the inner torment was greatest, it was not the cosmic companionship that gave King solace as much as it was the voice in the kitchen.

Certainly this was the case for King's most bitter and personal agony during these years—the stubborn persistence of a sense of personal sinfulness that could be ameliorated only by the belief that God might understand and help. When the issue was fear of death or conflict between the personal desire to retreat and the call of a higher cause, the relationship between King as a private citizen and King as an instrument of God was one thing. When the issue was repeated surrender to carnal temptation and personal betrayal of loved ones, the relationship between King the individual and God the personal protector took on a different dimension. Throughout his life, King had been a lover of sensuality and celebration. When he became "de Lawd," however, his behavior became a subject of political as well as personal attention. Especially when the FBI and its director, J. Edgar Hoover, became involved, the political dimensions of King's flaws and temptations took on overriding importance. Here, as in his effort to reconcile individual preference with collective responsibility, King shared his anguish and articulated his pain—finding solace only in the belief that the God who resolved his doubts and fears about the movement would also absolve his personal sinfulness.

King had always loved women and prided himself on his ability to attract those deemed by society to be most desirable. For many black men, that meant women with straight hair and pale complexions. At Morehouse, one friend recalled, "M.L. could get involved with girls, and most of the girls he got seriously involved with were light, . . . very fair-skinned." At Crozer the pattern continued: in an environment where one-third of the students were African American, King was most attracted to a young German woman, whom he wanted to marry. His attraction to women of diverse backgrounds continued, apparently even after his marriage, and when his colleague and closest friend Ralph Abernathy was accused of sexually exploiting a parishioner, a minister friend warned King that he was a "marked man": "All sorts of subtle attempts will be made to discredit you . . . One of the most damning influences is that of women. They themselves too often delight in the satisfaction they get out of affairs with men of unusual prominence. Enemies are not above using them to a man's detriment. White women can be lures. You must exercise more care. You must be vigilant indeed." The warning was prophetic.

Acutely sensitive to the reality of temptation in his life, King repeatedly expressed guilt and perplexity about how a sinner could be redeemed. "Each of us is something of a schizophrenic personality," he told his congregation. "We're split up and divided against ourselves. There is something of a civil war going on within all our lives." But King went beyond abstractions in sharing his plight with his parishioners. "I make mistakes morally," he admitted, "and get down on my knees and confess it and ask God to forgive me . . . We are unfaithful to those we ought to be faithful to . . . There are times that all of us know somehow that there is a Mr. Hyde and Dr. Jekyll in us."

In the eyes of many of his closest associates, King was particularly guilt-ridden because of the gap between his public persona of saintliness and the far different reality of his private self. There were two Martin Luther Kings, an old seminary friend said. One of the traits King admired in Mahatma Gandhi was the ability to avoid such a split through constant self-criticism and self-discipline. "There was no gulf between the private and the public," King wrote about Gandhi after a trip to India. Indeed, King's insistence on not accumulating material wealth or possessions represented an effort to live by Gandhi's example in one part of his life. But he could never achieve the same results in other parts of his life, and he was tormented as a result. "He never felt that he deserved all the accolades," his close associate Dorothy Cotton said. "He almost felt guilty that he got all of that praise and publicity and honor." Hence the sermons on the wrenching two-ness of the personal struggles of people like St. Augustine, turning from lustfulness to sainthood, or of St. Paul, transformed from a persecutor into an apostle—all of these revealing, in Taylor Branch's words, King's "turbulent conflict over the relationship between the public and the private person." He was, his parishioners said after hearing such sermons, "a God-troubled man."

As if his own conscience were not enough of a source of anguish, King soon had to face the FBI's determination to use evidence of his sexual behavior to destroy his reputation as a civil rights leader or even to push him to commit suicide. FBI agents first focused on King because of his close relationship with Stanley Levison, thought by the Bureau to be a highly placed Communist agent. FBI agents used wiretaps and listening devices in hotel rooms and offices to gather information about Levison's presumably subversive influence on King. They also found vivid evidence of King's womanizing, including tapes that suggested all-night orgies and drinking parties, as well as indications of longer-term affairs between King and women in various cities. Already committed to undermining King, J. Edgar Hoover became infuriated when King began to attack the FBI for failing to protect civil rights workers in the South. Hoover disseminated information about King's alleged behavior to reporters and editors, used public forums to denounce civil rights leaders as "moral degenerates" and as "soft" on Communism, and infiltrated the Southern Christian Leadership Conference (SCLC)— the umbrella organization that King and other ministers had formed after Montgomery—with informers who would help him weaken the organization.

Hoover plumbed new depths when the FBI sent King a composite tape that disclosed in detail King's sexual activities, along with a letter telling him that suicide was the only path open to him. Thinking the tape contained speeches King had made, the SCLC staff gave the package to Mrs. King to take home. There, with her husband, she played the tape and opened the letter. Nothing revealed more clearly how far the government was ready to go to destroy King and the movement. "You know you are a complete fraud," the letter said, playing on King's guilt at being portrayed as a saint. "You could not believe in God . . . Clearly you don't believe in any personal moral principles." Calling him a "dissolute, abnormal, moral imbecile," the letter continued: "King, like all frauds your end is approaching . . . You are done. Your honorary degrees, your Nobel prize (what a grim farce) and other awards will not save you . . . King, there is only one thing left for you to do. You know what this is . . . You better take it before your filthy, abnormal fraudulent self is bared to the nation." Stunned by the letter, King sank into even greater depression than before. "They are out to break me," he told a friend, "[to] harass me, break my spirit."

Once again the only solace King could find was in his relationship with God. He could try to justify his behavior on the grounds that he was under constant stress, traveled all the time, and did not always have the best relationship with Coretta. His indulgences, he told one friend, "were a form of anxiety reduction." But ultimately King knew that the answer—and the burden—rested within, and between himself and his faith. "When I delve into the inner chambers of my own being," he preached one day, "I end up saying, 'Lord, be merciful unto me a sinner'." He brooded on his inability to reform. "Year by year," he said, "you become aware of the terrible sin that [is] taking possession of your life," and resolve to end it, only to find that the next day or month it is still there. And so, finally, the sinner must prostrate himself and confess the weakness, the helplessness, and the depravity. "It can only be done," he said, "when we allow the energy of God to be let loose in our souls."

Perhaps the torment was part of the price of "stand[ing] up against entrenched evil," the "dark and agonizing moments" a penance. But in the end, all King could do was go back to the personal connection with God that he had established so many years before. "God does not judge us by the separate . . . mistakes that we make," he declared, "but by the total bent of our lives." That way one could avoid the polarity of saint and sinner, the risen and the fallen. "You don't need to go out [of church] this morning saying that Martin Luther King, Jr., is a saint," he told the Ebenezer congregation. "I want you to know this morning that I am a sinner like all of God's children, but I want to be a good man, and I want to hear a voice saying to me one day, 'I take you in and I bless you because you tried'." Only through that confession and testimony could the opposites be reconciled, the divided made whole.

Taylor Branch has observed that King felt authentic despair over his inability to live up to the standards he believed he should uphold. It was a "passion all too real," Branch wrote, "an empathy with evil that became relentless self-abasement, a cry for penance. Low and leveling, yielding to no one in keenness of feeling, this raging humility collided with high righteousness to produce a synthetic passion that was uniquely King's." Yet King's direct engagement with the polarity generated the purest expressions of the meaning of his faith. Alone and flawed, he had nowhere else to turn.

❖ ❖ ❖

Another reference point by which to chart King's journey was the tension that characterized his political thought, especially his struggle to find a course between reformism and radicalism. Notwithstanding the efforts of Ronald Reagan and others to portray King as a moderate who simply wanted Americans to obey the Constitution and support equality of opportunity, he was a complicated and nuanced figure. To be sure, King believed in and eloquently invoked the principal tenets of the American creed, but throughout his life—and especially toward the end—he also sought to restructure American society in the name of justice. "We are called upon to raise certain basic questions about the whole society," King declared just before his assassination. "We must recognize that we can't solve our problem now until there is a radical redistribution of economic and political power."

King had come to his initial skepticism about capitalism and materialism by viewing with distaste his father's attachment to worldly goods. Whatever benefits he had derived from his family's economic security and comfort, the younger King wondered about the consistency of preaching justice while craving possessions that separated people from one another. At Morehouse and especially at Crozer, King became familiar with Marxist thought and concluded, according to one classmate, that "the capitalist system was predicated on exploitation and prejudice," with a "new social order" the only solution. Like Gandhi, King renounced material wealth. "I don't want to own any property," he said, "I don't need a house." Indeed, it required a sustained campaign by family and friends to persuade him to purchase a modest home in Atlanta after taking the pulpit of Ebenezer Baptist. King told his wife: "It's so unfair that a small percentage of the population [should] control all the wealth . . . I don't believe in capitalism as it is practiced in the United States."

Nevertheless, much of King's early public career focused on achieving reform by working within the traditional values and institutions of American capitalism and democracy. The Montgomery bus boycott, although it used a technique considered radical by some, sought extremely modest changes, beginning with a demand for flexible seating within segregated buses (with the line between black and white passengers shifting as their relative numbers increased or decreased). Similarly, the early efforts of the Southern Christian Leadership Conference focused primarily on gaining the right to vote (the most traditional and conservative goal of social movements), securing the right of access to public accommodations like hotels and restaurants, and ending racial discrimination in the workplace and in schools. All of these were basic rights of citizenship—a theme sounded by King at the March on Washington in 1963, when he evoked the vision of an America where people would be judged "by the content of their character rather than the color of their skin."

Yet privately, and sometimes publicly as well, King continued to imagine more far-reaching change. King told a crowd in Chapel Hill in 1957: "I never intend to accommodate myself to the tragic inequalities of an economic system that denies necessities to the many in order to give luxuries to the few." Forgotten by most mass media recollections and popular histories is the fact that the March on Washington was for *jobs* and freedom, not just freedom, and that the goal—orchestrated by Bayard Rustin, the Democratic Socialist organizer of the event—was a domestic Marshall Plan that would have remade America's urban infrastructure through federal building and employment programs. Thus, even in the years when he was ostensibly committed to "reform," King entertained visions of radical change.

After Birmingham and the March on Washington, such visions increasingly predominated. As early as the "Letter from a Birmingham Jail," King declared: "We are engaged in a social revolution . . . [that seeks] to bring about certain basic structural changes in the architecture of American society." Focusing more and more on poverty as the heart of black America's dilemma, King called for a "massive assault upon slums, inferior education, inadequate medical care [and] the entire culture of poverty." He told a staff member in Selma: "If we are going to achieve real equality, the United States will have to adopt a modified form of socialism." And when he visited Los Angeles after the Watts riots, he observed: "[This] was a class revolt of the underprivileged against the privileged." Long before the sociologist William Julius Wilson started talking about the "declining significance of race," King recognized that maldistribution of wealth and income was as central to America's problems as the color of one's skin.

How to proceed with such an agenda was a huge problem. Bayard Rustin, in an article entitled "Protest vs. Politics" published in *Commentary* in 1965, argued that the time had come for the civil rights movement to move from demonstrations in the streets toward mobilization of a broad-based political coalition of the labor movement, liberal Democrats, urban leaders, and civil rights advocates to support the progressive political agenda he had outlined in his call for a domestic Marshall Plan. In 1965 King's close advisor Stanley Levison presented a version of the same theme. King, Levison argued, had attained unique political clout in America after Selma and Birmingham, while also "retaining his independence and freedom of action [and remaining] free of the taint of political ambition, wealth, power, or the pursuit of vanity." This was largely, Levison contended, because King's movement had been "basically a coalition for moderate change, for graduated improvements which are to be attained without excessive upheavals ... *It is militant only against shocking violence and gross injustice.* It is not for deep radical change." In Levison's view, the movement should continue along that moderate road. "America today," he said, "is not ready for a radical restructuring of its economic and social order," and were the movement to demand such restructuring, it risked being isolated and ineffective, since most Americans would prefer the status quo with discrimination to racial equality through social revolution. Trenchant, wise, and prescient, Levison appeared to understand well the pragmatic importance of not deviating too far from mainstream values and expectations.

Yet the 1960s were no ordinary time, nor was Martin Luther King Jr. an ordinary politician. Political expediency was not King's primary criterion for action. Never insensitive to political realities, he nevertheless based his decisions on moral grounds more than on the calculus of political success. In that context, two primary considerations altered the political equation. The first was King's growing realization, already articulated in his remarks on poverty and class, that civil rights alone meant little without the substance of economic power and resources. The second was the Vietnam war, which demonstrated that what was wrong in America was not only a domestic problem but a global one.

King had always had an international perspective. His trips to India, to Africa to visit newly liberated former colonies, to Sweden to accept the Nobel Prize—all these nourished his sense of the interrelatedness of freedom and justice everywhere on the globe. But it was Vietnam that galvanized his moral sensibility and pushed him away from the moderate course advocated by Levison and Rustin, and toward a more systemic, far-reaching, and ultimately radical demand for structural change. King had been opposed to the war in Vietnam for years, but had kept silent to avoid creating political problems for the movement. Then he saw in *Ramparts* magazine a photograph of a mother holding a dead child killed by Americans. "He froze as he looked at the picture," his friend Bernard Lee said, "then pushed the plate of food away from him." No longer able to set aside his revulsion, King joined the antiwar crusade. "I knew that I could never again raise my voice against the violence of the oppressed in the ghettos," he explained, "without having first spoken clearly to the greatest purveyor of violence in the world today— my own government." Change must be dramatic and basic, he said: "If we are to get on the right side of the world revolution, we as a nation must undergo a radical revolution of values. We must rapidly begin to shift from a 'thing-oriented' society to a 'person-oriented' society." King now talked more often of "our vicious class system," and urged a "radical refurbishing of the former racist caste order of America." For better or worse—and in the midst of intense harassment by the FBI—King had moved decisively toward a more radical view of what was required to achieve a society of justice and love. And issues of morality were central to his decision.

At the same time, however, King was racked with self-doubt and anxiety. Depression was not an unusual response to the kind of stress he was forced to endure. The pressure of constant travel and threats to his safety and his life was exacerbated by the FBI's campaign to destroy him, guilt over his marital infidelity and failure to live up to his image, and the battering intensity of people demanding from him solutions he did not have.

King felt keenly the burden placed upon him to come up with successful strategies for change. "People expect me to have answers," he commented, "and I don't have any answers . . . I don't feel like speaking to people. I don't have anything to tell them." Again, to a remarkable degree, he expressed his doubts and fears in public. In the midst of his campaign to establish a viable movement in Chicago, for example, he confided his despair to a negotiating committee that had been meeting for hours without reaching agreement: "There are moments when I doubt if I am going to make it through. I am tired of getting hit, tired of being beaten, tired of going to jail." Yet the very act of sharing these emotions evoked concern and commitment in the group, helping them find a way out of the impasse in their negotiations.

King also felt deeply the yawning gap between his hopes and expectations of great change and the reality of limited progress. "I am personally the victim of deferred dreams, of blasted hopes," he said in December 1967. Occasionally he felt his work had been a failure. "All I have been doing in trying to correct the system in America has been in vain," he told a colleague. King found himself making careless mistakes: "I know why I missed my flight," he told Coretta. "I really don't want to go. I get tired of . . . not having any answers." Sometimes he sounded self-pitying: "We often develop inferiority complexes," he said in a sermon, "and we stumble through life with a feeling of insecurity, a lack of self-confidence, and a sense of impending failure."

In perhaps the strongest display of depression, King seemed ever more preoccupied with death. In the past he had referred stoically to the threats on his life. When he was stabbed by a woman at a book-signing party in Harlem, or punched by a white fascist in the midst of a speech, King responded with calm and poise. According to Coretta, he "always talked about the fact that he didn't expect to have a long life . . . Somehow he always felt that he would die early." Indeed, King viewed acknowledging and confronting the threat of dying as a prerequisite to serving the cause. "One has to conquer the fear of death if he is going to do anything constructive in life and take a stand against evil," he said after Malcolm X was assassinated.

But now, according to King's close aide Andrew Young, "He talked about death all the time." "A profound sadness" had settled on King, noted the civil rights activist Roger Wilkins. Ralph Abernathy returned from a trip to find King "just a different person," and a Birmingham friend concluded that King "had a

death wish . . . I had a feeling he didn't know which way to turn."
Even Rustin and Levison became concerned about their friend's
preoccupation with death.

However haunted by his premonitions, King found the
strength to continue. His task, as he saw it, required a delicate
balancing act. "Somewhere there has to be a synthesis," he said.
"I have to be militant enough to satisfy the militant, yet I have to
keep enough discipline in the movement to satisfy white supporters and moderate Negroes." He recognized the polarization
in America: "You just can't communicate with the ghetto dweller
and at the same time not frighten many whites to death. There
must be somebody to communicate to two worlds." Yet he refused to back away from the systemic analysis of world problems
that had come to dominate his thoughts and speeches. In a series of lectures for the Canadian Broadcasting System, King articulated a vision that connected racism in America with colo-
nialism in Asia and poverty around the world. "We must see . . .
that the evils of racism, economic exploitation and militarism
are all tied together," he told his staff, "and you can't really get
rid of one without getting rid of the others." The only answer
was "a radical redistribution of economic and political power."

To that end, King settled on what would be the last crusade of
his life, the Poor People's Campaign of 1968. If only people living
in poverty—white and black, urban and rural, young and old—
could arouse the same national shock and outrage about their
condition that southern blacks had achieved in the early 1960s,
perhaps a national consensus could be mobilized to restructure
American life to eliminate poverty. A Poor People's Campaign
seemed the only way to strike at the economic roots of racism
and exploitation in America. In some ways this idea was as utopian and bold as anything King had ever conceived, but in oth-

ers it was no more utopian than the idea of a grassroots movement marching across the South must have seemed in the mid-1950s.

This last crusade crystallized all the tensions of King's life. Buffeted by conflicting pressures, "a profoundly weary and wounded spirit" (in Roger Wilkins's phrase), yet compelled to search for solutions to the disparities between rich and poor, black and white, King invested his faith in this struggle "to move this sick nation away from at least a level of its sickness." The means would be a national march to Washington led by mule-driven wagons, followed by an encampment on the National Mall until Congress agreed to enact a $30 billion program to provide full employment, a guaranteed annual income, and public housing.

It was both consistent and appropriate that King's journey to the Poor People's Campaign was interrupted by an unplanned detour to Memphis, where a strike by sanitation workers highlighted all the issues of race and poverty that the Poor People's Campaign was about. Memphis also reflected the divisions within America between the poor and the comfortable, black and white, young and old, militant and moderate, with tensions threatening to explode. In this setting, King spent his last days trying once more to make nonviolence and love work as catalysts for change and justice. Perhaps inevitably, the pressures of division triumphed. When King led a protest march in downtown Memphis in late March 1968, violence broke out, and he was whisked away for his own safety. An editorial in the Memphis *Commercial Appeal* declared: "King's pose as leader of a nonviolent movement has been shattered." "Maybe we just have to admit," King told Ralph Abernathy, "that the day of violence is here, and maybe we have to just give up and let violence take its course." Never, Abernathy said later, had he seen King so depressed.

Once again, as so often in the past, King refused to submit to his depression. Instead, he convened his staff and spoke to them for hours on the necessity of retaining nonviolence—not just as a tactic, he insisted, but as a fundamental principle. He also made plans to lead another march on behalf of the Memphis sanitation workers, this one scheduled for early April 1968. His flight to Memphis on April 3 was delayed because of a bomb threat. Nevertheless, in the speech he gave that night he reaffirmed his commitment to nonviolence: "It is no longer a choice between violence and nonviolence in this world; it's nonviolence or non-existence." Acknowledging how divided even black Americans were, he yet emphasized once again his belief in the transforming power of nonviolent love. At the end of his sermon, after describing his nearly fatal stabbing by "a demented black woman" ("if I had sneezed, I would have died") and mentioning the bomb threat that had delayed his plane, he concluded: "It doesn't really matter with me now, because I've been to the mountaintop . . . Like anybody, I would like to live a long life. Longevity has its place. But I'm not concerned about that now. I just want to do God's will. And he's allowed me to go up to the mountain, and I've looked over, and I've seen the promised land. I may not get there with you. But I want you to know tonight, that we, as a people, will get to the promised land." Even his closest friends, who had heard King say these words a dozen times before, found them particularly moving that night. The next day King was assassinated.

◆ ◆ ◆

Over the thirteen-year span of Martin Luther King's public political leadership, he was remarkably open and candid about the
conflicts that preoccupied him, willing to share with audiences
ranging from a few staff members to thousands of followers the
anguished choices that he confronted. To be sure, only a relatively small number of people knew of his torment over his marital infidelities, or of the FBI's attempts to use these against
him—yet in retrospect his references to this torment are crystal
clear, and even at the time parishioners commented after such
sermons about King being a "God-troubled" man. We have then,
in King, a rare instance in which a political leader has allowed us
inside the thought and belief processes by which he made the
decisions that charted his life course.

Those processes were both intellectual and spiritual, although
always rooted in a religious and moral framework. King's approach to the problems of race and society emerged from his
combination of Niebuhr's pessimism about the sinfulness of
humankind and social institutions with the optimism of the Social Gospel's conviction that society could be remade in Christ's
image. Mediated by King's own meditations about *eros, filios,* and
agape, this understanding of social dynamics enabled him to
maintain a constant tension between the demands of justice and
those of love. It was a tension that kept him always on course, on
the one hand insistent on the centrality of nonviolent love as the
prerequisite for engagement, on the other informed by a devotion to justice that permitted no compromise with evil. Witness
King's determination to proceed in Memphis—and the terms of
nonviolence on which he insisted.

That tension, in turn, created the structure within which King conducted his unending internal dialogue about just how sick American society was, and the degree to which the sickness called for radical rather than reformist solutions. The ingredients of a radical critique had always been present in his thought, as had an awareness that many of the issues of racial inequality were rooted as much in economics and class as in prejudice based on skin color. Yet, with his commitment to both love and justice, King was prepared to give American society a chance to bring about change by reform. Hence his tactics of seeking legal and governmental change, of working within the existing political system, and of using a broad-based coalition that was fundamentally moderate. At the same time, King was sufficiently secure in his own politics and in his faith that he could listen and understand when others in the movement called for a more militant posture. Moreover, his own reading of what was and was not changing in America propelled him to a more systemic critique. When the Vietnam war made him feel he could no longer in good conscience remain silent, King became a prophetic proponent of acknowledging that capitalism, racism, and militarism were all part of one problem and seeking strategies for addressing all three. Whether or not his chosen instrument for beginning this—the Poor People's Campaign—would have succeeded, the choice itself spoke to a logical conclusion of abiding concerns that had been there for years.

At the heart of all of this was King's religious faith. It is never easy for an observer to determine when or whether a person referring to religious belief is speaking with sincerity. Yet it seems impossible that Martin Luther King Jr. could have endured the constant demands and threats of being at the forefront of the nation's greatest social movement had not his faith sustained and empowered him. No one knows whether the night in his kitchen, when, he claimed, in the midst of despair he reached out for and received God's commitment, was actually the turning point in King's personal journey of faith. The story may well have been embellished over time, made into the stuff of legend both by King himself and by historians and movement colleagues. Yet it is inconceivable that some such experience did not enter into King's life and create the deeply emotional conviction that was at the core of his faith. That conviction, along with the sense of having been called to a divinely ordained mission, enabled King to accept the many sacrifices he made—putting his own safety at risk to serve the cause, giving up the retreat and contemplation he craved to persevere in the grinding life of pressure and danger on the road. At the heart of this story, then, is a sense of there being a personal covenant between a preacher and politician and his God. There appears to be no other possible explanation of what took place in this remarkable life. Flawed, ever aware of his own sinfulness, and never sure he deserved the praise he received, King nevertheless found the strength to persist in risk and engagement—confident that he was acting in partnership with a higher force.

3

JOHN F. KENNEDY
From Detachment to Engagement

Three days in June 1963 suggested that John F. Kennedy might have found a new voice. The first came on June 10, when the president, in a speech at American University, asked that Americans and Russians together have the courage to cast aside the shibboleths of the Cold War and start anew on a quest for peace. "We must re-examine our . . . attitudes as individuals and as a nation," he declared, because in the end, "our most basic common link is that we inhabit this small planet." The next night, in an impromptu televised speech, Kennedy for the first time embraced civil rights as a moral issue. "Who among us," he asked, "would be content to have the color of his skin changed and stand in [the Negro's] place?" Then, on a third day, Kennedy ordered his staff to draft plans for a federal assault on poverty, acknowledging the links between racism and economic inequality and recognizing that a fundamental flaw existed in American society. Three straws in the wind—signaling a potential new direction in the Kennedy presidency.

❖ ❖ ❖

For more than four decades John F. Kennedy has symbolized to the American people youth, activism, vibrancy, energy, and tragedy. The first president born in the twentieth century and the first to speak for "a new generation of Americans," Kennedy exhorted his countrymen to "ask not what your country can do for you, but what you can do for your country." With almost palpable urgency, he conveyed a sense that anything was possible if only people willed it to happen. Urging the nation to pick up the "torch of the American revolution," Kennedy seemed like a Roman tribune, galvanizing the best minds of his era to confront the challenges of a world which, he said, faced its hour of maximum peril. "We can do better," he insisted.

The promise proved more luminous than the performance. Notwithstanding his extraordinary capacity for ennobling rhetoric, Kennedy's idealism rarely translated into programmatic initiatives. Although it became a truism that the 1960s represented a break with the past, the reality is that most of the changes came from below and were due primarily to the civil rights movement; only in the middle of the decade did they translate into a significant shift in the activities and aspirations of government. As generations of political observers and historians have since told us, Kennedy's forte was more style than substance. Washington became a glamorous place, full of arts, culture, intellectual triumphs, and smart sophistication. But all too often there seemed little beneath the glittering surface.

At least until the last year or so of Kennedy's life. In that period, whether the issue was civil rights, poverty, or the ultimate dilemma of peace and war, Kennedy's actions began to provide manifestations of creative vision where before there had only been words. Now, with the benefit of hindsight and the scholarship of numerous historians, it may be possible to separate the superficial from the real, and to ask whether there was, in this hero of a thousand days, a core identity that gave coherence to the array of images associated with Camelot.

Depending on one's perspective, the Kennedys were either the most loyal, affectionate family in Boston, dedicated to public service; or they were one of the most dysfunctional group of individuals ever assembled, committed to unhealthy competition, lack of respect for women, suppression of truth about family relationships, and self-aggrandizing manipulation. Supportive of the first view are the legendary closeness of the Kennedys and the fact that four of the nine siblings held high public office. Supportive of the second view are the womanizing of so many Kennedy men, Joe Kennedy's treatment of his wife Rose, and the efforts of both parents to hide their daughter Rosemary's mental retardation and her secret lobotomy operation and institutionalization. In reality, both views were correct, and the future president spent his early childhood in the midst of these powerful and contradictory competing forces.

Joseph P. Kennedy, the patriarch of the clan, trusted almost no one except his immediate family. Consumed by ambition, he dedicated his life to proving, by whatever means necessary, that an Irish-American family was every bit as good as any WASP family whose forebears arrived on the *Mayflower*. Kennedy made his fortune by wheeling and dealing his way through the shipping industry, manipulating the stock market to drive up the price of stocks he owned and then dumping them, monopolizing the Scotch whiskey trade, and eventually becoming a force in the motion picture industry. "For the Kennedys," he told his friend Arthur Krock, "it is the shithouse or the castle—nothing in between." Turned down for membership in a prestigious club as an undergraduate at Harvard, Kennedy determined to become part of America's political and economic elite. He parlayed his business successes into an appointment as the head of the Securities and Exchange Commission in Franklin Roosevelt's administration, and then was awarded the diplomatic plum of being named ambassador to Great Britain. He even aspired to be president. Yet throughout he was driven by the fear of not belonging. "When," his wife Rose once asked a friend, "are the nice people of Boston going to accept us?"

Joe Kennedy was a brazen philanderer, flaunting his relationships with many women, including the starlet Gloria Swanson and the socialite Clare Booth Luce. Swanson described her initial sexual encounter with Kennedy as almost a rape. "He was like a roped horse, rough, arduous, racing to be free." He took Swanson home to meet his wife and children, and then on a trip to Europe along with Rose. "Was [Rose] a fool," Swanson wondered, "or a saint? Or just a better actress than I was?" The children could not help being aware of the affair, and, more generally, of their father's nonstop extramarital adventures. He even made advances to some of his daughters' friends.

By contrast, Rose Kennedy appeared committed to living a life as close to the Roman Catholic ideal as possible. The daughter of Boston's mayor, she attended a church school, and her parents sent her to a convent rather than to Wellesley College, where she wanted to go. Conceiving and bearing children appeared to be her primary responsibility. Managing her ever growing household through their multiple family moves provided her second major task. Yet Kennedy's mothering technique was cold and distant. She rarely touched her children or kissed them. Indeed, she often ignored them. Leaving behind extensive written instructions for how they should be treated and what they should do, on seventeen different occasions when her children were young, Rose took ocean trips to Europe which lasted six to eight weeks. It was Joe, not Rose, who visited Jack at prep school. Speculating on Jack's relationship with his mother, Betty Spalding, one of Kennedy's few female confidantes, declared: "Jack hated physical touching . . . which I assume must go back to his mother . . . I never saw her with her arms up, outstretched . . . I doubt if she ever rumpled the kid's hair in his whole life." Spalding added: "What is touch? It must come from some deeper maternal security—arms, warmth, kisses, hugs."

The Kennedy home, therefore, was a household of many demands, enormous contradictions, and oftentimes very little affection or emotional support. Joe was the dominant presence, injecting competition into every aspect of family life. Dinnertime conversations were run like seminars, each of the children being quizzed on public affairs and expected to make significant contributions to dinner-table debate. Athletic contests were a family trope, with touch football battles becoming legendary. Everyone, one associate recalled, was expected to "show our guts, fall on your face now and then, smash into the house once in a while." Those who did not participate were suspect. Yet both Joe and Rose were often absent, Rose perhaps even more than Joe, and despite the motif of togetherness, trust, warmth, and honesty were profoundly missing.

John Fitzgerald Kennedy—Jack—was the second-oldest of nine children. His brother Joe Jr., two years older, aspired to emulate their father, exhibiting the same ambition, competitiveness, and bravado. He seemed to accept without question the manners and morals that governed the family. Bright, keenly athletic, energetic, Joe Jr. occasionally tried to intimidate Jack even while looking after him as a brother. Joe did his father's bidding, seemingly without question. The family ambition for him was that he become president of the United States and the richest, most powerful Catholic in the country. Setting out to achieve these goals, Joe Jr. went to Choate, an elite prep school, and to Harvard, where he gained a letter in football, and then—with the outbreak of World War II—into the army air force.

Jack was a different story. He too emulated the masculine mystique of his father, engaging throughout his life in multiple affairs with women, seeming not to care what impact his behavior had on others (including, eventually, his wife). He also could be cold and calculating in advancing his own interests. But he was more complicated than Joe Jr., more intellectual, more questioning, less satisfied with simply imbibing the family's values.

Jack spent much of his childhood sick in bed, often requiring hospitalization. As his brother Robert later noted, "at least one half of the days that [Jack] spent on this earth were days of intense physical pain." He almost died from scarlet fever as a child, at one point was diagnosed as having leukemia, and repeatedly struggled to finish a normal school year without extensive diagnostic tests. In addition, his back was a chronic problem. As a result, Jack spent much more time reading than his brothers and sisters did and learned to love the life of the mind. Although he often got up out of a sickbed to play touch football, the experience of being physically fragile enabled Jack to develop more nuanced responses to the world around him. Literature and history gave him an alternative frame of reference to the one-upmanship of family competition, freeing him to think larger, more skeptical thoughts.

Partly as a consequence of his illnesses, Jack Kennedy developed a certain remoteness. He looked from the margins inward, refusing to become engaged, emotionally attached, or committed to particular causes. His was a self-protective isolation, allowing him to move in and out of family affairs as he saw fit. Examining the world from the periphery, he developed a wry sense of humor, a sharp wit, and a sense of skeptical irony that helped make his attitude toward himself, as well as toward others, one of detached and bemused analysis. Throughout his prep school years, first at Canterbury, then at Choate, his intelligence was evident. He was "a complete individualist in theory and practice" according to one of his Choate instructors, so that "the ordinary appeals of group spirit and social consciousness . . . [had] no effect." One of his roommates, Charlie Houghton, characterized Jack's intellect as "razor sharp" and said he was "a very stimulating person to live with, very argumentative in a nice way. He questioned everything. I think the depth of his intellectual curiosity was shown in that he challenged anything you said." Another friend offered a similar characterization: "[Jack] was a person who would ask questions of you, who would challenge your assumptions . . . you got the impression that here was a mind that was learning from other people . . . The questioning was never ruthless, . . . but he wanted to know what you knew . . . He was decidedly not a superficial person."

Kennedy's intellectual independence went hand in hand with a willingness to challenge authority, a rebelliousness largely unthinkable for Joe Jr., or later for Bobby. He created a club at Choate called the "muckers" dedicated to tearing down everything a traditional elitist prep school exemplified. One of his teachers called the club "a colossally selfish, pleasure-loving, unperceptive group—in general opposed to the hard working, solid people in the school." So outrageous was the behavior of the "muckers" that it resulted in a confrontation between the headmaster and Jack, with Joe Kennedy present.

The same rebelliousness surfaced in Jack's sense of humor. His close friend Lem Billings recalled: "I've never known anyone in my life with such a wonderful [capacity] to make one laugh and have a good time . . . boys who are as full of fun and joie de vivre as he was can't help but irritate teachers." His humor was honed during his frequent illnesses, when making jokes may have been the only way he could tolerate all the medical care he was receiving. "They gave me five enemas until I was white as snow inside," he wrote, "then surrounded by nurses, the doctor first stuck his finger up my ass. He wiggled it suggestively and I rolled them in the aisles by saying 'you have a good motion.'" In his teen years, his letters both to and from his closest friends were packed with sexual and scatological references.

Sex, of course, was another adolescent preoccupation. All Jack wanted to do, Billings remembered, was go after girls. He wrote to his friends about women he had slept with, trivializing all but the sense of conquest. One missive was entitled "Travels in a Mexican Whorehouse with Your Roomie." Almost every trip away from Choate involved some sexual escapade.

Jack was the pivot around which a community of friends revolved. He animated people, and he used his sparkling wit to create a band of young men who shared an attraction to independence, women, and camaraderie. Yet at the heart of his personality, as Billings saw it, was a lack of emotional engagement or commitment. In thirty-two years Billings never saw Kennedy shed a tear. "Anytime you were with Jack Kennedy you would laugh," Billings said, but "he was never emotional . . . and never showed any great affection for anybody." Jack was a paradox—

funny, loyal, and warm, but also detached, skeptical, and always observing from the outside.

Kennedy's college years further honed his intellectual sharpness, while bringing him for the first time face to face with the intrigue and subtlety of foreign affairs. He initially attended Princeton, but subsequently, after another long hospitalization, dropped out and transferred to Harvard. On a trip to Europe in 1937 with Lem Billings, he explored cathedrals and the battlefields of the Spanish civil war, and indulged his appetite for digging deep into cultural and political questions. "He wanted experience to be intense," Joseph Alsop reflected about that summer. "What I'm really talking about is a matter of style, intellectual style, a viewpoint of what you care about most." Kennedy's diary entries reflected the rapid maturing of his sense of world affairs. "Isn't a chance of war less as Britain gets stronger?" he asked. "Or is a country like Italy liable to go to war when economic discontent is rife?" At Harvard he took courses on fascism, communism, and imperialism, and when he returned to Europe in the summer of 1939, he focused on the ways people under different regimes were being mobilized for war.

Throughout this period Jack's father was ambassador to the Court of St. James. Joseph Kennedy supported a policy of appeasement toward Nazi Germany. He argued that Britain should strike an economic deal with Germany, and he consistently lobbied Prime Minister Neville Chamberlain and other cabinet members against military confrontation. Kennedy went so far as to draft a speech for delivery in Scotland in which he planned to declare: "For the life of me, I cannot see anything involved which could be remotely considered worth shedding blood for." Not surprisingly, the U.S. state department ordered him not to give the speech.

◆ ◆ ◆

Because of his first-hand experience of these tensions, Jack Kennedy chose to write a senior thesis entitled "Why England Slept." Using his father's access to documents as a source of information, Kennedy argued that the British had failed to rally as a democracy to the challenge of fascism. He traced Britain's reluctance to fight to the pacifist experience of the 1920s and the need to win elections. From the point of view of his professors, the thesis was solid but not distinguished. Awarding it a cum laude grade, one professor commented: "Fundamental premise never analyzed. Much too long, wordy, repetitious." Harold Laski of the London School of Economics called it a work of "a lad with brains, [but] it is very immature, it has no real structure, and draws almost totally on the surface of things. In a good university, half a hundred seniors do books like this as part of their normal work." But Jack Kennedy was not a "normal" student, and his father was intent on securing publication of the thesis. With his friend Arthur Krock, a correspondent for the *New York Times,* as a chief resource, the elder Kennedy had the thesis edited thoroughly, and Krock's literary agent found a publisher. It was not the first or the last time that Jack Kennedy would succeed because of his father's influence, and perhaps only his capacity for self-deprecation prevented him from taking seriously the assumption that anything he wanted in the world could be his.

In fact, Jack's intellectual detachment and skepticism were what enabled him to cope with the tensions in his relationship with his parents. He often talked with friends about his father's infidelities, and how Joe would lavish expensive presents on Rose as a way of making her feel better. One associate said: "It seemed to me that his father's obvious rather low opinion of his wife in the way he treated her . . . rubbed off on Jack. He wasn't mean or anything about his mother, but I think that the denigration, that came from the father, rubbed off on the son." While dutiful to his mother, Jack had little patience for her strong religiosity. Sometimes, his impatience and anger with his mother became manifest, as when he wrote to her from prep school making fun of the long letters she sent to the family. "I'm saving them to publish—that style of yours will net us millions," he said acerbically. "With all this talk about inflation, when I think of your potential earning power—with you dictating and Mrs. Walker [Rose's secretary] beating it out on that machine—it's enough to make a man get down on his knees and thank God for the Dorchester High Latin School which gave you that very sound grammatical basis which shines through every slightly mixed metaphor and each somewhat split infinitive."

Jack's relationship with his father was equally complicated. Joe Kennedy was relieved of his ambassadorial position in London because of his disagreement with Roosevelt's policy of support for British confrontation of Hitler; more and more, Jack seemed to agree with the president rather than his father. When his father asked him to draft an article defending the senior Kennedy's position on appeasement, Jack instead wrote a piece arguing that the danger of not giving aid to Britain was far greater than the danger of war. Nigel Hamilton, one of Kennedy's biographers, considers this decision to oppose his father directly "the most crucial and influential [moment] of John F. Kennedy's early life."

If Jack broke with his father in politics, however, he emulated his father's attitude toward women and sexuality. With his quick wit, his charm, his humor, and his good looks, Jack entranced women. One woman said he was "unbelievably handsome" with a "remarkable animal pull." He used these advantages to accomplish a series of sexual conquests. "Expect to cut one out of the herd and brand her shortly," he wrote from California to a friend, "but I'm taking it very slow as do not want to be known as the beast of the East." Echoing what Betty Spalding called his hatred of physical touch, one woman he was involved with noted that Jack "didn't enjoy cuddling" after making love, but he did "like to talk and had a wonderful sense of humor—he loved to laugh." According to Lem Billings, Kennedy "knew he was using women to prove his masculinity, and sometimes it depressed him. I think he wanted to believe in love and faithfulness and all that but what he had seen at home didn't give him much hope. So he sort of bumped along."

Except for one time. When Jack met Inga Arvad, a reporter working in Washington, he opened up to a woman in a manner he had never come close to before. Danish by birth, Arvad had spent much of her early life in Europe. Kennedy met her when he was in Washington to join the Naval Intelligence Service. He had used his father's connections to get accepted into the armed services during the war, notwithstanding his physical disabilities. A naval intelligence report described him as "an exceptionally brilliant student who has unusual qualities and a definite future in whatever he undertakes. Being son of a prominent father has not in the least affected [him]. He is a clean, ambitious, and likeable young American—anxious to make his own way in life . . . at no time in [our] investigation was there any trace or evidence of moral turpitude, gambling, drinking to excess, or philandering." In Washington Jack dated a number of women, sometimes double dating with his sister Kathleen, who was, like him, seeking to establish her independence from their parents. On one such double date, he met Inga Arvad.

Inga, who was married but separated from her husband, found Jack mesmerizing. "When he walked into a room," she wrote, "you knew he was there, not pushing, not domineering, but exuding animal magnetism." She told their friend John White: "Jack knows what he wants. He's not confused about motives and those things. I find that refreshing. I like it—and furthermore, I like him." Jack reciprocated. What enchanted him, beyond sex, John White said, was that "she was totally woman. She wasn't handsome, she was gorgeous. Luscious, luscious is the word." Inga had a European charm, a worldliness, that made Jack start to think, perhaps for the first time, of a serious relationship with a woman.

Even as the relationship intensified, however, both Joe Kennedy and the FBI were watching. Federal officials, concerned that Arvad might be a Nazi agent (she had once been photographed sitting with Adolf Hitler at a sporting event), followed all of her activities. Joe Kennedy, meanwhile, hired a detective to watch the couple, and persuaded the columnist Walter Winchell to announce in his column on January 12, 1942, that "Pa Kennedy no like" the relationship. Within twenty-four hours the navy transferred Jack from Washington to Charleston, South Carolina. He later told a reporter: "They shagged my ass down to South Carolina because I was going around with this Scandinavian blonde, and they thought she was a spy."

But the transfer did not end the affair. On repeated occasions, Inga visited Charleston, or Jack went to Washington. Once she wrote about leaving him behind at the train station in Charleston: "The further the train pulled away, the less visible was the young handsome Boston Bean . . . there was the good old feeling of stinging eyes and a nasty pull at the heart strings which always show us when too great a distance is put between us." If she could ever indulge her fantasy to go west and write and read books, she told Jack, "I would make sure I had your baby along with me." FBI tape recordings of one of their weekends together disclosed that they discussed in detail the possibility of her going to Reno for a divorce so they could marry. One of Jack's sister's friends commented that most of Jack's girlfriends were cheerleader types, but "this was a very different relationship."

The two clearly shared something special. Nigel Hamilton concludes: "No woman in his life would ever come close to Inga's mix of licentiousness and wit, talent for gossip, and adventurous ambition." Only with Inga did Jack share an "admission of profound love." They seemed to trust each other, and to speak with both candor and mutual respect. Inga wrote in the spring of 1942: "As I told you yesterday, I [understand] you pretty well, and still I like you. You know, Jack, that is a hell of a compliment, because anyone as brainy and Irish-shrewd as you can't be quite like a white dove. But by golly you have a strong hand, one I like to shake, and it ain't bad looking into that steady left twinkling eye either. You will get there . . . you have more [going for you] than even your ancestors and yet you haven't lost the tough hide of the Irish potatoes. Put a match to that smoldering ambition and you will go like a wildfire." This might not mean being together on "the ranch out west," she concluded, "but it is the unequalled highway to the White House."

And then it ended—or at least appeared to. Inga had sensed the power of Jack's father to affect their future. "Big Joe," she wrote, "has a stronger hand than I." Joe telephoned Jack to tell him the FBI had a complete file on his relationship with Inga, and that it was imperative that he break it off. Inga understood.

"You belong so wholeheartedly to the Kennedy clan," she wrote, "and I don't want you to ever get into an argument with your father on account of me." But she was devastated. For a brief few months, she told Jack, the birds had sung and she had refused to listen to reason. "It took me the FBI, the U.S. Navy, nasty gossip, envy, hatred and Big Joe before the birds stopped [singing]. In the beginning I was just stunned darling [when you broke it off]. Then I slowly woke up. Hard to start and realize that you are a living corpse."

In the meantime, Joe pulled more strings to get Jack an assignment on a patrol torpedo (PT) boat in the Pacific. One more time, the medical records were suppressed, and in April 1943 Kennedy took command of a vessel that, by most accounts, was a floating suicide mission. PT boats were supposed to get within five hundred yards of enemy ships, barges, or shore batteries and fire their torpedoes, then zip away without themselves being destroyed. The entire enterprise was fraught with risk for the PT boat crews.

Following orders, the newly minted Lieutenant Kennedy took *PT 109* out into the middle of the Blackett Straits off the Solomon Islands one night when a convoy of Japanese warships was coming through. A Japanese destroyer, the *Amagiri,* came speeding toward Kennedy's boat and split it in two. Since no other PT boats remained in the area, Kennedy was left alone with his surviving crewmen. His heroism on that occasion has become legendary, with justification. Refusing to give up, he saved a wounded comrade by gripping the man's life preserver rope in his teeth and swimming to an island. He also mobilized the remainder of his crew to remain calm and follow him. For days thereafter, he swam to other islands until finally he was able to get a message to naval headquarters about where he and his crew were stranded.

It was an extraordinary adventure, one that displayed tenacity, courage, and powerful leadership. It also caused serious physical injury. Kennedy's back was severely hurt, and all his other physical weaknesses were exacerbated. He entered into a lengthy period of rehabilitation, with months in the hospital. "There was a hole in his back that never closed up after the operation he had during the war," a friend noted. "You could look into it and see the metal plate that had been put into his spine." Enduring constant pain, Kennedy went through test after test. The doctors finally concluded that he had Addison's disease, a deficiency in the supply of adrenal hormones that can be treated only by massive daily doses of cortisone. At the time the disease was believed to be terminal, and Jack told a friend: "I'll probably last until I'm 45." For the rest of his life, Kennedy would have to take medication, oral or injected, every day to keep the disease under control.

❖ ❖ ❖

His combat experience in the Pacific strongly influenced Kennedy's subsequent views on war and violence. The sinking of *PT 109* caused him to question the wisdom of the military and its attitudes. He understood the riskiness of the PT missions, and he resented the navy's inadequate efforts to send rescue teams to search for survivors. Looking back at the event, he said: "How do we ever win wars anyway? You know the military always screws up everything."

Kennedy's *PT 109* experience inspired some of the most revealing and emotional letters of his life. Earlier he had resumed correspondence with Inga, telling her he needed to know how she felt about him "so I will know if this whole thing is worth fighting for." He also told her: "A number of my illusions have been shattered, but you are one I still have, although I don't believe illusions is exactly the word I mean." Now he shared with her his deepest reflections about war, peace, and life. "We get so used to talking about billions of dollars and millions of soldiers," he wrote, "that thousands of casualties sound like drops in the bucket. But if those thousands want to live as much as the ten that I saw, the people deciding the whys and wherefores had better make mighty sure all this effort is headed for some definite goal, and that when we reach that goal we may say it was worth it, for if it isn't the whole thing will turn to ashes." Reflecting on the comrade whose life he had saved, he mourned his compatriots who had failed to survive. The experience made him question the rationale for war: "This thing is so stupid that while it has a sickening fascination for some of us, myself included, I want to leave it far behind me when I go."

He also acknowledged that Inga was special to him: "You are the only person I'd say [this] to anyway. As a matter of fact, knowing you has been the brightest point in an extremely bright twenty-six years." Whatever else Jack Kennedy's relationship with Inga Arvad signified, it evoked in him remarkable qualities of engagement, emotion, and thoughtfulness, and a level of commitment that was new in his life. The relationship was a pivotal moment of self-discovery in his personal history.

◆　◆　◆

The Kennedy story took a dramatic turn upon the young veteran's return to the United States. Celebrated as a hero, he for the first time outshone even his handsome and boisterous older brother. "It was written all over the sky," a fellow officer said, "that he was going to be something big. He just had that charisma." Then the popular author John Hersey chronicled Jack's heroic exploits in a book about *PT 109* that was serialized in the *New Yorker* and the *Reader's Digest*. However cynical Kennedy may have been about the military, and however ironic and skeptical his portrayal of his own role, he quickly had come to epitomize the dash and daring of a traditional American military hero.

Meanwhile, his older brother—the one whom Joseph Kennedy Sr. had always expected to become president of the United States —was a navy pilot based in England, flying bombing missions across the English Channel. After Joe Jr. had flown enough missions to finish his tour of duty, he volunteered to stay on with his squadron. Indeed, he offered to pilot a highly dangerous flight on a secret mission. He was to fly a plane packed with explosives to a designated position, then bail out over England, with the plane set to be guided by remote control to its target in France. Yet, as subsequent research has shown, British radar was not told about the mission and remained active instead of being turned off. In all likelihood the radar sent out electrical waves that caused the bombs on Kennedy's plane to explode in midair. He died immediately. Whatever Joe Jr.'s reasons for undertaking such a risky mission—and some have speculated that he was jealous of Jack's celebrated heroism—the son destined to realize his father's dreams was now gone.

The news devastated the Kennedy family. In typical fashion, Joe Sr. told the children about Joe Jr.'s death and then urged them to continue about their daily routines. No one had been more like his father than Joe Jr.: arrogant, ambitious, single-minded, and intent on fulfilling his destiny. His loss crushed the Kennedy clan, puncturing their dreams of glory.

Joe Sr. now turned to his second son to carry out those same dreams. "I can feel Pappy's eyes on the back of my neck," Jack told a navy friend. "It was like being drafted. My father wanted his elder son in politics. 'Wanted' isn't the right word. He demanded it. You know my father."

Yet the interpretation of Jack Kennedy as a reluctant political warrior obscures the evidence of his own ambition. He and Inga had often talked about his own potential candidacy for the White House. His college classmates, friends, and naval comrades had detected a political ambition that would, in all likelihood, have surfaced no matter what happened to Joe. For example, Lem Billings noted: "A lot of people say that if Joe hadn't died that Jack might never had gone into politics. I don't believe this. Nothing would have kept Jack out of politics. I think this is what he had in him, and this would have come out, no matter what."

Jack's father wasted no time in generating a congressional candidacy for his son. He made a financial arrangement with James Michael Curley, a former mayor of Boston who was now a congressman, agreeing to pay Curley's personal debts if he would not run for reelection and promising to support him in a new run for the Boston mayoralty. With Curley's congressional seat vacated, Jack joined nearly a dozen other candidates in seeking election from the eleventh district, which included parts of Boston, Somerville, and Cambridge. Unaccustomed to campaigning, he nevertheless announced his candidacy in eloquent rhetoric that anticipated the speeches he would make more than a decade later on the way to the presidency. The United States and the world, he told his future constituents, stood at a crossroads: "What we do now will shape the history of civilization for many years to come." With a coterie of Irish pols at his side, Kennedy then set out to win over the voters, spending days and nights climbing tenement staircases to meet his prospective constituents. Jack's father later said of the election: "With the money I spent, I could have elected my chauffeur." And in fact the family's money made a difference. But so did the personality and appeal of Jack Kennedy. He was, according to a local newspaper, "the only candidate with an effective personal machine [which] was built overnight and . . . based on voters under the age of 35." Already John F. Kennedy was showing the qualities that would carry him beyond his six years in the House of Representatives to the Senate and then to the White House.

The most distinctive aspect of Kennedy's congressional record was his sophisticated approach to foreign relations. While for the most part embracing the traditional anticommunism of the Cold War, he showed a surprising sensitivity to the rising aspirations of developing nations. Kennedy was particularly prophetic in his approach toward Southeast Asia. There, he declared, "The fires of nationalism . . . now ablaze, [must] be heeded lest America fall into the trap of being aligned with colonialist oppression." Throughout the developing world, he said, there were "civilizations striving to be born." Nowhere did his warnings hold more relevance than in Indochina: "No amount of American military assistance," he told the Senate in 1954, "[can] conquer an enemy which is everywhere and at the same time nowhere, 'an enemy of the people' which has the sympathy and the covert support of the people." And: "To pour money, materiel, and men into the jungles of Indochina without at least a remote prospect of victory would be dangerously futile and self-destructive." Almost no other members of Congress displayed the same awareness of forces that were rapidly promising to take over the world.

On domestic issues, in contrast, Kennedy was moderate and mainstream. While supporting the bread-and-butter concerns of his working-class constituency—increased minimum wage, better veterans' benefits, public housing, organized labor—he shied away from bold social programs. "I'm not a liberal at all," he told one interviewer. Instead of fraternizing with progressives in the House or the Senate, he was most often seen around conservative southerners like Richard Russell of Georgia or John Rankin of Mississippi.

In 1952 Kennedy succeeded in the next stage of his quest for national leadership, defeating Henry Cabot Lodge for a seat in the U.S. Senate. Once again moderation characterized his politics. His lack of strong liberalism was evident in his ambivalence toward McCarthyism. Joseph Kennedy Sr. strongly supported McCarthy. Jack Kennedy liked him personally and enjoyed socializing with him. Jack's younger brother Robert went to work for McCarthy. Although the future president regretted McCarthy's excesses, he refused to condemn McCarthy's politics, and when the Senate voted to censure the junior senator from Wisconsin, Kennedy—who was hospitalized at the time with his recurrent back trouble—issued no statement, keeping his views to himself.

Kennedy's rise to national visibility continued. One of the most eligible bachelors in the capital, he courted a glamorous young newspaper photographer named Jacqueline Bouvier. Stylishly dressed, educated at the best private schools, and belonging to a prominent family from the elite enclave of Newport, Rhode Island, Bouvier seemed the perfect match for Kennedy. Married in 1953, the couple soon appeared on cover stories of national magazines and were featured on network television.

Shortly after the wedding, Jack Kennedy's physical ailments recurred. While recovering from back surgery, he wrote *Profiles in Courage*, a book that portrayed the moral crises a phalanx of U.S.

senators had faced over the history of the Republic. The book, published in 1956, won a Pulitzer Prize. In fact, its publication was a repeat of Kennedy's experience with his Harvard thesis. Although the concept was his, and many of the perspectives in the book reflected his contribution, most of the research and writing was done by Ted Sorenson, his speechwriter, and Jules Davids, a professor of Jacqueline Kennedy's at George Washington University. Kennedy immersed himself in reading for the project and contributed a number of dictabelt recordings of notes, but a claim that he had written the book, the historian Herbert Parmet concluded, would be as "suspect as installing a Chevrolet engine in a Cadillac." Nevertheless the book won plaudits and enhanced Kennedy's reputation as an unusual kind of politician.

Kennedy gained national attention at the 1956 Democratic convention, with his speech nominating Adlai Stevenson for president. In response to the enthusiasm Kennedy's speech engendered, Stevenson opened the vice presidential nomination to all comers, and Kennedy put into place, almost overnight, a strikingly attractive campaign, arguing that placing a Roman Catholic on the national ticket would have a positive impact. Although Kennedy was narrowly defeated on the second ballot, in fact he was the real winner. As one columnist observed: "His was the one new face . . . His charisma, his dignity, his intellectuality, and in the end his gracious sportsmanship . . . are undoubtedly what those delegates would remember." For a person who had put so few markers on the political landscape in terms of policy, Jack Kennedy had come a long way. "You know," he told his personal aide Dave Powers, "if we work like hell the next four years, we will pick up all the marbles."

His prediction was accurate. With his brother Robert running a tight campaign, mobilizing city bosses like Chicago's Richard Daley and governors like Pennsylvania's David Lawrence, Kennedy put together a juggernaut that was hugely successful in the Democratic primaries in states from New Hampshire to West Virginia, rolling over announced opponents like Hubert Humphrey. Kennedy's liberal credentials were still in question, and he never persuaded people like Eleanor Roosevelt to be enthusiasts—largely because of his tepid stand on McCarthy. But by wooing labor leaders such as Walter Reuther and bringing on board intellectuals like Arthur Schlesinger Jr., he made significant inroads into left-of-center constituencies in the party. By the time of the Democratic convention in Los Angeles, Kennedy was in control, notwithstanding a dramatic last-minute wave of support for Adlai Stevenson.

What was less clear was what Kennedy stood for. Although his acceptance speech at the convention eloquently invoked the image of America standing on the edge of a "new frontier," Kennedy's rhetoric far exceeded his substantive programs. Over and over again he insisted that "we can do better," that the American economy was in the doldrums, that there was a missile gap with the Soviet Union, and that the country faced a crisis of credibility and confidence unparalleled in its history. In his televised debates with Richard Nixon, the Republican nominee, Kennedy demonstrated an assertiveness and mastery of facts that buttressed his case with the American people. Yet there were few specifics. In the end, his campaign was based more on image and gestures than on substance. The young Garrison Keillor, then a student at the University of Minnesota, later recalled the widespread impression that Kennedy was a new kind of candidate: "He had more keys on his piano. He had black keys and they didn't. There was playfulness in him; . . . he quoted Dante . . .

[and] made you believe that at one time in his life he'd sat down and read the *Inferno*." But his vision for the future remained opaque. In fact, had Kennedy not made the decision to phone Mrs. Martin Luther King Jr. when her husband was thrown into jail—a gesture that galvanized a previously uncommitted black community—he might not have won at all. Kennedy's overture to Coretta Scott King did more to swing African-American votes than any specific proposals he put forward on civil rights, and the black vote proved decisive to Kennedy's narrow victory.

If there were two attributes that most clearly identified the Kennedy approach as he prepared to take office in 1961, they were his obsessions with style and with foreign policy. As the historian and journalist Richard Reeves has noted: "[Kennedy] had little ideology beyond anti-communism and faith in active, pragmatic government . . . what he had was an attitude, a way of taking on the world, substituting intelligence for ideas or idealism, questions for answers." In Kennedy's view, the key to good government was putting the right people in the right places at the right times. Staff meetings, extensive consultation, hierarchy, and delegation of responsibilities did not matter. What counted was getting the best minds together under the leadership of the president himself. While Eisenhower had surrounded himself with corporate executives, Kennedy recruited academics, policy wonks, and young technocrats, with himself at the hub of the entire operation. "He wanted all the lines to lead to the White House," noted Hugh Sidey, a correspondent for *Time* magazine. "He wanted to be the single nerve center." Spontaneous, informal huddles took the place of well-prepared staff meetings. The British journalist Henry Fairlie described the administration's working style this way: "The Kennedy team lived on the move, calling signals to each other in the thick of the action . . . like basketball players developing plays while the game moved on."

It was an era, Robert Kennedy later recalled, "when we thought we were succeeding because of all the stories of how hard everybody was working." Pentagon staff members would feel the secretary of defense's car to determine by its temperature how many hours he had already been at work when they arrived. The energy and sense of urgency were intense. The Kennedy team, one correspondent wrote, "aspire to greatness, not just occasionally, but all the time . . . as the sun rose over the farthermost shores of Cathay and began its slow process across the heavens, it was [always] one minute to midnight somewhere, and something would happen; and . . . all over Washington, men would rise early to answer the bidding to crisis and to greatness."

The mood was one of exhilaration. "Washington seemed engaged in a collective effort," Arthur Schlesinger Jr. observed, "to make itself brighter, gayer, more intellectual, more resolute. It was a golden interlude." The wife of Kennedy's aide Walt Rostow said she had never seen her husband "more cheerful or effective. You're an odd lot. You are not politicians or intellectuals, you are the junior officers of the Second World War come to responsibility." The new generation of Americans, headed by the former PT boat commander, seemed always in a hurry, always ready for the next crisis. It was a team, in the words of the commentator Joseph Kraft, that "dazzled the nation by intellectual brilliance and social swank."

What seemed lacking was vision. James Reston of the *New York Times* wrote of asking Kennedy what he hoped to achieve by the end of his presidency: "Kennedy looked at me as if I was a dreaming child. I tried again: Do you not feel the need of some goal to help guide the day to day decisions and priorities? Again, a ghastly pause." Whatever their brilliance, and however refined their sophistication and style, those in charge of the New Frontier seemed to have little sense of where they wanted to go.

In fact, the only consistent focus in the early years of the Kennedy administration was the need to confront the Soviet Union and devise a strategy to win the Cold War. On domestic affairs, Kennedy was very much a part of what the British journalist Godfrey Hodgson has called the "liberal consensus"—a belief that capitalism was a superb economic system, that there were no fundamental problems in American society, that improvement could take place through incremental reforms rather than structural changes, and that rapid economic growth was the best means of improving people's lot. "A rising tide lifts all boats," Kennedy said: an economic boom would take care of most domestic inequities. Foreign policy, in Kennedy's view, offered a far greater challenge, particularly given the "great revolutionary transformations" that were occurring around the globe. "To be an American in the next decade," the candidate for president said in September 1960, "will be a hazardous experience. We will live on the edge of danger." The issue, he declared, was "the preservation of civilization": "The world cannot exist half slave and half free." It was the responsibility of the United States "to be the chief defender of freedom at a time when freedom is under attack all over the globe."

Nothing better illustrated Kennedy's priorities than his inaugural address. It was brilliantly written and delivered, and Kennedy used each sentence to evoke the conclusion that America was at a point of crisis. Despite a burgeoning civil rights movement that was challenging America at its domestic core, the new president made only one oblique reference to events at home. Instead, his message to America was that the issue before his countrymen was the survival of freedom in the world. "Let every nation know," he said, ". . . that we shall pay any price, bear any burden, bear any hardship, support any friend, oppose any foe, in order to assure the survival and the success of liberty." His was a call to action, with a new generation of Americans in command and prepared to take on the world.

As is now well known, two other features of Kennedy's life persisted during his thousand days in office. The first was his insatiable appetite for extramarital sexual encounters. Those around him were complicit in making such encounters possible—his secretary, cabinet members, journalists, even his wife, Jacqueline, who made occasional barbed comments about his philandering but never forced the issue. Kennedy once told the British prime minister, Harold Macmillan: "If I don't have a woman for three days, I get terrible headaches." He seems not to have had a headache problem. On inauguration night, he slipped off with a Hollywood starlet during an inaugural party. He had sexual relationships with two staff members, with his wife's press secretary, with a woman rumored to be an East German spy, with a nineteen-year-old White House intern, and—until J. Edgar Hoover put a stop to it—with Judith Exner, who was also involved with the Mafia boss Sam Giancana. At no point did the press reveal any of these encounters, although gossip about the president's sex life was rife.

The second feature of Kennedy's life that persisted in secret was his reliance on extraordinary levels of medication. His physicians injected him with mixtures of amphetamines, vitamins, and painkillers. The treatment for his Addison's disease involved pellets implanted in his thighs, regular cortisone injections, and a variety of pills. The medications often had an impact on his mood. Sometimes a cortisone rush created a feeling that almost anything was possible. Nevertheless, Robert Dallek, the preeminent biographer of Kennedy, who has had greater access to the medical records than anyone else, concludes that at no point was his performance as president affected by the drugs he was taking. But it is hard to disagree with Richard Reeves's remark that "in a lifetime of medical torment, Kennedy was more promiscuous with physicians and drugs than he was with women."

Fortunately, Dallek's conclusion seems corroborated by the president's behavior during foreign policy crises. The first disaster Kennedy faced was the Bay of Pigs fiasco, the abortive invasion of Cuba by anticommunist rebels. During the presidential campaign Kennedy had lambasted Richard Nixon and the Republicans for lacking a plan to oust Fidel Castro from Cuba— a country whose revolution in 1959 had brought the first communist regime to the western hemisphere. Now he discovered not only that a plan existed but that he was expected to implement it.

There are three views of the Bay of Pigs. The first holds that under no circumstances could the invasion have succeeded because it was based upon erroneous premises. A fighting force of 1,500 guerrillas had no chance of success, according to Maxwell Taylor's ex post facto review of the invasion plans, and even a force of 15,000 might not have succeeded given the lack of popular insurgency against Castro on the island. The second view holds that Kennedy was largely a hostage to the Eisenhower administration's plan and that any deviation from it would have been political suicide. The third view puts more of the blame on Kennedy himself, critiquing his failure to go through military channels, his refusal to consult Pentagon experts, and his infatuation with the daring counterinsurgency plans of Richard Bissell

of the Central Intelligence Agency. According to this third perspective, Kennedy became enthralled with the notion of striking
quickly and effectively. Garry Wills has noted: "It was a military
operation run without the military's control . . . The truth is
that Kennedy went ahead with the Cuban action, not to complete what he inherited from Eisenhower, but to mark his difference from Eisenhower . . . In all of this, he was the prisoner of his
own rhetoric."

All three of these perspectives have merit. From the beginning
Kennedy was fascinated by counterinsurgency, and with the
imaginative visions of people like Bissell and Edward Lansdale,
who helped to develop the notion of counter-guerrilla warfare
and started the Green Berets. Thus Kennedy saw a night landing
by an exile army as a dramatic example of bold new military tactics. At the same time, he clearly felt strong political pressure to
proceed with an operation that his four-star predecessor had ostensibly supported. What remains most impressive is the fact
that Kennedy resolutely refused to send American troops into
action once he faced the abundant evidence that the Bay of Pigs
invasion was failing. Drawing on his previous experience of mis-
trusting the advice of military officers, he pulled back to avoid
making even worse what he realized had been a terrible mistake.

The Bay of Pigs failure had serious repercussions. Kennedy
revealed an inclination to scapegoat members of his administration who had been skeptical about the plan. Perhaps more
important, the debacle encouraged the Soviet premier, Nikita
Khrushchev, to believe that Kennedy was too immature and too
insecure to be an effective foe. Although the ultimate importance of the Bay of Pigs rested in its reinforcement of Kennedy's
caution about reckless military action, it also helped precipitate
the Berlin crisis of the summer of 1961, Khrushchev's decision to

place offensive missiles in Cuba, which led to the missile crisis of 1962, and Kennedy's decision, in the face of widespread doubts about U.S. credibility, to commit troops to Vietnam as a way to demonstrate America's determination to fight communism.

The first evidence of these repercussions of the Bay of Pigs came when Kennedy met with Khrushchev at a summit meeting in Vienna in June 1961. Kennedy, who had barely avoided a confrontation over communist advances in Laos by negotiating the creation of a neutral regime in that country, hoped to begin a dialogue with Khrushchev about how the two superpowers could resolve many issues, including suspension of nuclear tests, reduction of offensive missiles, and other peacekeeping arrangements. Kennedy traveled to Vienna from Paris, where he and his wife had enjoyed a stunning political and diplomatic success, becoming the toast of the town. In Vienna the mood changed dramatically, with Khrushchev launching blistering denunciations of capitalism, predicting the military and economic triumph of communism, and announcing his determination to sign a separate peace treaty with East Germany and to end American access to Berlin. Although Kennedy understood the pressures under which Khrushchev was operating—East Germany had lost 20 percent of its doctors and 17,000 teachers to the West through escape from East Berlin to West Berlin—he also recognized that Khrushchev's plan struck at the heart of the professed U.S. commitment to defend freedom anywhere and everywhere, and that it was especially important to honor that commitment in the city that had become a worldwide symbol of democracy.

"[Khrushchev] savaged me," Kennedy told James Reston. "I think I know why he treated me like this. He thinks that because of the Bay of Pigs, that I'm inexperienced. He probably thinks I'm stupid; maybe more important, he thinks I had no guts."

Understanding the test he faced, Kennedy resolved to do whatever was necessary to counter the Soviet threat. "There are limits to the number of defeats I can defend in one twelve-month period," he confided to aides. "I've had the Bay of Pigs, and pulling out of Laos, and I can't accept a third."

Nevertheless, the crisis brought home to him the dangers of military confrontation and nuclear war. When his assistant secretary of defense proposed that the United States use nuclear weapons to defend Berlin, despite the projected cost of 70 million American lives and even more Soviet lives, Kennedy was shaken. "If Khrushchev wants to rub my nose in the dirt," he told the editor of the *New York Post,* "it's all over." The president was appalled by the ease with which his generals talked about their readiness to use atom bombs. On one occasion, when he saw a pregnant woman, he said: "I question whether it's really right to bring children into this world right now."

In the end, Kennedy succeeded in deflecting Khrushchev from his immediate plan to sign a peace treaty and deny Americans access to Berlin. Sending a convoy of troops through East Germany to Berlin, he reaffirmed America's treaty guarantees. In the meantime he spoke to the American people in a televised address, asking for a ten percent increase in the army's strength, a major program to build civil defense shelters, authority to mobilize reserves, and a tripling of draft calls. Although Khrushchev's decision to build the Berlin wall eventually defused the crisis, providing a humiliating but effective way of preventing East Germany from hemorrhaging its brainpower, the fragility of peace between the superpowers had been made terrifyingly clear.

Nothing brought that fragility home more graphically than America's confrontation with Russia a year later, when U.S. reconnaissance photographs revealed that the Soviet Union was installing intermediate-range ballistic missiles—capable of hitting Washington, D.C.—in Cuba. With this bold and risky step, Khrushchev believed, he could both protect Castro's regime from U.S. attempts to topple it and raise the Soviet Union to a new position of nuclear deterrence to American military initiatives. The Soviet premier and his associates denied that they had any intention of deploying offensive weapons in Cuba, but the photographic evidence confirmed that they were within days of being able to activate the IRBMs.

Without letting on that he knew what the Soviets were doing, Kennedy mobilized his closest advisors to form an executive committee—dubbed the ExComm—to assess the situation and come forward with recommendations. Kennedy maintained his own schedule of speeches and meetings, and members of the ExComm performed their public functions as well, meeting secretly in the White House. Attorney General Robert Kennedy even sat on someone else's lap to minimize the number of cars seen coming and going at the White House and thus keep reporters from suspecting that something was wrong.

Almost immediately the ExComm reached an overwhelming consensus in favor of military action. Some members, including all those from the military, urged a full-scale invasion to eliminate Castro's rule forever. Others opted for an air strike designed to knock out the missiles. Only a few urged negotiation. Everyone agreed that quick action was needed. Time was running out.

The president viewed the military options with skepticism. His brother Robert, perhaps speaking for him, compared the possible air strike to the surprise Japanese attack on Hawaii in 1941: "I now know how Tojo felt when he was planning Pearl Harbor." Such an attack, the attorney general said, would destroy the moral position of the United States in the world. More-

over, it would kill Russian troops, thereby almost inevitably trig-
gering a military response from the Soviets that would escalate
into nuclear war. At first other ExComm members were upset by
the allusion to Pearl Harbor, but some began to recognize the ac-
curacy of the parallel.

The president, on numerous occasions during the deliberations, stepped in to deflect the growing momentum in support
of military action. His own preferred alternative was to create
what he called a "quarantine," a blockade around Cuba that
would prevent Soviet ships from carrying missile supplies and
aircraft to the island. Such a step, he believed, would both signal
America's determination not to tolerate the presence of missiles
in Cuba and also give the Russians time to reconsider their reckless policy and find a way to defuse the crisis. In a televised
speech on a Sunday evening, the president disclosed to America
and the world what the Soviets were attempting, and demanded
that the missiles be removed.

On the one hand, Kennedy gave the Soviets an ultimatum
that the missiles must go. On the other, he proceeded cau-
tiously, choosing to avoid confrontation where possible. For example, he allowed the first two ships that encountered the blockade to pass after they identified themselves. "I don't want to put
[Khrushchev] in a corner," he said. "We don't want to push him
into a precipitous action." The world nevertheless came to the
brink of war when a Soviet missile shot down a U.S. spy plane
over Cuba and pressure mounted for Kennedy to authorize an
immediate response. But then good news started to come
through. Russian ships backed away from the quarantine zone.
A Soviet official approached an American reporter with the suggestion that the Russians would remove their missiles if the

United States would pledge not to invade Cuba. Then, twelve days into the crisis, came a rambling letter from Khrushchev, disjointed but clearly suggesting that it was time to pull back from the brink. "We are of sound mind and understand perfectly well," the Soviet premier wrote, "that if we attack you, you will respond the same way . . . only lunatics and suicides, who themselves want to perish and to destroy the world before they die, could do this. We, however, want to live and do not at all want to destroy our country."

Khrushchev then made the proposal that would become the basis for a solution. The Soviets would withdraw their missiles from Cuba in return for a U.S. pledge not to invade. "Mr. President," he wrote, "we ought not now pull on the ends of the rope in which you have tied the knot of war, because the more the two of us pull, the tighter that knot will be tied. And a moment may come when that knot will be tied so tight that even he who tied it will not have the strength to untie it." Secretary of Defense Robert McNamara declared that Khrushchev was "scared." But so was Kennedy. He understood the dimensions of the crisis, and because of this awareness, repeatedly overruled his advisors' proposals for military action. Kennedy even was ready to trade withdrawal of American nuclear missiles from Turkey for the withdrawal of Soviet missiles in Cuba.

In the end, Kennedy and Khrushchev came to an agreement. As many interpreted the outcome, Kennedy had faced down his opponent and won. Secretary of State Dean Rusk told a journalist: "Remember when you report this that eyeball to eyeball, they blinked first." Prime Minister Macmillan of Great Britain predicted that Kennedy would achieve greatness in history for his handling of the crisis; and Arthur Schlesinger Jr. called the president's leadership "a combination of toughness and restraint, of will, nerve and wisdom, so brilliantly controlled, so matchlessly calibrated, that [it] dazzled the world."

In fact, what Kennedy had done was to go back to the fundamental understanding of war and peace he had gleaned from his experience in the Pacific during World War II. Throughout the crisis, his actions had been consistent with the sentiment he expressed to Inga Arvad in his letters after the sinking of *PT 109*: that only fools would intentionally bring the world to the brink of catastrophe. Although his own decisions regarding the Bay of Pigs and other issues had been partly responsible for the missile crisis, at critical junctures during the deliberations of the executive committee, President Kennedy and his brother were the only voices arguing against launching a general air strike on Cuba. Instead, Kennedy insisted on seeking a peaceful solution. Like Kennedy, Khrushchev seemed to have a deep personal understanding of the stakes for both sides. The two men together walked to the precipice and then turned back, dreading what would happen if, in Khrushchev's words, the "terrible forces" of their countries were used against each other. It was the closest the world had ever come to mutual assured destruction, and something in the background and character of these two men prevented it from happening.

The Cuban missile crisis proved to be a turning point in Kennedy's presidency. If the Bay of Pigs initiated a series of miscalculations and misperceptions, the missile crisis created a foundation upon which Kennedy, Khrushchev, and other world leaders could build to create a different and better kind of world. Kennedy had gained self-confidence by presiding over a brilliant resolution of near nuclear disaster. At the same time, he had stood up to the military and had prevailed. General Curtis

LeMay of the air force might lament that "we lost" by not destroying the Soviets. But Kennedy knew better, and never again would he be intimidated by military judgments. In the missile crisis he had abandoned his usual position of detached observation and returned to the kind of emotional engagement and commitment that he had displayed as the skipper of *PT 109*.

With this moment of mature triumph behind him, Kennedy became a different kind of leader, more ready to be engaged, more ready to commit, more ready to provide hands-on leadership. The most visible manifestation of this change occurred in the area of civil rights. Although Kennedy's rhetoric had always been supportive of civil rights, he had remained conservative, and even indifferent, toward the more passionate demands of the black community. He had voted on the "wrong" side on two critical issues in the 1957 civil rights bill, in particular supporting an amendment that would substantially diminish the chances of gaining convictions of white southerners who violated black civil rights. Marjorie Lawson, a black Kennedy advisor in his 1960 campaign, insisted that Kennedy take steps to overcome his image of detachment from black Americans. "Somehow," she wrote, "some warmth has to be added to this image of intellectual liberalism . . . A candidate who wins [blacks] will be the one who is most able to make them feel, not only that he understands, but that he cares about human dignity . . . nothing short of a national *gesture* will erase the doubts in the minds of rank and file Negro voters."

Kennedy appeared responsive to Lawson's advice. Not only did he intervene forcefully and effectively in the case of Martin Luther King Jr.'s arrest. He also promised that if elected he would propose new civil rights legislation and use executive action to advance civil rights. In one of the campaign debates he spoke in favor of "equality of opportunity in the field of housing, which could be done on all Federal supported housing by a stroke of the President's pen." When Kennedy noticed at his inaugural that the coast guard honor troops had no blacks in their midst, he ordered his aides to correct the omission.

Yet for the most part the Kennedy administration's early record on civil rights was characterized as much by ambivalence as by forceful commitment. In spite of his words in the debate, for example, Kennedy delayed signing an executive order banning discrimination in housing. To protest his slowness, civil rights supporters organized an "Ink for Jack" campaign, mailing pens and bottles of ink to the White House. He also backed away from ordering the integration of the National Guard out of fear that southern senators and congressmen would be offended. Although Robert Kennedy's justice department significantly expanded the number of black attorneys and the number of lawsuits introduced on voting rights cases, the Kennedy administration also supported the appointment of segregationist judges in critical southern states. The president and the attorney general actively supported the right of African-American freedom riders to take public transportation through the Deep South—especially after one of Robert Kennedy's aides was brutally attacked—but at the same time they criticized civil rights demonstrators for embarrassing the president on the eve of his first trip abroad. In an effort to "cool down" civil rights demonstrations, Robert Kennedy promised federal protection for voting rights workers, but the FBI and the justice department proved notoriously reluctant to intervene against local authorities who interfered with efforts to register black voters. Notwithstanding Kennedy's positive actions, including his support for James Meredith's entry into the University of Mississippi in the fall of

1962, most civil rights leaders were bitterly disappointed in his failure to provide persistent and courageous leadership on the issue. The students in the movement, in particular, were not willing to wait any longer.

In 1963 Kennedy finally responded. With student demonstrations across the south, and with Martin Luther King Jr.'s Southern Christian Leadership Conference focusing national attention on the brutal racism of Birmingham, Alabama, "freedom now" became a clarion call that Kennedy could no longer ignore. As national television showed police dogs attacking terrified women and children in downtown Birmingham, the Kennedy administration took action. Every cabinet member was urged to contact business officials in Birmingham. The White House sponsored behind-the-scenes negotiations for a settlement of the conflict. The two Kennedy brothers pressured Alabama governor George Wallace to admit two black students to the University of Alabama. And for the first time civil rights became the administration's number one priority.

At long last, in June 1963, Kennedy put his own prestige and moral authority on the line, publicly embracing the civil rights message. In a speech to the nation delivered largely extemporaneously, the president proclaimed that civil rights was above all "a moral issue . . . as old as the Scriptures and . . . as clear as the American Constitution." America, he declared, had been founded on "the principle that all men are created equal." Are we about to say, he asked, that black Americans were not included in that promise? "We preach freedom around the world, and we mean it, and we cherish it here at home, but are we to say to the world, and much more importantly to each other, that this is the land of the free except for the Negroes; that we have no second-class citizens except Negroes, that we have no class or caste system, no ghettos, no master race except with respect to Negroes?" For the first time showing passion and commitment on the issue, Kennedy asked: "If an American, because his skin is dark, cannot eat lunch in a restaurant open to the public, if he cannot send his children to the best public school available, if he cannot vote for the public officials who represent him, if, in short, he cannot enjoy the full and free life which all of us want, then who among us would be content to have the color of his skin changed and stand in his place? Who among us would then be content with the counsel of patience and delay?" Announcing his introduction of a comprehensive new civil rights bill that would provide equal access to public accommodations as well as support for desegregating school systems throughout the south, Kennedy said: "A great change is at hand, and our task, our obligation, is to make that revolution, that change, peaceful and constructive for all." For someone who had through most of his political life avoided engaging the central issue of America's domestic politics, the time for commitment had finally come.

That same month—June 1963—Kennedy launched a peace initiative that revealed a perspective radically different from the one he had enunciated in his inaugural address. Scheduled to speak at American University's commencement, he drafted his speech without input from state and defense department officials, who would not have approved of his message. In that speech, Kennedy turned on its head most of the rhetoric he had been using for the previous two years. For too long, he declared, Americans had envisioned a "Pax Americana enforced on the world by American weapons of war." Yet it was not enough to blame the Soviet Union or other enemies. Rather, Americans had to examine their own preconceptions, "for our attitude is as essential as [that of the Soviet Union]." In the past, he observed, both sides had been "caught up in a vicious and dangerous cycle in which suspicion on one side breeds suspicion on the other, and new weapons beget counterweapons." Now it was important "not to see only a distorted and desperate view of the other side" but rather to recognize that accommodation, communication, and reciprocal respect could lead to a very different kind of world. "No government or social system," he pointed out, "is so evil that its people must be considered as lacking in virtue." Acknowledging Soviet sacrifices during World War II, he focused on what the two countries had in common: "We all breathe the same air. We all cherish our children's future. And we are all mortal." It was as if the lessons Kennedy had learned from World War II and the Cuban missile crisis had all come together in a determination to reverse the momentum leading to confrontation and create a new momentum leading to world peace.

In this speech Kennedy moved beyond abstraction and rhetoric to specific changes in policy. To move toward more open communication with the Soviet Union as well as significant disarmament, he proposed immediate new negotiations for a comprehensive ban on nuclear tests, and he pledged that the United States would not "conduct nuclear tests in the atmosphere so long as other states do not do so." No treaty, he admitted, could "provide absolute security," but it could offer more security than "an unabated, uncontrolled, and unpredictable arms race."

Responding almost immediately, the Kremlin authorized publication of the text of Kennedy's American University speech by Izvestia, and stopped blocking the Voice of America broadcast so that the Soviet public could hear the speech in translation. Less than two months later the chief U.S. negotiator, Averell Harriman, initialed the test ban treaty, which President Kennedy himself had helped to draft in daily communication with

Harriman in Moscow. Announcing the signing of the accord, Kennedy told the American people:

> In an age when both sides have come to possess enough nuclear power to destroy the human race several times over, the world of communism and the world of free choice have been caught up in a vicious circle of conflicting ideology and interest. Each increase of tension has produced an increase of arms; each increase of arms has produced an increase of tension . . . Yesterday a shaft of light cut into the darkness . . . Let us, if we can, step back from the shadows of war and seek out the way of peace. And if that journey is a thousand miles, or even more, let history record that we, in this land, at this time, took the first step.

On this issue as on civil rights, Kennedy had moved from a posture of detached observation to one of engaged commitment.

The third major step Kennedy took in the summer 1963 was to order his administration to draw up plans for a new war against poverty. Over and over again during the 1960 campaign, he had noticed the disparity of conditions under which different groups of Americans lived. Now he had learned as well the relationship between the moral focus of the civil rights movement and the economic needs of those who had long been left out of the American dream. As a consequence, Kennedy ordered a review by all federal agencies to determine whether blacks were being hired on the same basis as whites. The results were shocking, disclosing that black teenagers were unemployed at twice the rate of white teenagers, and that nearly half of whites but only seventeen percent of African Americans had white-collar jobs. At the same time, Kennedy's economic advisors started to focus on the inequities revealed in Michael Harrington's exposé *The Other*

America, with its observation that more than twenty percent of the population lived in poverty. The result was a broad new initiative ordered by Kennedy to develop a comprehensive plan to fight poverty through job training, education, nutrition, and other programs.

In each of these areas—civil rights, détente with the Soviet Union, and the war on poverty—it seemed that Kennedy was ready, for the first time, to commit himself and his political future to causes that were not necessarily destined for success. Jack Kennedy appeared to have found a voice that previously had been quiescent. Now taking risks for peace, for civil rights, and against the inequalities of the American economy, he set forth a new vision. As Robert Dallek has suggested, Kennedy may also have been ready to begin disengaging the United States from Vietnam. In a move consistent with his perception that forces of nationalism were on the rise, Kennedy urged Secretary of Defense McNamara to make plans to withdraw a significant portion of American troops by 1964, and seemed to suggest that once reelected he would begin the process of leaving South Vietnam to its own fate.

Tragically, the country never discovered whether Kennedy would complete the new vision he had set forth. With his new sense of direction and purpose, he devoted a significant portion of his last six months to lobbying congressmen and business leaders on behalf of civil rights. His last major speaking tour focused on issues of world peace. On a personal level, the birth and death of his third child, Patrick, affected him deeply, renewing his sense of the fragility of human life. Those were the circumstances surrounding his decision to intervene in the internecine political battles of Texas in November, in an attempt to prepare the party for a successful presidential campaign in 1964. It was as

he journeyed to the final speech of that trip that he was struck
down by an assassin's bullet in Dealey Plaza in Dallas, Texas.

After the passage of more than four decades, it is hard to recapture the sense of loss that gripped America and the world. "I have lost my only true friend in the outside world," Sekou Touré, the president of Guinea, declared. Khrushchev mourned the death of his new partner, recalling that the two had acted as a team to avert nuclear holocaust. Clearly, Kennedy had been the beneficiary of wealth, power, and an extraordinarily effective political machine. Accustomed to winning, he had sometimes seemed unaware of, and unconcerned about, the plight of ordinary men and women. Yet there was another side as well—the side that revealed itself in his ability to give African Americans hope that their government might finally be responsive, in his articulation of a world vision that turned around the self-destructive assumptions of the Cold War, in his ability to convey to young Americans a sense of possibility, of renewal, and of confidence that they too could make a difference.

The life of John F. Kennedy reflects as much as that of any person in public life the dynamic tension between the personal and the political. Kennedy's entire political style—his mode of operation and his way of interacting with others—reflected his unease with the role models provided by his egotistical, power-driven father and his distant, moralistic mother. Kennedy's way of coping with these contradictory models was to avoid emotional engagement, to adopt a wry, humorous, detached posture toward the world. For the most part, that stance kept him from committing himself to a person or a cause.

Yet throughout his life he had the potential for such commitment. It had burst to the surface in the South Pacific when he came to a profound understanding of the consequences of war. It also emerged in his relationship with Inga Arvad, freeing him to write letters of personal self-discovery unlike those he had penned to anyone else. Now, in the last year of his presidency, he seemed to have discovered an ability to announce in a firm voice his commitment to change, even on issues that seemed most intractable. If Kennedy had lived most of his life trying to preserve his options and avoid risking commitment, he now had the confidence and emotional engagement to become a different kind of leader. But that was not to be. His death cut off that possibility. In James Reston's words: "What was killed was not only the President but the promise . . . The death of youth and the hope of youth, of the beauty and grace and a touch of magic . . . he never reached his meridian: we saw him only as a rising sun."

4

ROBERT F. KENNEDY
Despair and Commitment

Robert F. Kennedy was a tough and loving father. He tousled his kids' hair, challenged them to be competitive at sports, and took them with him to the office to play under his desk while he worked. Children brought out a side of his personality that others did not always see. When as part of a Senate committee he visited the homes of poor sharecroppers in Mississippi, he held malnourished children in his arms, their bodies bloated because of poor food and covered with infected sores. The children evoked in him a passion—and a compassion—as powerful as any he had ever experienced in politics. This from the same man whose reputation as a sharp-edged, ruthless politician knew hardly any equal.

◆ ◆ ◆

Few political figures have been more surrounded by controversy than Robert F. Kennedy. As epitomized in a famous cartoon by Jules Feiffer, Kennedy seemed to embody two contradictory personae, the "bad Bobby" and the "good Bobby." He was, on the one hand, opportunistic, unfeeling, hard, calculating, and cruel; on the other hand, passionate, caring, a tribune for those without power, a spokesman for the underclass, a romantic idealist who felt the pain of hungry children and acted to save them. Two warring souls in one human being. At those times when Kennedy was at his most calculating, there still existed the occasional grace note; and even in those moments when he embodied compassion, a hint of ambitious self-interest remained.

For Robert Kennedy, as for Franklin Roosevelt, Martin Luther King Jr., and John Kennedy, there was a turning point, a crisis. If for Roosevelt the crisis was polio, for John Kennedy the sinking of *PT 109,* and for King the night of terror when he found a personal relationship with God, for Robert Kennedy, the event that forever changed his life was the assassination of his brother Jack. Bobby's life had been wrapped up in his brother's political career. And so when Jack Kennedy died, Bobby's life was transformed. To make the transformation even more complicated, Bobby had reason to fear that he himself had planted the seeds of his brother's assassination through his relentless pursuit of organized crime. This fear made all the more striking his subsequent plunge into self-examination and reflection, and his reaching out to the poor and disenfranchised of the world.

In fact the two Bobbys were never completely separable. Although it is easy in retrospect to create a fault line between the period before November 22, 1963, and the years afterward, the clean division does not work. Kennedy's two instincts existed side by side, in different proportions, throughout his life. The proportions did change dramatically, with 1963 constituting a pivotal turning point, and the interaction between the competing personae shifted over time.

The story of the two Bobbys cannot be separated from the

story of the two brothers, Bobby and Jack. Coming from the same family, subjected to the same bizarre behavior by both father and mother, they might have grown up to be very much alike—and in some ways they were. But their differences stand out more sharply than their similarities. It was those differences that shaped Bobby's life, creating for him, in the aftermath of his brother's death, a set of choices that would have been inconceivable for his brother. The mystery, fascination, and tragedy of the decisions Robert Kennedy made reveal much about the human condition and especially the complex role that personality plays in determining our fate.

In the eyes of many, the course of Robert Kennedy's life was shaped almost as much by the timing of his birth into the Kennedy family as by the family itself. Robert Francis Kennedy was the seventh of nine children. Joe Jr. and Jack were ten and eight years older than Bobby, with a cluster of girls—Rosemary, Kathleen, Eunice, and Patricia—born in between, and sister Jean and brother Ted to come after. Joseph P. Kennedy focused most of his energy and attention on Joe Jr. and Jack. Wealth, power, and fame had already become daily features of the elder Kennedy's existence. What still eluded him was acceptance—the wish that Brahmin Yankees would finally recognize him and his family as part of the entitled elite—and the legitimacy that accompanied acceptance, including the right to hold the highest offices of the nation, and above all the presidency.

Joe Sr. doted on his elder sons, especially Joe Jr. Bobby, by contrast, felt ignored both by his father and his older brothers. Jack later said he did not remember Bobby until Bobby was almost four. Like his brothers, Bobby learned some of the family's basic

lessons. "We don't want any losers around here," he later recalled, "in this family we want winners. A Kennedy learns not to
be a loser at the age of two." Emulating his brothers, he vigorously pursued athletics, driving himself to win letters both in
high school and in college. But he did not have the same active
engagement with his father that the older boys had. "I wish
Dad," he wrote from college, "that you would write me a letter as
you used to Joe and Jack about what you think about the different political events . . . as I'd like to understand what's going on
better than I do now."

Bobby grew up reflecting more the influence of his mother.
Deeply religious, she instilled in him a pattern of obedience, discipline, and faith that set him apart from his older brothers.
Trying to find his own path, he became, in one biographer's
words, "dependent and obsessively obedient . . . [He] developed a
precocious conscience, and emerged from childhood less self-re-
liant yet more loving, cooperative and morally judgmental than
his older brothers." Joe Kennedy Sr. exhibited his penchant for
philandering for everyone to see, including his children. Jack
quickly became known for the same kind of behavior. Bobby was
different: shy, retiring, known as a sexual prude, and tending to
perceive the world as starkly divided between right and wrong,
good and evil. "What I remember most about growing up," he
noted, "was going to a lot of different schools, always having
to make new friends, and that I was very awkward . . . I was
pretty quiet most of the time. And I didn't mind being alone."
Bobby was the only Kennedy son to win his father's offer of a
$2,000 prize for not smoking or drinking before age twenty-one.
Clearly, if Robert Kennedy had absorbed the competitive spirit
and intensity of his older brothers, he also came to adulthood
with a measure of seriousness, discipline, and conservative morality that distinguished him significantly from both of them.

◆ ◆ ◆

The early ethic that guided Robert Kennedy's political involvement came down to three basic tenets: loyalty and service to family; commitment to individuals based on personal ties rather than political ideology; and pursuit of Manichean, good-versus-evil crusades. All three ultimately existed in service to Bobby's determination to advance the ambitions and goals of his brother Jack.

The confluence of these three tenets—and their contradictions—appeared vividly in Bobby's relationship to Senator Joseph McCarthy. Notorious for his anticommunist demagoguery, McCarthy clearly portrayed himself as a crusader for good against evil. He also had a powerful patron in Joseph P. Kennedy, who admired his gutsy, anti-establishment tactics and embraced the moral absolutism of anticommunism. The senior Kennedy's endorsement proved enough to garner Jack's support for McCarthy: "I [know] Joe pretty well," he told one college audience, "and he may have something." Bobby followed suit. After managing Jack's successful candidacy for the U.S. Senate seat from Massachusetts in 1952, Bobby had his father call McCarthy and get Bobby a position on McCarthy's staff. Bobby began to work for McCarthy in January 1953 and resigned seven months later, largely in anger and protest against Roy Cohn, McCarthy's chief investigator. He had conducted only one investigation, into allied shipping practices during the Korean War. But in February 1954 he went back as minority counsel, this time playing the role of prosecutor in the Army-McCarthy hearings, and focusing most of his attention on Roy Cohn, whom he blamed for the excesses of the McCarthy period.

Robert Kennedy never turned his back on McCarthy (nor did Jack). Kennedy and his wife Ethel had invited McCarthy to be godfather to their oldest daughter, Kathleen. Always respectful toward McCarthy, he said that when McCarthy died "I felt that I had lost an important part of my life." On an issue that became a litmus test for liberals, both Kennedy brothers failed miserably, refusing to attack a family friend simply to be on the "correct" side of the civil liberties issue. It was one of those issues that in the 1950s created reciprocal suspicion between liberal Democrats and the Kennedys. Perhaps thinking back to such tensions, Bobby later said: "What my father said about businessmen applies to liberals . . . They're sons of bitches." Liberals returned the sentiment, with one, who subsequently became a close friend, describing Bobby in this period as an "arrogant, narrow, rude young man . . . insufferable."

In the aftermath of the Army-McCarthy hearings and the Senate vote censuring McCarthy, Robert Kennedy pursued with even greater zealotry a campaign against the organized crime connections of big labor unions. Working as counsel to the Senate Committee on Improper Activities in the Labor or Management Field (better known as the McClellan Committee), Kennedy marshaled a brilliant staff—the largest ever assembled for a Senate committee up to that time—and initiated a series of hearings focused on corruption within the Teamsters Union headed by Jimmy Hoffa. The Kennedy-Hoffa relationship displayed all the rancor and absolutist combat of the Kennedy-Cohn engagement, only this time with a far clearer sense that issues of good and evil were paramount and that Hoffa embodied venality. The two men came to hate each other. Hoffa described Kennedy as a "damn spoiled jerk" and tried to disconcert him by winking at him from the witness chair. Kennedy, in turn, saw Hoffa as "worse than anybody said he was." Kennedy's pursuit of Hoffa and his Mafia connections knew no bounds and demonstrated neither subtlety nor nuance.

Kennedy's reputation for ruthlessness achieved its greatest credibility during this period. *The Enemy Within*, Kennedy's book on the alliance of organized labor and the Mafia, demonstrated his most moralistic qualities. Kennedy pursued Hoffa with singular intensity, occasionally using questionable legal and investigatory tactics. "If we do not on a national scale attack organized criminals with weapons and techniques as effective as their own," he declared, "they will destroy us." Alexander Bickel, a distinguished Yale University law professor, chastised Kennedy for "relentless, vindictive battering" of witnesses. Although Hoffa's lawyers outwitted him in Hoffa's first trial for bribery and conspiracy, Kennedy would not desist, carrying his vendetta into the early 1960s. In the course of his McClellan Committee investigations, Kennedy also developed a personal revulsion toward such gangland figures as Sam Giancana, Joey Gallo, and Carlos Marcello, whom he saw as pernicious enemies, even worse than communists. Indeed, when Kennedy became attorney general in 1961, his obsession with the Mafia took highest priority, with indictments of mob figures growing from 121 in 1961 to 615 in 1963.

Kennedy's reputation as a bully and an unprincipled tactician solidified during the 1960 presidential race, when he again managed his brother's campaign. Like any campaign manager, Bobby frequently took the blame for hard decisions made by the candidate himself. Thus when Franklin D. Roosevelt Jr. suggested that Hubert Humphrey might have dodged the draft in World War II, the low blow was attributed to Bobby. Adlai Stevenson called Bobby Jack's "Black Prince," while another observer said he looked like "the hit man in a prep school gang." The role of a campaign manager was neither to be lovable nor to be seen as soft or easy. Robert Kennedy fit the part.

Yet he proved to be brilliant at his task. He talked hard numbers and threatened reprisal if big-city bosses failed to deliver their delegates. He created a highly disciplined campaign team that knew how to organize rallies, turn out the voters, and maximize the candidate's romantic appeal. Moreover, he orchestrated the right decisions at critical moments. If the campaign manager deserved criticism for being "hard eyed, hard faced, hard minded and hard lipped," as one reporter had described him during a previous campaign, he also deserved credit for shaping John Kennedy's strategies for handling the issue of religion (he should wrap himself in the First Amendment) and for reaching out to African-American voters. Although Bobby initially criticized his brother-in-law Sargent Shriver for urging President Kennedy to call Coretta Scott King when her husband was arrested and sent to jail, it was Bobby himself who the next day telephoned the judge in the case and secured Martin Luther King Jr.'s release—an act that by itself transformed black voting patterns and in large measure provided the margin of victory for John Kennedy's election.

Bobby Kennedy thus emerged from the decade of the 1950s with a reputation clearly tilted toward the "bad Bobby" side of his internal dichotomy: fanatically loyal to his family, especially his brother Jack, intensely moralistic, singular in the energy with which he pursued his goals, and more simplistic than nuanced in his appreciation of public policy issues. It remained to be seen whether the image represented a portrait or a caricature, and whether a different setting, with different circumstances, might generate behavior and responses of greater complexity and subtlety.

◆ ◆ ◆

It had become clear to John Kennedy that his brother was an indispensable presence if his presidency was to be successful. Bobby served as Jack's alter ego, his confidant on all matters—including sexual ones—his political eyes and ears, his best friend, and his wisest advisor. Rather than make Bobby his personal assistant, he chose to appoint him attorney general—to give him a little "legal experience" before he had to practice law, the president joked. In that post, Bobby could exercise powerful influence, nominating judges, choosing cases to prosecute, dispensing patronage, and also providing the weight among other powerful cabinet officers to facilitate, and monitor, the president's policies. Moreover, the office of attorney general exerted central government authority in the areas of civil rights and control over organized crime, two of the most significant issues confronting the country. And although foreign policy lay outside the purview of the attorney general, as the president's close advisor Bobby played a central role in that domain as well.

Kennedy's involvement in civil rights issues suggested the degree to which he might be capable of growth and change. Although Jack Kennedy failed to make civil rights a major issue in either his acceptance speech as the Democratic nominee or in his inaugural address, race had been instrumental to his electoral victory. The Greensboro sit-ins of February 1960 had sparked demonstrations in fifty-four cities in nine states, and like a grass fire, the movement for racial justice was sweeping the nation. "The candidate who wins [the black vote]," wrote Marjorie Lawson, one of Jack's African-American advisors, "will be the one who is most able to make [blacks] feel, not only that he understands, but that he cares about human dignity." The Kennedy brothers heeded the advice, with Jack Kennedy's call to Coretta Scott King and Bobby Kennedy's intervention with the trial judge to secure Dr. King's release from jail constituting precisely the kind of engagement that Lawson had called for.

Still, Robert Kennedy admitted that until the campaign, he had never stayed awake at night worrying about Negro rights. To be sure, he had urged his classmates at the University of Virginia Law School to integrate the audience for a guest lecture by the United Nations leader (and distinguished African-American scholar) Ralph Bunche. But he had never been in the forefront of civil rights activism, and he had not shown any personal sensitivity to the scourge of American racism. Now that began to change.

Reflecting his reputation as a stickler for the rules, the new attorney general, outraged that the justice department had done so little to enforce existing civil rights legislation, set out immediately to change the status quo. Surrounding himself with skilled lawyers who shared his passion for law enforcement, Kennedy presided over a fivefold increase in federal voting rights cases. The justice department petitioned the interstate commerce commission to desegregate all public accommodations affecting travel across state lines, and became a "friend of the court" in suits involving hospital segregation, employment discrimination, and police brutality. When Kennedy learned that there were only ten black attorneys in the justice department, he wrote to law school deans seeking their best black recruits, and increased the number of black lawyers at justice to one hundred within two years.

As Kennedy's involvement in issues of civil rights deepened over time, the moral side of his commitment—clearly related to his concern with right versus wrong—often existed in tension with his political commitment to his brother's image and agenda. Kennedy's passion for doing the right thing brought him quickly to the fore of the freedom ride struggle in the spring of 1961. Unbeknownst to Washington (itself an indication of just how far off the radar screen civil rights issues were), civil rights activists embarked on a challenge to segregation on interstate buses, pledging to ride from Washington to New Orleans in integrated groups. Racist mobs ambushed the buses, firebombing one outside Anniston, Alabama, and meeting its replacement with brutal attacks carried out by gangs wielding iron pipes in Birmingham and Montgomery.

The attorney general, personally affronted by the notion that armed mobs would deprive citizens of a fundamental right, quickly took personal charge of the federal response. Working the phones, he exhorted the governors of Alabama and Mississippi to guarantee the safety of the civil rights protestors, and then, convinced that their promises were hollow, called out U.S. marshals to do the job. "After all," he argued in one phone call, "these people have tickets and are entitled to transportation." Kennedy even personally tried to persuade a reluctant bus driver to take the wheel and continue the journey. His commitment intensified when Assistant Attorney General John Siegenthaler, his personal representative on the scene, was knocked unconscious by a pipe-wielding attacker.

But Kennedy had by no means become part of the movement, or even its unequivocal advocate. Repeatedly, he urged demonstrators to take their crusade out of the streets and into more established legal channels. He seemed indifferent to the decision by Mississippi officials to incarcerate hundreds of freedom riders in the notorious Parchman Prison; and he became indignant when it seemed civil rights demonstrations might embarrass the president as he took his first major trip abroad to meet European leaders and confer with Soviet premier Nikita Khrushchev. "This is too much," he told one associate. "I wonder whether the [freedom riders] have the best interest of the country at heart. Do you know that one of them is against the atom bomb—yes, he even picketed against it in jail! The president is going abroad and this is all embarrassing him."

Yet, during his years as attorney general, Kennedy developed an ever deepening understanding of the centrality of race in America. Beginning with a simple belief in playing by the rules and enforcing the law—a basic moral credo consistent with his upbringing—he moved to a level of engagement that was more mature, more complicated, and more profound than any he had previously experienced. No other issue received as much of his energy, time, or emotional and intellectual resources. Often, as with the freedom rides and the court-ordered integration of the University of Mississippi, a crisis required a federal response because a federal law or court edict was at issue. Other times, as in Birmingham, Alabama, and countless voting-rights protests, civil rights demonstrators created local confrontations that became national news stories, flashing across network TV news and dominating the front-page headlines of newspapers across the country. Frequently, the Kennedy administration responded too little and too late, pursuing a version of federalism that left too much authority in the hands of local officials, despite the surveillance presence of FBI agents. But as Robert Kennedy slowly but surely became more actively involved, he gradually shifted the perspective of the entire administration, and most important, that of the president, toward one of moral commitment.

The events in Birmingham highlighted the growth that Bobby had undergone in these years. He had earlier developed a relationship of trust and respect with the Reverend Fred Shuttlesworth, a Birmingham church leader and civil rights activist. When the Southern Christian Leadership Conference (SCLC), under Martin Luther King Jr.'s direction, chose, in the face of defeats in Albany, Georgia, and elsewhere, to gamble on a huge campaign to desegregate Birmingham in coalition with Shuttlesworth, Kennedy understood how high the stakes were. The Birmingham demonstrations could be seen as a quintessential confrontation between the forces of good and evil—King, with his eloquent appeal to the principles of Christianity articulated in his famous "Letter from a Birmingham Jail"; Bull Connor, with his police dogs and high-pressure hoses attacking demonstrators. The photographs of German shepherd dogs attacking children and fire hoses blasting students against walls told the story.

While Kennedy was involved in the crisis as the chief spokesman for the federal government, he played a far more complicated role, coordinating lobbying efforts on behalf of civil rights. The administration sought to mobilize white moderates in Birmingham in order to fashion a compromise that would advance the cause and calm the crisis. Hundreds of phone calls went out from federal officials to bankers, corporate executives, and community leaders. It was not the kind of moral courage displayed by activists on the scene in Birmingham; yet it reflected an unprecedented degree of commitment on the part of the Kennedy administration. And it culminated in the decision—largely fashioned by the two Kennedy brothers—to have the president make a nationally televised speech directly addressing the civil rights revolution for the first time, and proposing major federal civil rights legislation to secure the right of black Americans to equal protection under the law.

John F. Kennedy's speech in June 1963 represented an historic breakthrough. Delivered largely extemporaneously, the president's address reflected not only his own perspective but the passion that his brother had conveyed to him about the situation. The NAACP's Roy Wilkins and SCLC's Ralph Abernathy both traced the administration's change of heart to Bobby, who had developed "a very strong fire" on civil rights. The attorney general's own position was clear in his testimony before Congress on the proposed civil rights legislation. "The question is," he declared, "whether we, in the position of dominance, are going to have not the charity, but the wisdom to stop penalizing our fellow citizens whose only fault or sin is that they were born."

Kennedy even proved to be able to learn from confronting the anger, hostility, and contempt of black activists who perceived him, not as a white ally, but as part of the institutional structure that was the core of the problem. The author James Baldwin, the psychologist Kenneth Clark, and ten other black activists, including militant students, arranged a conversation with Kennedy at Harry Belafonte's New York home in May 1963. Clark later described the meeting as "a series of violent, emotional verbal assaults." One participant told Kennedy he was nauseated to be in the same room with him. Others spoke of giving guns to blacks to help them kill whites. "Nobody even cared about expressions of goodwill," Clark said. "[It was] the most intense, traumatic meeting in which I've ever taken part." The participants attacked the complacency of liberals, who thought they deserved praise for their views even as blacks were being beaten and their churches burned.

Kennedy responded with his own form of anger. The participants in that meeting knew nothing about how politics worked, he told his friend Arthur Schlesinger Jr. They had no right to attack him or his brother, and they should feel grateful for all the Kennedy administration had done. But within a few days his perspective altered. He had seen the face of black anger and alienation, and he did not ignore it. Soon he was telling an aide at the justice department that if he had been born a Negro he would feel the same way Baldwin did. The confrontation, which in earlier times might have guaranteed Kennedy's eternal anger toward those who dared to question his or his brother's goodwill, instead became a transformative experience. It was, one civil rights ally said, "a climactic point in his education."

Inconceivable a few years earlier, Kennedy's response to the meeting with Baldwin suggested the degree to which the one-dimensional simplicity of his moral outlook was giving way to a broader, more complex view. Indeed, by 1964, as the historian James Hilty observed, Kennedy's language on civil rights was "laced with activist jargon and criticism of those who had lagged behind the civil rights movement."

A similar transformation in Kennedy's outlook occurred in the area of foreign relations. There, too, one might have anticipated hard-line, black-and-white judgments in the pattern of his earlier and fairly strident anticommunism. Once again, however, actual engagement of the issues generated far more sophisticated, wise, and careful judgments.

Kennedy's involvement with foreign policy matters grew out of the humiliation his brother experienced over the Bay of Pigs fiasco. Poor advice, ill-conceived tactics, and a failure to interrogate the odds of success or failure led to a botched invasion of Cuba. Eschewing the temptation to deflect blame onto others, Jack Kennedy accepted total responsibility. He also learned the importance of candor, of having confidants one could trust to raise any and every issue, especially the most difficult ones, and of taking time to make critical decisions. Bobby became his chief confidant on foreign policy, as he already was on domestic issues. There ensued an extensive reassessment of foreign policy, not only toward Cuba but around the world. Much of that reassessment led to bolder and stronger tactics, presumably as a signal to the Soviet Union that defeat in one enterprise did not mean surrender in other arenas. Hence the Kennedy administration's strong stance on Berlin, development of the Special Forces (Green Berets) in the army, and tougher talk—and action—on Indochina.

Earlier crises paled into insignificance, however, when the Soviets started to place offensive ballistic missiles in Cuba. Suddenly the specter of World War III and nuclear holocaust became a realistic possibility. President Kennedy established an executive committee—the ExComm—of military and diplomatic advisors to brainstorm about America's response. From the Pentagon as well as the state department came strong support for a preemptive military strike. Robert Kennedy alone stood in opposition. A sudden attack, he argued, would destroy America's moral credibility in the world, compel a Russian military response, and quite possibly trigger escalation into nuclear war. Largely because of those admonitions, as well as the president's own preference for a less radical response, a new ExComm consensus developed around the idea of a naval blockade, which John Kennedy announced to the world.

In the next few days, the passage of time without any resolution of the crisis brought armed confrontation ever closer. After an American surveillance plane was shot down over Cuba by Soviet anti-aircraft guns, the urge to retaliate became almost uncontrollable. Bobby, who was engaged in back-channel conversations with representatives of the Soviet embassy, suggested that the president respond affirmatively to the first of two letters from Khrushchev, the one offering withdrawal of the missiles in return for an American pledge not to invade Cuba. The strategy worked. Khrushchev accepted the president's pledge, and proceeded to dismantle the missiles in Cuba, reassured in a secret codicil that the United States would, six months later, begin to do the same with its missiles in Turkey.

In those tense days, Bobby Kennedy's intervention—along with his poise and good judgment—proved pivotal to securing peace and starting the process that eventually led to the nuclear test ban treaty of August 1963. "I had always had the feeling," Undersecretary of State George Ball later observed, "that Bobby had a much too simplistic and categorical position toward things—either you condemn something utterly or you accept it enthusiastically." But Ball now saw a different person, one who thoughtfully explored ambiguities and avoided hard-line positions, one who, in the midst of countless people losing control of their emotions, represented "a force for caution and common sense." When the attorney general opposed air strikes, another ExComm member noted, he "spoke with an intense but quiet passion [and] as he spoke, I felt that I was at a real turning point in history."

The burdens of power had generated in Robert Kennedy new perspectives and a deeper appreciation of the complexities of issues of good and evil. He carried with him into the exercise of his new responsibilities much of the moral core, founded on his Catholic faith and the injunctions of his mother, that had informed his earlier life. But he now developed richer, more nuanced understandings of the issues, both in the world of domestic politics and race relations and in the world of international diplomacy and superpower confrontation. In both arenas, he displayed compassion, intelligence, a shrewd ability to discriminate between alternative courses of action, and a capacity to think—and listen—beyond the narrowness that had once characterized his way of engaging the world. Kennedy changed significantly during his years as attorney general. He would change even more afterward.

◆　◆　◆

November 22, 1963, altered forever Robert Kennedy's assumptions about life. If ever he had believed that wealth and power gave the Kennedys anything they wished for, that illusion dissolved with the deadly bullets that ended his brother's life. "Why, God, why?" he was heard to moan that night at the White House, where he had accompanied the president's widow after her return from Dallas with her husband's body. Stunned by what had happened, angered by the cold, uninflected way FBI director J. Edgar Hoover had delivered the news, moved by the grace of his sister-in-law Jacqueline as she presided over arranging the funeral, Robert Kennedy struggled to find some meaning in this tragedy. He had devoted his life to his brother's career, sharing with him both the exhilaration of his successes and the humiliation of failures like the Bay of Pigs. Now the focus of his life was gone. There existed only a vacuum, and he had to find some way to put purpose into nothingness.

Like most people engulfed in grief, Robert Kennedy could not stop brooding about what had happened, fixating on the tragedy, poring over all its details, eventually coming back, over and over again, to the basic questions of existence. "He was virtually non-functioning," one aide recalled. "He would walk for hours by himself." He seemed in constant pain, another aide said. Rose Kennedy noted that Bobby, her third son, had gone into a "state of almost insupportable emotional shock." No one could reach him, even his wife. He appeared overcome by melancholy, consumed by sadness.

One explanation that may illuminate Bobby's descent into despair is the possibility that he believed he was responsible for his brother's killing. His determined pursuit of gang figures like Giancana, Marcello, and Gallo might have set in motion a plot to get the Kennedys before they could get the mob. "I thought they would get one of us," he told a friend, "but Jack, after all he'd been through, never worried about it . . . I thought it would be me." Supportive of this explanation is the fact that Bobby's campaign against organized crime ended the day his brother was killed. Never again did he speak about the issue or call together the task force he had established to work on the problem. Lending further credence to the theory, when the House Select Committee on Assassinations released its report in 1978, fifteen years after President Kennedy's death, it explicitly stated that some of the gang members whom Kennedy had pursued most vigorously possessed both the means and the motivation to have carried out the assassination. What could have been worse for Bobby than to live with the guilty suspicion that his own actions had led to the murder of his beloved brother?

Such feelings possessed Kennedy, fueling his quest to understand the deepest mysteries of life. "The innocent suffer," he wrote in a journal; "how can that be possible and God be just?" Devouring books about philosophy, tragedy, and religion, he sought to plumb the depths of what the Greek poets and tragedians had to reveal. He was especially drawn to the insights of

Aeschylus and of the French existentialist Albert Camus, who—in his allegorical treatments of fascism and his explorations of mankind's fall from grace—helped provide some clarity on the paradoxes of good and evil. Writing in his notebook, Kennedy quoted a passage from Camus that seemed prophetic for what he himself would later become: "Perhaps we cannot prevent this world from being a world in which children are tortured, but we can reduce the number of tortured children. And if you believers don't help us, who else in the world can help us do this?" The question framed a new set of possibilities: even if there was no cure for madness or evil, it was possible to take a stand and try to make a difference, however small.

There is no way to understand Kennedy's subsequent political journey apart from the spiritual and emotional crisis he experienced after his brother's death. Where he chose to travel, whom he decided to visit, what he said in his statements and speeches—all reflected a new sensitivity to the dimensions and variety of human suffering. To be sure, he retained a strong streak of self-interest and political expediency, but more often than not it was overshadowed by a sense of moral urgency and a reflective compassion that bespoke a commitment to the voiceless, the disenfranchised. Kennedy sought out victims of hunger and oppression, using his personal contact with them to inform and reinforce his analysis of what might be done politically to bring about change. While still a politician, always mindful of the impact of his words, he increasingly took on issues that offered no political payoff, and with a boldness that defied political common sense.

Not surprisingly, Kennedy's involvement with black Americans was one of the first sites where his new sensibility revealed itself. After being elected United States senator from New York in 1964, Kennedy chose to serve on a subcommittee that investigated rural poverty. He used exposure to the people and their problems—and the press coverage it received—to highlight the need for action. "He did things I wouldn't do," said the activist Marian Wright Edelman, who would later found the Children's Defense Fund. "He went into the dirtiest, filthiest, poorest black homes . . . and he would sit with a baby who had wet open sores and whose belly was bloated from malnutrition, and he'd sit and touch and hold those babies . . . I wouldn't do that! I didn't do that! But he did." While most public figures continued to focus their attention on racial oppression in the South, Kennedy turned his attention as well to "the brutalities of the North." "I have been in tenements in Harlem," he said, ". . . where the smell of rats was so strong that it was difficult to stay there for five minutes, and where children slept with lights turned on their feet to discourage rat attacks." Kennedy proposed private and public programs to assist those trapped in a northern version of racist oppression. Observing this, the psychologist Kenneth Clark, one of the participants in Kennedy's encounter with James Baldwin and others in 1963, commented: "You know, it is possible for human beings to grow. This man had grown."

Kennedy also reached out to Native Americans and Chicanos. Holding hearings into Native American poverty in the southwest and in New York, he convinced the Indians he talked to that this was a different kind of politician. "Loving a public official for an Indian is almost unheard of," one Seneca tribesman said, "[but] we trusted him . . . we had faith in him." Chicanos felt the same, especially after Kennedy became one of the few national political figures to embrace the United Farm Workers strike, led by Cesar Chavez, against the grape growers of California. Defending the strikers against the accusation that they were communists and radicals, Kennedy helped bring legitimacy to the national campaign that eventually produced victory. "Robert didn't come to us and tell us what was good for us," a farm worker said. "He came to us and asked two questions . . . 'What do you want? And how can I help?' That's why we loved him." Facing the risk of being denounced by powerful interests who opposed the grape pickers, Chavez said, Kennedy "did not stop to ask whether it would be politically wise for him to come . . . nor did he stop to worry about the color of our skin . . . We know from our experience that he cares, he understands, and he acts with compassion and courage."

Experience—in so many cases that seemed the key. Kennedy placed himself in contact with those who felt ignored and disrespected, empathized with their plight, voiced their grievances. Kennedy, Chavez said, was "able to see things through the eyes of the poor . . . It was like he was ours." That kind of personal connection fulfilled Kennedy's hunger for a constituency that would justify his existence, and reinforced his belief that he could make a difference. It was the quality, the newspaper columnist Murray Kempton wrote, that made Kennedy "our first politician for the pariahs, our great national outsider, our lonely reproach, the natural standard held out to all rebels."

Kennedy's identification with rebels and dissenters had its most profound impact, though, in foreign policy. He used his travels abroad to fashion a rhetoric that seemed pervasively anti-establishment. Emerging from a primitive and unsafe mineshaft in Chile, Kennedy announced to a reporter: "If I worked in this mine, I'd be a Communist too." In a discussion about how the Alliance for Progress had deviated from its democratic agenda for social change, a journalist asked Kennedy what he thought of Che Guevara. "I think he is a revolutionary hero," Kennedy responded. Placing himself on the side of youthful insurgencies around the world, he told an audience of Peruvian students: "The responsibility of our time is nothing less than a revolution—peaceful if we are wise enough, humane if we care enough; successful if we are fortunate enough. But a revolution will come whether we will it or not."

Vietnam, of course, proved the point of greatest contention, with every critical statement made by Kennedy against the war widening even further the bitter personal relationship between Kennedy and President Johnson. Starting in 1965, well before most Democratic senators turned against the war, Kennedy urged a negotiated settlement, defended the integrity of those who had burned their draft cards to protest the war, and endorsed the idea of Americans donating their blood for the North Vietnamese as well as the South Vietnamese. Kennedy always recognized the degree to which he and his brother bore responsibility for America's Vietnam policy; but he went on to question the foundation of that policy, particularly on the grounds that the war in Vietnam took resources away from pressing social problems at home. To give the war priority, he told an audience in 1965, "would be to invite the very internal conflagration of which we have been warned—to invite a society so irretrievably split that no war will be worth fighting, and no war will be possible to fight." By early 1966, before the first major congressional campaigns in which Vietnam was the central issue, Kennedy had called for recognizing the National Liberation Front and negotiating a settlement that would involve a coalition government.

What remained most remarkable about Kennedy's pronouncements on Vietnam was their tone of moral urgency, and the repeated attention he gave to the suffering of children. It was almost as though his own engagement with children—reflected in the quotation he wrote down in his notebook from Camus,

his focus on babies with bloated bellies in Mississippi, his attention to the youngsters threatened by rats in Harlem—had become the moral focal point of his universe. When he asked his
fellow citizens to confront the horror of the war in Vietnam, he
specifically evoked for them "the vacant . . . and amazed fear as a
mother and child watch death by fire fall from an improbable
machine sent by a country that they barely comprehend." Righteousness, he said, "cannot obscure the agony and pain those
acts bring to a single child."

By the end of 1967 Kennedy returned to the same theme, explicitly yoking his imagery of suffering to a searing sense of religious sensibility. He asked one audience:

> Are we like the God of the Old Testament, that we can de-
> cide in Washington, D.C., what cities, what towns, what
> hamlets in Vietnam are going to be destroyed? . . . Do we
> have a right, here in the United States, to say that we are
> going to kill tens of thousands, make millions of people
> refugees, kill women and children? . . . I very seriously ques-
> tion whether we have that right . . . Those of us who stay
> here in the United States must feel it when we use napalm,
> when a village is destroyed, and civilians are killed. This is
> also our responsibility.

And when students at Catholic University voted in a straw ballot
for more rather than less bombing, Kennedy asked: "Don't you
understand that what we are doing to the Vietnamese is not very
different than what Hitler did to the Jews?"

Kennedy had struck upon a mode of presentation that fused
an existentialist sensitivity to moral choice with a philosophical
reflectiveness about the limits and possibilities of human courage and goodness. In June 1966, in what amounted to a public
meditation, Kennedy presented the most mature statement of

his political philosophy in a speech at the University of Cape Town in South Africa. Reformers in South Africa had wanted to invite Martin Luther King Jr., but the apartheid regime would not allow King to come. They could not refuse to let a United States senator, the brother of a martyred president, come to their country.

And Kennedy seized the moment. Joining his audience in denouncing the scourge of apartheid, he urged them not to become discouraged out of concern that "there is nothing one man or woman can do against the enormous array of the world's ills—against misery and ignorance, injustice and violence . . . Few will have the greatness to bend history itself; but each of us can work to change a small portion of events, and in the totality of all those acts will be written the history of this generation." Kennedy then moved from this echo of Camus's statement about reducing the number of tortured children to the larger political lesson of what might happen if everyone accepted moral responsibility. "It is from numberless diverse acts of courage and belief," he said, "that human history is shaped. Each time a man stands up for an ideal, or acts to improve the lot of others, or strikes out against injustice, he sends a tiny ripple of hope, and crossing each other from a million different centers of energy and daring, those ripples build a current that can sweep down the mightiest walls of oppression and resistance." There, in one simple statement, lay the philosophical core of Robert Kennedy's growth since his brother's assassination.

◆　◆　◆

If Kennedy had followed his instincts, he would have become a candidate for president by the end of 1967. His convictions led him in that direction, as did his impulse to challenge actions he had come to see as immoral. But he did not, for two primary reasons: Lyndon Johnson and the politics of realism. Johnson was the sitting president—someone who had carried on John F. Kennedy's agenda with brilliance, moving even further than the New Frontier to create the Great Society legislation that featured Medicare, a war on poverty, model cities, and federal aid to education. Even Johnson's escalation in Vietnam could be seen as consistent with his predecessor's policies.

But Johnson and Robert Kennedy had never gotten along. From the 1960 convention when Bobby three times visited Johnson's suite to try to persuade him not to accept second place on a Kennedy ticket, to the White House where President Johnson viewed every move by Kennedy as part of an East Coast conspiracy to deny him his presidency, there was little but friction and hostility between the two. On occasion they treated each other with the appearance of warmth: Johnson vigorously campaigned for Bobby when he was a candidate for the U.S. Senate in New York in 1964; Bobby introduced Johnson at a New York fundraiser in 1967 with what the *New York Post* described as "a surprisingly warm and unqualified endorsement." Yet beneath the surface suspicion reigned. Kennedy's freedom of political maneuver was constrained by the certainty that any step he took to oppose Johnson's reelection because of disagreements over Vietnam would be interpreted as a crass and ruthless attempt to usurp Johnson's political legitimacy.

Political realism posed the second barrier. Virtually all of Kennedy's senior advisors counseled him that 1972 would be "his" year to run for president, and that any alienation of the Democratic establishment before that time might destroy his chances in 1972. To be sure, the brilliant young people Kennedy had recruited to his staff, such as Peter Edelman, Adam Walinsky, and Jeff Greenfield, pushed him fervently to challenge the president. Their arguments appealed to his own deepest impulses. But then there were the veteran politicos—Ted Sorenson, Arthur Schlesinger Jr. (at least initially), Fred Dutton—who predicted disaster were he to follow such a course. The Kennedy family friend and nationally syndicated columnist Joseph Alsop wrote to him: "You must really give more weight to the support of what people call 'the establishment' than I think you now do . . . Adam's kids [Walinsky's people] are wonderfully attractive and stirring supporters, but as an old uncle, I have to point out that they have neither the money nor the votes." The *New York Post* publisher Dorothy Schiff made the same point: "Who is for you? The young, the minorities, the Negroes and the Puerto Ricans." That combination, she said, would not suffice. Paralyzed by the opposing opinions even among his own friends, Kennedy confessed on national television: "No matter what I do, I am in difficulty."

Kennedy was torn in opposite directions by his conscience and his political pragmatism. "All of his own convictions, all of his own statements, all of his own feelings came back to really haunt him," one friend said. How could he be the person he felt he had become, if he refused to live up to his beliefs? Richard Goodwin, who had been an aide to Presidents Kennedy and Johnson, wrote to him: "Your prospects rest on your qualities. The less true you are to [those qualities] and the more you play [the political game] the harder it will be." What made the dilemma all the more acute was that political pragmatism was also an essential part of Kennedy's character—the quality that had made him such a superb campaign manager in 1952 and 1960, that had earned him the reputation for being shrewd, disciplined, ruthlessly efficient. "If one more politician on [the national level] asks me to run," Bobby said, "I'd do it. [But] the politicians who know something, they say it can't be put together." He confided in a friend, the columnist Anthony Lewis: "I wonder what I should be doing . . . everyone I respect with the exception of Dick Goodwin and Arthur Schlesinger have been against my running. [But] my basic inclination and reaction [is] to try, and let the future take care of itself."

Kennedy's initial decision to forgo the race—largely out of deference to the political realism of his senior advisors and his reluctance to be portrayed as conducting a personal vendetta against Johnson—ran the risk, as Arthur Schlesinger said, of making Kennedy "the anti-hero of countless Democrats across the country disturbed by the war." Moreover, if he were later to change his mind, "there might well be serious resentment on the ground that you were a Johnny-come-lately." By allowing himself to be immobilized—by, in effect, making a choice, this time not to run—Kennedy seemed to corroborate the judgment of those who believed he had always been, at bottom, a calculating opportunist, prepared only to move when the political currents were running in a favorable direction.

That impression was only underlined by the Minnesota senator Eugene McCarthy's courageous decision to step out and take on the president. In the fall of 1967 Allard Lowenstein, a brilliant, charismatic, and peripatetic antiwar organizer, asked Kennedy, his favorite politician, to become the tribune for the "Dump Johnson" movement. The two sat together for hours, Kennedy acknowledging that all his instincts propelled him toward running, and even speculating that "Johnson might quit the night before the convention." But instead it was Kennedy who backed off, eventually declining Lowenstein's invitation.

When Lowenstein took his crusade to McCarthy, he got a different response. "There comes a time," McCarthy said in announcing his decision at the end of November 1967, "when an honorable man simply has to raise the flag." McCarthy's words, intentionally or not, cast in bold relief the contrast between his willingness to seize the moral issue and Kennedy's withdrawal from the fray. The thousands of young people and antiwar dissenters who had been ready to rally to Bobby's candidacy now flocked to McCarthy instead, further emphasizing the loss Kennedy had suffered because of his immobility. But Kennedy had made his decision, and now he had to live with it.

Or so it seemed until late January 1968, when the Vietcong and the North Vietnamese launched what became known as the Tet offensive. Through December 1967 and January 1968, McCarthy worked to mount a respectable campaign in New Hampshire, the state with the earliest presidential primary, where he was challenging Johnson. The polls showed Johnson well ahead, the war seemed to be proceeding according to plan, with the Pentagon issuing regular pronouncements about how another corner had been turned and America could now see the "light at the end of the tunnel"—a phrase that political humorists like Art Buchwald and Russell Baker soon would make memorable. Then on January 30, during an agreed-upon truce in honor of the Vietnamese holiday of Tet (the lunar new year), Vietcong soldiers blasted into the courtyard of the U.S. embassy in Saigon, while across the countryside, other Vietcong and North Vietnamese fighters attacked sixty-four district capitals, thirty-six provincial capitals, and five major cities. From Saigon to Hue, the war raged door to door, especially in the areas that once had been perceived as safest for Americans and their allies. More than sixteen hundred Americans were killed. It took three weeks to put down the offensive, and whole cities were left burning hulks. "What the hell is going on?" the venerable CBS news anchorman Walter Cronkite asked. "I thought we were winning the war." Acerbically posing the same query, the *Washington Post* cartoonist Herbert Block depicted an American embassy surrounded by Vietcong, with the American spokesman saying "Everything's okay—they never reached the mimeograph machine."

The "Dump Johnson" campaign immediately took on new life, with thousands of college volunteers rushing to New Hampshire, shaving their beards and donning neckties, styling their hair and wearing skirts, to "be clean for Gene." A few weeks earlier, polls had given McCarthy under 10 percent of the vote. Now his popularity skyrocketed, or perhaps more accurately, Johnson's plummeted. By the day of the state's primary in March, McCarthy's share had become a powerful 42 percent. He won 20 of New Hampshire's 24 delegates to the Democratic convention, and created the impression across the nation that politics had taken a new turn. Although later surveys showed that half of McCarthy's votes came from pro-war citizens who were simply fed up with Johnson, there now seemed a realistic possibility that Johnson could be defeated and a new, antiwar Democratic coalition forged, ready for victory.

The Tet offensive had a similar galvanizing effect on Robert Kennedy. He had already experienced the personal disappointment of key aides, with Adam Walinsky and Peter Edelman raising the possibility of taking leaves to work for the antiwar cause. Kennedy became outraged when a network TV broadcast showed the chief of South Vietnam's security forces holding a gun to the head of a Vietcong suspect and executing him on the spot. "We are not fighting the Communists in order to become more like them," he observed. When Johnson portrayed Tet as a triumph, Kennedy noted "how ironic it is that we should claim a victory because a people [to] whom we have given 16,000 lives, billions of dollars, and almost a decade to defend, did not rise in arms against us."

Most fundamentally, Tet prompted Kennedy to reappraise his stance toward running for president. As he had after his brother's death, Kennedy brooded, spending hours by himself. He spent more time listening to Walinsky and reading the countless letters he was receiving from anti-war activists, including G.I.'s in Vietnam, and paid less attention to the political realists, who in any case were reconsidering their own stance in light of New Hampshire. In his first major speech after Tet, Kennedy left intact all the harsh criticisms of Johnson and the war penned by Walinsky and Edelman, whereas in the past he had deleted them. "It is a much more natural thing for me to run than not to run," he told associates. "When you start acting unnaturally, you're in trouble. I'm trusting my instincts now, and I feel freer." The problem, as Schlesinger had foreseen, was that changing his mind made Kennedy look even more opportunistic than before—in Schlesinger's words, as if he were "trying to cash in after brave Eugene McCarthy had done the real fighting."

Nevertheless, in mid-March 1968, Robert Kennedy made the decision he had not been able to make in December. However self-serving or calculated his timing might appear to be, he was ready to move forward. His announcement of his candidacy encapsulated most of the themes he had been articulating so forcefully over the past three years. "I run to seek new policies," he declared, "policies to end the bloodshed in Vietnam *and* in our cities, policies to close the gaps that now exist between black and white, between rich and poor, between young and old in this country and the rest of the world." Kennedy referred specifically to the "inexcusable and ugly deprivation which causes children to starve in Mississippi, black citizens to riot in Watts, young Indians to commit suicide on their reservations because they have lacked all hope." It may not have been a speech conceived with the moral purity and coherence that a similar pronouncement would have had in December, but it still represented a vision significantly different from that articulated by any other public figure at the time—one rooted in the direct experience and personal identification he had developed with the children, the poor, and other underrepresented people of America over the previous three years.

The next weeks brought a staccato series of surprises, tragedies, highs and lows. Initially, as if driven to overcome his own guilt over how long it had taken him to declare his candidacy, Kennedy barnstormed the country exhorting audiences with intensity about the evils of Vietnam. Occasionally, as in a speech to students in Kansas, his shrillness became almost demagogic. Then, on March 31, Lyndon Johnson stunned the world and threw U.S. politics into disarray by announcing that he would not be a candidate for reelection. Suddenly the campaign required a different kind of rhetoric and strategy, less focused on demonizing Johnson, more on putting together a workable coalition of reformers. Then, on April 4, Martin Luther King Jr. was assassinated in Memphis, Tennessee, as he tried to fuse the oppressions of class and race by leading Memphis garbage workers on a strike that, in many ways, encapsulated what he hoped to achieve for the nation as a whole in his nascent Poor People's Campaign.

At that point Robert Kennedy regained his focus and found once more the voice he had lost, the deep insight and prophetic vision of his University of Cape Town speech. Kennedy and King had never established a deep personal tie. For political reasons, neither could afford to be seen as too close to the other. But they had much in common, from the ironic fact that FBI director J. Edgar Hoover hated each of them with a passion, to their similar views about poverty, race, the war, and the burdens of leadership. When Kennedy heard the news of King's assassination, he was en route to Indianapolis to address a rally in the black community. A reporter on the plane observed that Kennedy "seemed to shrink back as though struck physically." Urged to cancel his speech, Kennedy insisted on going directly to the rally, where most people still knew nothing of what happened. Extemporaneously, Kennedy then spoke to the crowd in words that suggested just how much he had learned in the forty months since his brother's death, and how far he had progressed in his own sense of what mattered and of the bonds that could unite humankind.

"I have some very sad news for all of you," Kennedy told the assembled throng, "and, I think, for all of our fellow citizens, and people who love peace all over the world . . . Martin Luther King was shot and killed tonight." As the audience gasped, Kennedy continued:

> Martin Luther King dedicated his life to love and to justice
> between fellow human beings. He died in the cause of that
> effort. In this difficult day, in this difficult time for the
> United States, it is perhaps well to ask what kind of nation
> we are and what direction we want to move in . . . For those
> of you who are black and are tempted to be filled with ha-
> tred and distrust of the injustice of such an act, against all
> white people, I would only say that I can also feel in my
> own heart the same kind of feeling. I had a member of my

family killed, but he was killed by a white man . . . We have to make an effort to understand, to go beyond these rather difficult times. My favorite poet was Aeschylus. He wrote: "In our sleep pain which cannot forget falls drop by drop upon our heart until, in our own despair, against our will, comes wisdom, through the awful grace of God." What we need in the United States is not division; what we need in the United States is not hatred; what we need in the United States is not violence and lawlessness, but is love and wisdom, and compassion toward one another, and a feeling of justice toward those who still suffer within our country, whether they be white or whether they be black . . . Let us dedicate ourselves to what the Greeks wrote so many years ago: to tame the savageness of man and to make gentle the life of this world. Let us dedicate ourselves to that, and say a prayer for our country and for our people.

Kennedy had spoken to the crowd directly from his own pain and the wisdom he had gained from it—the pain that they all would feel, "which cannot forget" and which "falls drop by drop upon our heart until, in our own despair, *against our will*, comes wisdom, through the *awful* grace of God" (italics added). Never before had he spoken of his brother's death in public. Now he bared his soul, and the lessons he had learned from his own meditations on violence, tragedy, and humanity. And because he found within himself the ability to share that with his audience, they understood the bonds that united him with them. They departed quietly, in sadness, while elsewhere in the country riots erupted in a hundred cities.

The next day, in Cleveland, Kennedy took a further step, making the link between the personal violence that had taken the life of Dr. King and the institutional violence that pervaded American society. "This," he said, "is the violence that afflicts the poor, that poisons relations between men because their skin has different colors. This is the slow destruction of a child by hunger . . . Only a cleansing of our whole society can remove this sickness from our soul." These were not ordinary words in a campaign. This was not politics as usual. To be sure, the politics was still there. But something more was happening, bringing to a level of public expression and discourse a sensibility that was deeply personal, based upon a profound reassessment of the human condition and what human beings could and could not accomplish.

After King's death, Kennedy focused on putting together a coalition of rural farmers, inner-city blacks, and white ethnics. "We have to convince the Negroes and poor whites that they have common interests," he told a reporter. "If we can reconcile those two hostile groups, and then add the kids, you can really turn this country around." Kennedy had become a hero to black Americans. "He had this fantastic ability to communicate hope to some pretty rejected people," one black leader said. "No other white man had this same quality." To white factory workers, he carried the appeal of his fallen brother and his own commitment to law and order as well as racial justice. Some accused him of articulating different messages to different audiences, and to some extent the criticism had merit. But Kennedy also continued to break the political mold, especially in his willingness to challenge white complacency. Speaking to a hostile group of medical students in Indiana, he said: "Let me say something about the tone of these questions. As I look around this room, I don't see many black faces who will become doctors . . . You are the privileged ones . . . It's the poor who carry the major burden in Vietnam. You sit here as white medical students, while black people carry the burden of the fighting in Vietnam." Those students were "so comfortable, so comfortable," Kennedy later observed angrily. These kinds of comments were surely not made by one whose primary concern was political expediency.

Kennedy never could overcome, in his own soul or in the view of his critics (who were also often his friends), the nagging sense that he had betrayed his fundamental instincts when he declined to become a candidate in the winter of 1967. Riding back on a bus from Albany, New York, one night that same winter, he had written a note to Al Lowenstein, the antiwar crusader who had pleaded with him to run: "For Al, who knew the lesson of Emerson and taught it to the rest of us: 'they did not yet see . . . if a single man planted himself on his convictions and then abide, the whole world would come round to him.' From his friend, Bob Kennedy." Yet even if he could never wipe out the shame of that earlier decision, or the credence it gave to all the caricatures of the "Bad Bobby," he could move on—as he did in Indianapolis on the night of King's murder, or the next day in Cleveland, and do what one person might try to do, to make a difference and reduce the number of innocent children killed.

The tragedy was that Kennedy himself was the next victim of an assassin's bullet. He had put together, in Indiana, the kind of coalition of blacks, white ethnics, farmers, and factory workers that might have moved beyond the polarizations of racial conflict and the war in Vietnam. In Nebraska he had done the same, winning 85 percent of the black vote, 60 percent of the working-class vote, all the white ethnic areas. And although he failed in Oregon, a predominantly white, middle-class, suburban state ("Let's face it," he told a reporter, "I appeal best to people who have problems"), he moved forward to California, the most populous state in the nation, where blacks, Chicanos, and a host of dissidents resided. There, once again, Kennedy put together the coalition that had carried him to victory in Indiana and Nebraska. To those who had given up hope, Kennedy was, in the words of one radical, "the last of the great believables." And then, ten minutes after declaring victory in the California primary and repeating his contention that blacks and whites, rich and poor, old and young, could work together, he was shot in the head. He would never have the chance to show what could have been accomplished by the difference he might have made.

◆ ◆ ◆

The brilliance of Robert Kennedy's life lay less in what he achieved, although in the areas of civil rights and the avoidance of nuclear war his achievements were considerable, than in what he embodied about the complexity and richness of the political process. The notion of a dichotomy between "good Bobby" and "bad Bobby" says less about Kennedy himself than it does about the spectrum that exists in all political figures between their passion to attain certain ideals or programs and the short-term accommodations they must reach in order to retain power. In Kennedy, the two sides became caricatured.

Robert Kennedy had undergone considerable change and growth before November 1963. But he changed more dramatically after President Kennedy's assassination, and in that change lies the compelling fascination of Robert Kennedy's life. Plunged into depression and guilt after November 22, 1963, Kennedy plumbed the depths of despair. What had he done wrong? How could this have happened? How could what seemed so right turn out so wrong? And from that immersion came a new understanding about the human condition, about tragedy, and about the limits and possibilities of what one person might accomplish that transformed Kennedy's conceptualization of politics. Moreover, he shared that understanding with the public—most poignantly in his speech in Indianapolis the day of Dr. King's murder. He did so as well in his speech to the students at Cape Town, spelling out with nuance and inspiration his mature understanding of the calling of reformer, politician, and human actor in history.

This was the genius of Robert Kennedy—the knowledge he had gained through suffering and despair, and his ability to share that knowledge, especially the importance of directly experiencing the suffering of others as a means of moving to corrective action. Robert Kennedy's "most tenaciously maintained secret," Richard Goodwin wrote, "was a tenderness, so rawly exposed, so vulnerable to painful abrasion, that it could only be shielded by angry compassion to human misery, manifest itself in love and loyalty toward those close to him, or through a revelatory humor." But Goodwin was only partly right. For in the final years of his life, Kennedy managed to disclose that secret. In the process, he showed that beneath the supposed split between a good Bobby and a bad Bobby existed a whole person, capable of short-sighted and ill-considered calculating behavior, but also capable of a grace and a candor that gave hope to a people.

5

LYNDON BAINES JOHNSON
A Need for Consensus

The *New York Times* columnist Russell Baker called Lyndon Johnson "a human puzzle so complicated nobody can ever understand it." Robert McNamara, secretary of defense for seven years, declared that he had "never work[ed] with a more complicated man than Lyndon Johnson." The historian Robert Dallek concluded: "There was no trusting anything he said or did on a given day." And the Johnson biographer Robert Caro observed that while liberal senators like Paul Douglas and Hubert Humphrey "spoke of truth and honor, [Johnson] was deceitful and proud of it." Yet Caro also described Johnson as "the greatest champion that . . . black Americans had had since . . . a president named Lincoln."

How to make sense of this walking paradox? By all accounts the politician who did more legislatively to free American blacks than any white leader in history, Lyndon Johnson used "nigger" as a casual term of reference as late as 1968. A giant physically, conveying an impression of power with his hovering, ever active body, he also cowered under the bedclothes in paroxysms of self-doubt at critical junctures of his life. Deeply dependent on the presence, strength, and support of his wife, Lady Bird, he was also a profligate womanizer who publicly humiliated her. Perhaps the most consummate political tactician of the twentieth century, he ignored the necessity of sharing information about major military issues with the Congress and the American people. And the most powerful man in the nation, he reacted with fear and paranoia to anyone who disagreed with his policies. Lyndon Johnson was a person destined for great accomplishments; he was also condemned by the contradictions of his own personality to tragic failure.

Johnson provided his own account of his life in a series of early morning interviews with Doris Kearns, a former White House Fellow who taught history at Harvard University and whom he had recruited during his post-presidential years to help with his memoirs. "Terrified of lying alone in the dark," Kearns wrote, "he came into my room . . . I would awaken at five and get dressed. Half an hour later, Johnson would knock on my door, dressed in his robe and pajamas." While Kearns sat by the window, notebook in hand, Johnson "climbed into the bed, pulled the sheets up to his neck, looking like a cold and frightened child." Subsequently he told Kearns that she reminded him of his dead mother: "In talking with me, he had come to imagine he was also talking to her, unraveling the story of his life."

Lyndon Johnson did not grow up in a happy household. His parents could hardly have been more different. His mother, Rebekah, reared in a middle-class family accustomed to gentility and fine manners, aspired to a life in which literature, art, and culture would be part of everyday existence. When she was forced to leave college because of a family financial disaster, she ended up marrying Sam Johnson, a farmer and politician, raucous, brash, and more given to glad-handing visits with prospective voters than to evenings of cultural refinement. Rebekah felt she had married beneath her, but hoped to revive her dream of a civilized existence through her children, teaching them the poetry of Tennyson, training them in music, dressing them in Little Lord Fauntleroy suits. Sam, in contrast, wanted Lyndon to be rough, tough, and masculine, to follow in his footsteps, mixing with the crowds.

Johnson's childhood became a war between his parents over who would control his future. While Rebekah curled his hair like that of a girl and signed him up for violin lessons, Sam wanted to take him out on the hustings to court voters. The young Lyndon was torn, attracted to both options. He liked his mother's attention, and her ambitions for him. "She made me believe I could do anything in the whole world," he told Kearns. He also thrived on visiting constituents with his father, glad-handing, eating their homemade snacks. "Christ," he later said, "I wished it could go on forever." But there was no middle ground. His mother, frequently beset by depression, felt victimized in a life she had not envisioned for herself. And when Lyndon did not do exactly as she wanted, she withdrew her affection, making him feel abandoned and alone. When his mother prevailed, in turn, Sam would go off and pursue his political business, and Lyndon would endure a different kind of loneliness. Caught between two self-absorbed, strong-willed, and intensely antagonistic forces who happened to be his parents, Lyndon became, in Robert Dallek's words, "an emotional orphan."

Johnson's response, then as throughout his life, was to try to forge unity out of disharmony, to rise above the battles and make himself an instrument for creating peace. That process often involved his cultivating and venerating "father figures," older, wise men who by their stature stood above conflict. Consensus, bringing people of opposite persuasions together, massaging agreement out of division—this was the motif of Johnson's political and personal life. A young child with warring parents will have no higher mission than to bring together those who are apart, feeling both somehow to blame for the discord and responsible for resolving it. No passion can be greater, no obligation more unconditional than securing the family and the home. The pressure to transcend and unify brings with it a presumption of self-importance—no one else can do it—and an inability to engage with the reality of conflict, since to do so inevitably requires making a choice, casting one's lot with one side or the other.

Lyndon could not resolve the conflict between his parents. Instead, he chose the path of physical escape, going to California after high school, ostensibly to find work, but in reality because he could not stand the pressure of staying at home. Eventually he followed his father's example, thriving on the banter and wheeling and dealing of politics, using crude language, enjoying the masculinity of the legislative cloakroom. Perhaps he felt he could never measure up to his mother's standards. When he went to Washington, he had staff members write Rebekah gossipy letters for him to sign, as if he could not stand to engage her himself; and his ambivalence toward intellectuals and artists may have reflected some of his unease with his mother's demands. Yet he never ceased to crave the approbation of the intellectual and cultural elite; and it was perhaps no accident that the person to whom he chose to reveal his deepest feelings was Doris Kearns, a Harvard graduate, who reminded him of his mother.

Johnson shaped the model for his future political career while a student at Southwest Texas State Teacher's College in San Marcos. Recognizing that success rested on cultivating those in power, the young Johnson became an indispensable aide to Cecil Evans, the college president. He used that position to dispense jobs, favors, and college resources to other students, who then became part of his extended network. Before long, Johnson had generated a political coalition whose candidates won virtually every major campus office. He courted student support through his editorials in the campus paper—editorials that sounded the themes of paternalism and patriotism, unifying values that eschewed conflict and confrontation. Johnson was in the process of creating a political philosophy centered on building consensus around sacrosanct values such as the responsibility of the strong to care for the weak, the rich for the poor. "The enduring lines of my life lead back to this campus," Johnson subsequently noted, and indeed, the pattern he set there of cleaving to authority figures, using patronage to build loyalty, and transforming that loyalty into political and personal power would characterize his style from that time forward.

The young graduate's career soon skyrocketed. At age twenty-three he became secretary to a Texas congressman, replicating in his Washington boarding house and on Capitol Hill the network-building he had demonstrated in college. He organized other congressional aides, impressed powerful people (including executives of big construction companies back in Texas) with his efficiency in getting things done, and honed his skills of identifying whom to cultivate and on what issues. "The astonishing thing," recalled a more experienced aide about the newcomer, "was that Lyndon made us feel as if we were the pupils and he were the teacher."

Two years later Johnson returned to Texas as director of the National Youth Administration (NYA) for the state. He rapidly gained a reputation as an innovative and shrewd administrator, making the Texas NYA a force for reform and education and himself a well-regarded rising star among the political luminaries of Washington. When a local congressman died in 1936, Johnson put himself forward as a candidate. Although the youngest and least known of the field, he soared to victory by arguing, falsely, that he was the only candidate in the race who supported President Roosevelt and the New Deal. With the administration's help, Johnson won the race, as well as the additional prize of an invitation to join the president on his train ride through Texas as he returned from a fishing trip on the Gulf of Mexico.

Throughout his life Johnson would refer to Roosevelt as his political "daddy," the man he venerated because of his political skill and sought to emulate as a transcendent unifier. Cultivating the president as he did other powerful men, Johnson secured special access to the White House, and used that access to deliver goods to his constituents, including huge construction projects for his primary bankroller, the Brown and Root Construction Company. Go ahead, Roosevelt told an aide in response to Johnson's importuning, "give the kid the dam." Roosevelt predicted that Johnson would become president one day, and remarked with keen insight: "That's the kind of man I could have been if I hadn't had a Harvard education." When Roosevelt died, Johnson declared that he felt as if he had lost his father.

In 1941, after four years in the House, the thirty-two-year-old Johnson ran—with Roosevelt's blessing—for the Senate. With strong financial backing from Texas oilmen and contractors, he seemed likely to win, but then Pappy O'Daniel, the sitting governor and Johnson's opponent in the election, held back his strongest counties until after Johnson's best areas had reported their votes, and brought in enough additional ballots to defeat the two-term congressman. Johnson ran again for the Senate in 1948 in what one historian has called an "all or nothing gamble," this time against the legendary Coke Stevenson, a fellow Democrat who had been successively speaker of the Texas House, lieutenant governor, and governor. Having learned from his loss to O'Daniel, Johnson stole the votes this time. Six days after the party primary, with the race still too close to call, Johnson forces produced a late-reporting precinct that recorded 202 votes for Johnson, cast in alphabetical order, all in the same handwriting. As Robert Caro has observed, Johnson "went further than anyone had gone before, violating even the notably loose boundaries of Texas politics." But "Landslide Lyndon," as they called him after he won the primary by 87 votes, easily defeated his Republican opponent, became a U.S. senator, and set about to become the most powerful legislator the U.S. Congress had ever seen.

◆　◆　◆

The Senate was made for Johnson. Unlike the House, with its cavernous chamber and hundreds of members, the Senate was small enough to feel intimate. In five terms in the House Johnson had introduced just eleven bills—fewer than any of the members he came in with in 1938—and had spoken hardly at all. The Senate was a different stage, a different drama, with different characters, pace, and resonance. Watching Johnson sit in silent contemplation of his new workplace one afternoon, Walter Jenkins, his trusted aide, heard the new senator from Texas say, "just the right size, just the right size." It was a place that prized civility, nurtured the instinct for compromise, and provided ample room for a person of Johnson's towering ego and endless ambition to exercise his talent for interpersonal persuasion.

As he had in the past, Johnson began by cultivating his elders. "When I was a boy," he told Kearns, "I always liked to spend time with older people, . . . telling them what I had done during the day, asking what they had done, requesting advice. Soon they began to feel as if I, too, was their son." While some derided Johnson's penchant for deferring to his elders (one called him a "professional son," another a "Uriah Heep from Texas"), his aide Horace Busby recognized Johnson's skills at work: "He was learning, studying," Busby said. The respectful listener was getting to know his fellow senators intimately, their likes and dislikes, flaws and virtues, weak points and strengths. "They craved attention," Johnson told Kearns, "and when they found it, it was like a spring in the desert; their gratitude couldn't adequately express itself with anything less than total support and dependence on me."

Johnson paid extra attention to certain pivotal Washington figures, whose backing would open doors, silence enemies, and create allies. One of these was Speaker of the House Sam Rayburn from Texas. Almost every day Johnson would go to Mr. Sam's suite of offices in the House. He would waltz in, Robert Caro writes, kiss Rayburn's bald head, and say, "How are you my beloved?" The two would drink, often with others, Rayburn his bourbon, Johnson his Cutty Sark and water, and discuss the politics of the day. Often Johnson took Rayburn, a bachelor, home to dinner with him, alerting Lady Bird at the last minute to set another place at the table. The two men formed a father-son friendship that endured until Rayburn's death.

The other giant on Capitol Hill was Richard Russell of Georgia. Elected to the Senate in 1933, Russell had become the most highly esteemed senator from the South since Henry Clay and John Calhoun. Johnson knew that whatever his ambitions, he needed a home-base from which to pursue them. The South was that base, and Russell, who enjoyed all the perquisites of long membership in Congress such as the committee chairmanships that came with seniority, was widely regarded as the person in control of the South. With Russell, Johnson pursued the same kind of patient, persistent cultivation he had demonstrated with Rayburn. "He flattered him outrageously," Johnson's assistant Bobby Baker said; if Russell had been a woman, "he would have married him." Johnson learned to love baseball so the two could go to Washington Senator games together. Each Sunday Russell went to the Johnsons' for brunch. Both men wanted to be president, but Russell was convinced that if he could not achieve that ambition, Johnson could. And Johnson made a point of consulting Russell frequently and reassuring him that the senator from Texas stood resolutely at his side in defense of the Solid South.

As the congressional leader of the South, Russell wrapped his commitment to the racial status quo in the civilized rhetoric of constitutionalism, advocating states' rights and insisting on the age-old rule of the Senate that free and open debate should continue unless two-thirds of the members voted for cloture, or termination of discussion. Not surprisingly, therefore, Lyndon Johnson made a ringing defense of the filibuster in his opening speech in the Senate in March 1949, opposing President Harry Truman's bill to establish a Fair Employment Practices Commission to prevent economic discrimination against blacks. Such a bill, Johnson declared, "would inflame the passions and prejudices of a people to the extent that the chasm of our differences would be irreparably widened." The speech cemented the bond between Russell and Johnson, convincing the Georgian that Johnson was "with us" on preserving southern traditions. Within two years of taking his Senate seat, Lyndon Johnson had successfully wooed the two most important men on Capitol Hill.

Within the Senate, Johnson continued to reach out to his peers. Almost a model of what the sociologist David Riesman called the "other-directed personality"—someone so attuned to the moods and desires of others that he can pick up the slightest nuance of affection or wariness—Johnson sought to develop close relationships with his colleagues. He "operated best in small groups," Walter Jenkins said, "the smaller the better." Expressive and intense, regaling people with Texas stories, Johnson captivated his audiences. "He could dominate a room with his charm," one Washington hostess said. But it was his physicality that stood out most. Meeting Johnson, the *Washington Post* editor Ben Bradlee said, "You really felt as if a St. Bernard had . . . pawed you over . . . He never just shook hands with you. One hand was shaking your hand, the other hand was always somewhere else, exploring you, examining you." Hubert Humphrey used a botanical image: "He'd be kind of looking down on you . . . He was like a plant reaching out for water. Like a tree. And his whole demeanor was one great big, long reach." When Johnson approached a person, he was like a preacher intent on making a convert. "What convinces is conviction," he told Kearns. "You simply *have* to believe in the argument you are advancing; if you don't, you're as good as dead." "He was like a psychiatrist," Humphrey said. "He knew how to appeal to every single senator and how to win him over. He knew how to appeal to their vanity, to their needs, to their ambitions."

Deploying all those skills, Johnson created a network of loyalists, using his charm, his physical presence, and his sheer energy to bind together the components of personal and political coalitions. Humphrey called him "a born political lover." "Many people look upon Johnson as the heavy-handed man," Humphrey said. "That's not really true. He was sort of like a cowboy making love . . . He'd come on like a tidal wave sweeping all over the place. He went through walls. He'd come through a door, and he'd take the whole room over. Just like that."

One of the chief purposes of the Johnson approach was to arrive at understandings and commitments that were private, not public; personal, not collective. Using his behind-the-scenes maneuvering, Johnson extracted from his colleagues promises that were exclusive to the two parties involved. These private—and secret—commitments would enable him to bring together in a common vote people who would otherwise never have taken the same position. Moreover, he was able to get away with telling each person something different, playing to each individual's biases, then holding those persons to the commitments they had made to him. He could tell liberals he was with them but they needed to vote his way to move forward, while convincing conservatives that he shared their commitment to preserving tradition and that making a minor concession was the best way to further their goals. A master dissembler, Johnson used these behind-the-scenes deals to create majority coalitions and prevent the public airing of divisions, meanwhile creating the impression that he was indispensable, the only person who could forge unity out of division.

The success of Johnson's legendary tactical skills depended on his avoiding taking irrevocable positions that might prevent compromise and consensus. Johnson detested ideologues who trumpeted their purity in support of "causes"; that was one of the reasons for his lifelong grudge against classic liberals. "It's not the job of a politician to go around saying principled things," he argued. For him the only standard that counted was winning every battle he fought. For Johnson, according to his longtime aide George Reedy, "discussions of goals and ethics were merely exercises in posturing, and he had no patience with such goings-on. He abhorred dissent to a point where he sought to quell it long before protagonists had talked themselves out." Hence the private deals, the obsession with forging unanimous agreements in the Senate: he was determined to be in control. "He would just wear you down," one observer noted. "Finally you'd agree—anything to get it over with . . . One way or another, he just refused to have a single vote against him." A Senate aide commented: "There's nothing wrong with being pragmatic. But you have to believe in *something*. Lyndon Johnson believed in *nothing* but his own ambition."

◆ ◆ ◆

In order to realize his ambition, Johnson had to cultivate both conservatives and liberals. It was vital to sustain his conservative base in the South, and in particular his reciprocally profitable relationship with Texas oil, gas, and construction interests. For years Johnson had been an effective advocate for those interests, particularly for the Brown and Root Construction Company, whose corporate plane was available for his private use, and whose paper bags full of money helped support not only his own campaigns but those of his friends, who would then vote the right way as well. Whatever chance Johnson had of winning the presidency rested on cementing his ties with those who would bankroll his campaign, as well as sustaining his reputation with conservatives.

Both of those constituencies had a particular interest in blocking President Truman's nomination of Leland Olds in 1949 for a second term as chair of the Federal Power Commission. An ardent liberal and a persistent advocate of government ownership of public power, Olds had a thirty-year history of dedication to reform ideals. Johnson's role in destroying Olds's nomination indicates both the darker side of his penchant for manipulation and the effectiveness with which he used his legislative legerdemain to reward his conservative allies. First Johnson got himself named chair of the subcommittee to hold the confirmation hearings; then he arranged for the subcommittee to be changed and enlarged so that it consisted almost entirely of people unsympathetic to Olds's views on public power. Using his behind-the-scenes skills, Johnson structured the hearings to begin with an all-out attack on Olds by a Texas congressman using reams of material gathered by attorneys affiliated with Brown and Root. Most of the evidence went back thirty years and had been deemed irrelevant in previous confirmation hearings. It featured writings by Olds in his twenties for a federated labor press syndicate, some of which the communist *Daily Worker* had reprinted (as had various other papers).

All the while, Johnson continued to pose as a friend of Olds, who believed Johnson agreed with his views on public power. Although Johnson arranged for all the committee members to have copies of the evidence that the Texas congressman used in his testimony, he failed to supply copies to Olds, who was shocked by the attack. Nor did Johnson, as chair, allow Olds to read his prepared statement without interruption, which would have constituted an effective rebuttal of the attacks against him. Instead, he encouraged members of the subcommittee to interrupt with questions, most of which focused on whether Olds had ever appeared on the same platform as the communist leader Earl Browder, and on the articles that had been reprinted in the *Daily Worker.*

By the time Olds's liberal supporters became aware of what was happening, the battle was over and Johnson was delivering his subcommittee's unanimous rejection of the nomination. The hearing, Senator Thomas Connally said, "would prove [to the oil and power people] whether Lyndon was reliable, that he was no New Dealer. This was his chance to get in with dozens of oilmen—to bring very powerful rich men into his fold who . . . were still suspicious of him . . . This was the way to turn it around." Johnson himself gave the concluding speech in the Senate debate, accusing Olds of having chosen "to travel with those who proposed the Marxian answer." Johnson's friends from the New Deal days were horrified. It was "shameful," Benjamin Cohen said. "I thought it was the rottenest thing he'd ever done," Tommy Corcoran added. And Jim Rowe, one of Johnson's oldest allies, observed: "He grabbed onto the goddamned Commie thing and just ran with it . . . Just *ran* with it. Ran it into the ground for no reason we could see." Of course Johnson had a reason—getting in line the conservative forces whose support would be critical if he ran for the presidency.

◆ ◆ ◆

Johnson was far too smart to believe that having a conservative base and a wallet packed with oil money would be sufficient. He had to cultivate liberals as well. Ruling the Senate was one thing; ascending to national political leadership was another thing entirely. Johnson had seen both the strengths and the limitations of Richard Russell's power. Universally respected in the Senate, Russell wielded no influence in national party councils precisely because he was perceived as personifying the South, with its anti-labor conservatism and, above all, its racism. Russell had sought the Democratic presidential nomination in 1952 and learned the hard way that he could get nowhere. Now he looked

to Johnson to carry the southern banner, all the while recognizing that Johnson would also have to reach out to a larger constituency. Johnson, in turn, understood both how essential the
southern base was to his power in the Senate and how debilitat-
ing it was to his national aspirations. Thus he refrained from
signing the Southern Manifesto—a document written by southern congressmen and senators protesting the Supreme Court's
1954 decision that racial segregation in public schools was unconstitutional—using the rationale that it was inappropriate for
the majority leader to do so; and he went in and out of Russell's
Southern Caucus, creating the impression among some northerners that he had freed himself from the racial conservatism of
the South, even as Russell reassured southerners that Johnson
was "with us in his heart" on race. In the end, Johnson knew, he
would need to establish national credibility on the issue of race
to have any chance at all of winning party support and a presidential nomination.

Although Johnson recognized, in Robert Caro's words, that
"there was only one way to change his image in liberals' eyes
[and] that was to support the cause that mattered to them above
all others," it was not clear how he could make that happen. His
legislative record certainly gave no reason for optimism. Johnson
had opposed anti-lynching legislation, fought Truman's fair employment bill, and refused to do anything about enforcing voting rights. In a speech during his 1948 Senate campaign he
had denounced Truman's civil rights program as "a farce and a
sham, . . . an effort to set up a police state in the guise of liberty,"
trotting out all the negative stereotypes about Reconstruction
that meant so much to the white South. Moreover, he consistently defended Rule 22 in the Senate, the provision that gave the
South its greatest weapon against civil rights, the filibuster.

Johnson's biographers point to a number of experiences in his life that suggest a more progressive position on race. Robert Caro, for example, argues persuasively that Johnson's experience teaching Mexican-American children in Cotulla, Texas, in 1928–1929 foreshadowed his later liberal activism. As a teacher, Johnson worked tirelessly to help his students, arriving early, staying late, organizing field trips and sports teams, teaching a janitor to read English, going into the hovels of his poor and malnourished students. It was at that time, Johnson was later to say, that "my dream began of an America . . . where race, religion, language and color didn't count against you." In addition, while he was the Texas director of the NYA, Johnson won significant applause from Washington administrators, as well as from blacks in Texas, for reaching out to black youths and institutions.

Ample evidence exists from the same biographers, however, for a less positive reading of Johnson's racial attitudes. Despite the praise he received from some quarters for his NYA tenure, Johnson refused to put an African American on the organization's state advisory board (many other southern states had done so), had no black counselors or assistants, and named as head of the state board a racist who once compared blacks to mules, saying "Look, I like mules, but you don't bring mules into the parlor." Moreover, the proportion of aid given to blacks by the state NYA under Johnson was far below their numbers, blacks receiving only about ten percent of school aid even though they constituted about twenty-eight percent of the young people in the state. One assistant at the NYA office described Johnson's anger at a black porter who had made a mistake: "Lyndon would just keep calling him 'boy,' 'boy,' 'You understand that, *boy*? You got it now, *boy*? Do this, *boy*. Do that, *boy*.'"

One such story of racist paternalism might be dismissed, but not when put beside the pattern detailed by a longtime Johnson employee and driver, Robert Parker. Never, Parker said, did Johnson call him by his name. Instead, Parker was "nigger," "chief," or "boy." When Johnson asked Parker if the refusal to use his name bothered him, and Parker said yes, Johnson replied: "Let me tell you one thing, nigger. As long as you are black, and you're gonna be black till the day you die, no one's gonna call you by your goddamn name. So no matter what you are called, nigger, you just let it roll off your back like water, and you'll make it." Such accounts cast doubt on the emphasis by biographers and historians on Johnson's capacity for empathy with the poor and oppressed, notwithstanding the later changes in his actions.

Whatever his private attitudes, Johnson recognized that if he aspired to higher office he would have to take steps to counteract what the *Washington Post* publisher Phil Graham called "a growing public impression that you are the leader of the Southern Conservatives." That meant supporting civil rights legislation. "One thing had become absolutely certain," Johnson later said. "The Senate simply had to act, . . . the issue could wait no longer . . . I knew that if I failed to produce on this one, my leadership would be broken into a hundred pieces [and] everything I had built up over the years would be completely undone." Thus was the stage set for consideration of the Civil Rights Act of 1957, a process that illustrates both Johnson's brilliance in forging a national coalition on race and the severe limitations of his tactic of halving differences in order to achieve consensus.

❖   ❖   ❖

Much of the history of the 1957 civil rights bill would have been different if Rule 22 protecting the filibuster had been eliminated.

Herbert Brownell, Eisenhower's attorney general, had crafted legislation in which section 3 would have authorized the federal government to intervene forcefully on behalf of desegregation in schools, restaurants, hotels, and other public accommodations, and section 4 would have permitted the justice department to seek court injunctions against voting discrimination. Vice President Richard Nixon, as the presiding officer of the Senate, was prepared to issue a judgment that at the start of a new session a majority vote alone was sufficient to change Senate rules—in other words, that the rules could be changed without having to go through the process of filibuster and cloture. Plans to request such a judgment were in place. Had the judgment been issued, Rule 22 would have been discarded, and the civil rights bill as submitted would have had an excellent chance of passage.

However, Johnson, as majority leader, had priority for recognition over all other senators, and using that advantage he moved to table the motion before Nixon could rule on it. Whatever his commitment to do something on race, Johnson was clearly unwilling to alienate his base of support in the South. Instead, he would pursue the tortured route of protecting the filibuster—the South's major weapon against civil rights—while crafting other means to forge a compromise that would permit both northerners and southerners to vote yes on a civil rights bill. That task, which Johnson eventually accomplished, in his eyes established his credentials with northerners on race; yet it also required manipulation and dissembling that even by Johnson's standards reached new heights, producing in the end a bill that even supporters came to see as being without substance.

Johnson's tactics were brilliant. With the threat of a filibuster still in place, Johnson could tell northerners that if they failed to agree on weakening section 3 and adding an amendment to sec-

tion 4, the South would talk the bill to death. To the southerners, in turn, Johnson argued the converse. "These Negroes," he
said, "they're getting pretty uppity these days and . . . they've got
something now they've never had before, the political pull to
back up their uppityness . . . We've got to give them a little something, just enough to quiet them down, not enough to make a
difference. For if we don't move at all, then their allies will line
up against us, . . . we'll lose the filibuster, and there'll be no way
of putting a brake on all kinds of wild legislation. It'll be Reconstruction all over again." The maneuver was vintage Johnson.

With patience and tactical genius, Johnson pieced together
working coalitions to achieve both his objectives. Arguing that
no bill would pass as long as section 3 authorized federal intervention on behalf of desegregation, he persuaded two moderates, the Democrat Clinton Anderson and the Republican
George Aiken, to introduce an amendment that eviscerated section 3, and he secured 52 votes for it. ("This is not a compromise," Pennsylvania's liberal senator Joseph Clark declared. "It is
an abandonment by the Senate of the United States of all effort
to assist in the enforcement of the equal protection . . . clause [of
the Constitution]." Johnson then promoted an amendment requiring that federal court orders against individual counties for
voting discrimination must be tried by jury, a change that Roy
Wilkins, head of the NAACP, correctly said, could "only be intended to cripple the enforcement of the law by introducing into
the proceedings the very local prejudice against which protection is sought." Yet Johnson persuaded several labor unions as
well as some liberals that trial by jury was basic to the tradition
of freedom. He even persuaded the liberal senator Frank Church
to introduce the amendment. And as if that were not enough,
he engineered a back-door deal whereby five southern senators

would vote for the Hells Canyon dam project, which was of pivotal importance to a series of western states, while five western senators agreed, in a quid pro quo, to vote for the jury trial amendment. One more time, Johnson won.

With his two primary objectives now accomplished, Johnson put the revised bill before the Senate. It passed by a vote of 72 to 18. In the end, even the most ardent liberals, though disgusted with the emasculation of the legislation, supported the measure as a crucial first step that could be improved upon later. Southerners, in turn, could feel gratified that the filibuster remained intact, to be deployed later if needed against more threatening legislation. And Johnson had made it happen exactly *his* way, from his motion to table the proposed change to Rule 22 to his masterly configuration of tactical majorities on both the key amendments affecting sections 3 and 4. He had proved that he was not only a conservative southerner. And he had done so without losing his southern base.

What Johnson's triumph really meant was another question. While acknowledging that the 1957 Civil Rights Act changed nothing, failing even to lead to any gain in black voter registration, Robert Caro nevertheless concluded that the legislation was a breakthrough, both for blacks and for Johnson: "After decades in which the great dam [of the racial status quo] had been impenetrable, the sharp point of a wedge had now been hammered into it. The point could hardly have been tinier. But once the point of a wedge is hammered in, the rest of the wedge will, sooner or later, follow . . . The Civil Rights Act of 1957 was more than half a loaf, a lot more. It was hope." Others disagreed. The final legislation reminded Senator Paul Douglas of an old saying of Lincoln's: "It was like a soup made from the shadow of a crow which had starved to death." For the liberal columnist Thomas

Stokes, the act's passage was a "compliment, if of dubious character, for the ingenious and slick leadership of Senator Lyndon Johnson . . . he virtually compromised the civil rights bill out of existence in the zeal of exercising his talents of maneuver and behind-the-scenes negotiations . . . we might say that never was a strategy so brilliant used to bring about so evil a result."

In the end, the key question is whether the 1957 experience said more about Johnson's willingness to turn a new page on race, or about his obsession with sustaining consensus and presiding over a political process in which behind-the-scenes manipulation could be used to retain control and avoid the open engagement of conflict. The next decade suggested that each option contained a significant body of truth; one, however, remained dominant and ultimately worked to the destruction of the other.

◆ ◆ ◆

If, as Caro argues, Johnson's move on race was designed primarily to serve his ambition to become a national politician, the strategy worked. When Johnson announced his candidacy for the presidency in 1960, the possibility was taken seriously rather than dismissed as a hopeless gesture—the response Richard Russell had received in 1952 and Johnson himself in 1956. But Johnson made the critical mistake of believing the best way to advance his candidacy was to continue demonstrating his mastery of the Senate. In the meantime, other candidates—especially John F. Kennedy—were scouring the countryside seeking delegate votes and building a constituency among local voters and politicians. Johnson had little regard for Kennedy. "It was the goddamnedest thing," he told Doris Kearns. "Here was a whippersnapper [who] . . . never said a word of importance in the Senate . . . but somehow . . . managed to create the image of himself as a shining intellectual, a youthful leader who would change the face of the country." Yet, in the politics of the presidential nomination process, cloakroom kibitzing and lobbying stood little chance against cheering rallies, a handsome candidate's charisma and sex appeal, and the urban bosses who saw in Kennedy a bright new light who could guide the party back to popular acclaim.

When Kennedy offered Johnson the vice presidency, shrewdly recognizing that this was the only way he could win Texas and other key southern states, Johnson had little choice. Given his own focus on consensus and his desire for a future role in national politics, Johnson could ill afford to say no. Refusal would give the impression that he was more concerned with selfish interests than with party unity and victory; moreover, if he rejected the offer and remained as majority leader, there was a real possibility of his having to take orders from a president he had just rebuffed. Saying no, therefore, would mean two consequences that were anathema to Johnson: creating division and accepting subordination. Saying yes, in contrast, would mean reinforcing consensus, showing party loyalty, and keeping alive the possibility of ascending to the presidency when Kennedy's term was over.

Many who knew him could not believe that Johnson had agreed to take second place, and in fact he found the vice presidency insufferable. When he tried to get Kennedy's okay to see copies of all documents that went to the president, Kennedy ignored the request. In some ways, though, Kennedy showed sensitivity to Johnson's predicament. He instructed his chief of protocol to show Johnson appropriate recognition, and he sought to give Johnson important assignments, such as overseeing America's initiatives in space and chairing the committee on equal economic opportunity charged with making progress on race relations. "You are dealing with a very insecure, sensitive man with a huge ego," Kennedy told his assistant Kenneth O'Donnell, urging that O'Donnell do whatever he could to make Johnson feel good about his position. But nothing could change the reality that the vice presidency was primarily an honorific office. In Johnson's words, it was "filled with trips around the world, chauffeurs, men saluting, people clapping, chairmanships of councils but in the end it is nothing." Johnson appeared to enjoy his globetrotting, and made headlines comparing South Vietnam's Ngo Dinh Diem to Winston Churchill and offering a Pakistani camel driver an all-expenses-paid trip to the United States. But he was frustrated by his powerlessness, and in his view the Kennedy administration was "racing in neutral." Overall, he said later, "I detested every minute of [being vice president]."

◆ ◆ ◆

Then came November 22, 1963. Lifted by tragedy into the office he had always wanted, Johnson faced circumstances that would have been difficult for any mortal, but were particularly challenging for this giant from Texas. His aide Harry McPherson noted when the news came: "Dallas—insane city; insane, wide-eyed, bigoted Dallas bastards . . . A Texan become President after Kennedy is killed in Texas. There would be perilous suspicions." How to respond, how to find the right words, how to promote healing and a sense of national continuity. "I became president," Johnson said later, "but for millions of Americans, I was still illegitimate, a naked man with no presidential covering, a pretender to the throne, an illegal usurper." He recalled having been a "man in trouble," full of self-doubt and fearful that he might "become immobilized with emotion."

Yet in many ways his new role was the one Johnson had prepared for and craved from childhood on—the conciliator, the healer, the transcendent figure bringing people together, called to forge a feeling of national unity out of chaotic impulses toward fragmentation. In Robert Dallek's words, Johnson served as a "master therapist" to the nation. "We were all spinning around and around, trying to come to grips with what had happened," Johnson told Kearns. "We were like a bunch of cattle caught in the swamp, unable to move in either direction . . . I knew what had to be done. There is but one way to get the cattle out of the swamps. And that is for the man on the horse to take command, to provide direction. In the period after the assassination, I was that man." Rising above the clamor of recrimination and fear, the new president displayed a combination of humility, strength, calm, and direction. Expressing his awe at the responsibilities he had assumed, he offered himself as an instrument for redeeming the loss the nation had suffered. "Everything I had ever learned in the history books," he told Kearns, "taught me that martyrs have to die for causes. John Kennedy had died . . . [and now] I had to take the dead man's program and turn it into a martyr's cause. That way, Kennedy would live forever, and so would I."

Five days after Kennedy's death, Johnson addressed the Congress and the nation. "All I have," he declared, "I would have given gladly not to be standing here today." John F. Kennedy, he recalled, had said to the American people: "Let us begin." Johnson now said: "Let us continue." Emphasizing the message of continuity, he praised Kennedy's dreams for the nation's future and vowed: "And now the ideas and the ideals which he so nobly represented must and will be translated into effective action."

Johnson then focused on the crux of Kennedy's legacy. Invoking the words of another martyred president, he declared: "Let us here highly resolve that John Fitzgerald Kennedy did not live—or die—in vain." Seizing on the parallels between Lincoln's and Kennedy's leadership on issues of race, he urged the Congress to "continue the work of President Kennedy" by passing his tax bill, and then moved directly to a plea that the nation redeem its loss by acting on its most pressing social issue. "No memorial oration or eulogy," he said, "could more eloquently honor President Kennedy's memory than the earliest possible passage of the civil rights bill for which he fought so long." Lest anyone suspect that a Texan might not share Kennedy's commitment, Johnson embraced the civil rights cause with a passion never before heard in the halls of Congress. "We have talked long enough in this country about civil rights. We have talked for one hundred years or more. It is time now to write the next chapter—and to write it in the books of law." Whatever his previous views about race, Johnson now attempted to galvanize a new national consensus on behalf of racial equality—not only to fulfill Kennedy's mission, but also to correct the nation's most glaring injustice.

With tenacity and genius, employing the same skills with which he had so successfully weakened the 1957 Civil Rights Act, Johnson then wheeled and dealed to secure a victory for civil rights. He had almost daily consultations (and drinks) with the Republican Senate leader, Everett Dirksen, whose support for the bill and for cloture was indispensable. Pulling out of his hat another "Hells Canyon" deal, he promised support for a dam-building project in Arizona to get Arizona's Carl Hayden and the two Nevada senators on board. With his oldest friends from the South, he indicated that it was time to push substantive legislation on civil rights, not just the Kennedy bill but an even stronger one. In stark contrast to the eviscerated bill of 1957, the Civil Rights Act of 1964 outlawed employment discrimination based on race or sex, desegregated public accommodations such as restaurants, motels, and theaters, and gave the federal government new authority to intervene in states on behalf of integration. "You tell Lyndon," Richard Russell said to Johnson's aide Bill Moyers, "that I've been expecting the rod for a long time, and I'm sorry that it's from his hand the rod must be wielded, but I'd rather it be his hand than anybody else's I know. Tell him to cry a little when he uses it." Some southerners, like Herman Talmadge of Georgia, felt betrayed—"disappointed . . . angry . . . sick," Talmadge said—but Johnson, however deep his roots in the South, was now the national leader he had long aspired to be. He was running with a powerful wind, created by the new aura that surrounded him after Kennedy's death, and informed by an impulse to use immediately and decisively the mandate of carrying forward a martyr's cause.

Nor was civil rights the only legacy from Kennedy that Johnson pursued. Understanding that action on multiple items could have a synergistic effect, one victory leading to others, Johnson tried to create almost a stampede effect, insisting that action be taken on Kennedy's economic package, and telling Congress in his first State of the Union message that it was time to declare "an unconditional war on poverty." One after another victories were achieved: the tax cut of 1964, the Civil Rights Act of 1964, the start of antipoverty legislation. And then, in a masterly transition to an agenda of his own, Johnson started to articulate his own dream for a Great Society, a series of programs that would exceed the boldest expectations of the New Deal and would go beyond simple material progress to "build a richer life of mind and spirit." He challenged the nation to use its wealth "to enrich and elevate our national life, and to advance the quality of our American civilization," so that "the city of man [would serve] not only the needs of the body and the demands of commerce but the desire for beauty and the hunger for community." This was Johnson's dream, made possible by the legitimacy he had achieved by carrying forward so effectively Kennedy's legacy.

To a significant degree, the likelihood of Johnson's realizing his aspirations was enhanced by his good luck in having Barry Goldwater as the Republican nominee for president in 1964. Chronically beset by self-doubt, Johnson considered, briefly, the possibility of not being a candidate himself, angry that liberals were not giving him enough credit for getting *their* legislation passed. But such sentiments were of short duration, particularly because of Goldwater's views. Nothing could better serve as a Johnson foil than Goldwater's vote against the civil rights bill, his declared intention to privatize social security, abolish the income tax, sell the Tennessee Valley Authority, and give NATO commanders the authority to use tactical nuclear weapons. Goldwater was the radical, Johnson the voice of continuity and stability. While the Arizona Republican urged an American military victory in Vietnam, Johnson pledged: "We're not about to send American boys nine or ten thousand miles from home to do what Asian boys ought to be doing for themselves." Even Goldwater's bumper stickers worked to Johnson's advantage. "In your heart you know he's right," they declared. "Yes, far right," the Democrats responded. On election day Johnson won the popular vote by 61 to 39 percent. "For the first time in all my life," he would later tell Kearns, "I truly felt loved by the American people."

Not missing a beat, Johnson insisted that his aides proceed immediately with a massive legislative program to institutionalize the Great Society before his mandate started to erode. The administration had just one year to achieve its goals, he said. Each month, more of the 16 million votes they had won would turn against them. If the administration did not move now, a golden opportunity would be lost. A blizzard of legislative proposals ensued: the Elementary and Secondary Education Act, the Economic Opportunity Act (the war on poverty), Medicare, Model Cities, Higher Education, creation of the Department of Housing and Urban Development (HUD). Never had such an impressive body of laws been enacted in such a short period. "[Johnson] has outstripped Roosevelt," Senator Mike Mansfield said. "He has done more than FDR ever did, or ever thought of doing."

Most important, Johnson carried his crusade for civil rights and racial equality to new heights. All through the early months of 1965 the civil rights movement had been assaulting one of the strongest bastions of white racism in Selma, Alabama. Each day, as prospective voters sought to register, cattle prods and nightsticks were used to repel them. A planned protest march from Selma to Montgomery got only a few blocks, to the Edmund Pettus bridge, where armed cavalry of Alabama state troopers brutally attacked the demonstrators. As the public watched television's nightly coverage of the struggle, outraged citizens demanded action. And Johnson responded. On March 15, 1965, in what Robert Dallek has called "one of the most moving and memorable presidential addresses in the country's history," Johnson went before the nation and the Congress, comparing

Selma to Lexington and Concord as "a turning point in man's unending search for freedom." With a rhetorical power that exceeded even his speech after John Kennedy's assassination, he told the American people: "Rarely in any time does an issue lay bare the secret heart of America itself . . . The issue of equal rights for American Negroes is such an issue. And should we defeat every enemy, should we double our wealth and conquer the stars, and still be unequal to this issue, then we will have failed as a people and as a nation . . . Because it is not just Negroes, but really it is all of us, who must overcome the crippling legacy of bigotry and injustice." And then, in the most dramatic line he ever uttered, Johnson embraced the anthem of the civil rights struggle, declaring: "And we shall overcome."

This was a different Lyndon Johnson, one the nation had never seen before. The address not only identified Johnson totally with the cause of racial equality; it went beyond that to personalize, in vivid phrases, his individual experience with discrimination, and his aspiration to be *the* president who would save the poor and rescue the oppressed. Recalling the year he had spent teaching poor Mexican-American students, Johnson said: "They often came to class without breakfast, hungry. They knew even in their youth the pain of injustice . . . Somehow you never forget what poverty and hatred can do when you see its scars on the hopeful face of a young child." Now he was in a position to respond. "It never even occurred to me in my fondest dreams," he said, "that I might have the chance to help the sons and daughters of those students and to help people like them all over the country. But now I do have that chance—and I'll let you in on a secret—I mean to use it." Once more placing himself in a position of ultimate control and jurisdiction, Johnson shared with the American people his personal vision of who he might become: "I do not want to be the president who built empires, or sought grandeur, or extended dominion. I want to be the president who educated young children . . . who helped to feed the hungry . . . who helped to end hatred among his fellow men and who promoted love among the people of all races and all regions and all parties. I want to be the president who helped to end war among the brothers of this earth." It was a messianic vision, saying more about the man who enunciated it than about the politics of the moment. It also bespoke a transcendent paternalism that pledged to create unity in the entire world. Consistent with that vision, Johnson concluded: "God will not favor everything that we do . . . but I cannot help believing that He truly understands and that He really favors the undertaking that we begin here tonight."

Historians disagree about the meaning of Johnson's political leadership in the years 1963–1965. From one perspective, it is clear that Johnson had made a fundamental shift on civil rights. Leaving behind the tempered, compromise-building approach he had used during discussion of the 1957 Civil Rights Act, he now cast his lot, passionately and decisively, with dramatic and substantive change to the nation's laws governing race relations. No longer did he insist on preserving a southern base. Gone forever was his commitment to Rule 22, as well as his sense of obligation to people like Richard Russell and Herman Talmadge. Those who believe that all along Johnson was a true liberal, whose experience in Cotulla and the NYA shaped a fundamental commitment to the oppressed, see his maneuvering in 1957 as a way of doing all he could for civil rights, making possible the first civil rights legislation of the twentieth century. For them, the events of 1963–1965 reflect Johnson's real convictions, which he could at last reveal in the months after John F. Kennedy's assassination.

From another perspective, Johnson's wheeling and dealing in 1957 was a means of securing nearly unanimous support for the legislation, thus achieving his goal of giving something to each faction and creating the impression of consensus. In this view, Johnson's motivation was not a fundamental commitment to racial equality, but rather a wish to establish some credibility on civil rights as a way to further his ambition to become a national figure. According to this argument, the drive for consensus and power took precedence over a commitment to civil rights.

But how does that affect one's interpretation of Johnson in 1963–1965? First, it is important to recognize that Johnson had not always supported Kennedy's civil rights initiative. In memoranda and phone conversations with justice department and White House officials in June 1963, he argued against the initiative, contending that the bill Kennedy was proposing would cause his program "to go down the drain . . . he'll be cut to pieces, . . . and he'll be a sacrificial lamb." Instead, Johnson said, Kennedy should push through his tax cut, do more homework on civil rights, and only then—after much greater preparation— "go in for the kill." "I'd move my children on through the line," he said, referring to Kennedy's other legislative priorities, "and get them down in the storm cellar and get it, lock and key, and then I'd make my attack."

The assassination obviated the need for that kind of legislative strategizing and substituted a moral imperative to ensure that Kennedy had not died in vain. Under that rubric, all-out support for Kennedy's civil rights bill was a means by which people could both honor the martyred president's memory and simultaneously work to heal the nation's open racial wound. Brilliantly, Johnson wrapped himself in the emotionalism of that argument, using it to rise above the debate over specific issues and to adopt the posture of a transcendent leader, positioned above all divisions and dedicated to unifying the country at a time of national crisis. Within this framework, Johnson pursued civil rights so passionately not only because he believed in it—which he did—but also, and perhaps more important, because doing so allowed him to achieve two objectives: ensuring his legitimacy as the heir of Kennedy's presidency, and assuming a role of moral leadership that placed him above political conflict. In effect, his embrace of civil rights became a way to avoid politics as usual and to promote a presidential image more akin to a benevolent father, bringing unity, justice, and harmony to his people. Johnson's description of himself as feeding the hungry, helping the poor, educating the young, and bringing peace to people of all races fits such an interpretation. Under this argument, then, Johnson, whatever his deepest convictions on race, chose the path he did primarily because it was consistent with his lifelong quest to rise above the conflicts in his life, whether they be between his mother and father or between Richard Russell and Hubert Humphrey.

◆ ◆ ◆

A good way to test the validity of this view is to examine how Johnson dealt with other issues of potential conflict in his administration. Was he willing to adopt a strong position that might alienate some while pleasing others? Or did he always choose compromise and consensus? The most appropriate place to explore such questions is the Vietnam war, the other primary focus of the Johnson administration.

Just as with the question of race, Johnson did not enter the debate over Vietnam without preconceptions about the merits of the issue or the history involved. Whatever possibilities may have existed for a different relationship with Vietnam based on the close collaboration of the United States with Ho Chi Minh in the anti-Japanese resistance movement of World War II, by 1948 the United States had solidly aligned itself in support of the French colonial regime in Indochina. That choice had little to do with events in Southeast Asia, but instead reflected the priority America had given to the Cold War and the containment of communism. The United States needed French support in Europe, where the primary battles of the Cold War were being fought, and one price for securing that support was endorsement of French policies in Asia. Before long, however, Vietnam itself—like China and Korea before it—became a focal point for the policy of containment, with America assuming an ever larger role in bankrolling the French effort against the Vietminh and providing indispensable logistical and military support. By 1954, after the French collapse at the battle of Dien Bien Phu, the United States assumed primary responsibility for pursuing the policy of containment. Using the same rationale for Southeast Asia that had been used with regard to Poland, Hungary, and Czechoslovakia, President Eisenhower argued the necessity of an American presence there. "You have a row of dominoes set up," he declared. "You knock over the first one, and what will happen to the last one is a certainty that it will go over very quickly." Hence, he concluded, "the loss of South Vietnam would have grave consequences for us and for freedom."

Lyndon Johnson had come of age in a Congress consumed

by anticommunism. He had experienced firsthand the hysteria of the House Un-American Activities Committee, had seen the witch hunt to discover which communist sympathizers in the state department were responsible for "losing" China to communism, and had himself presided over the Leland Olds hearings, shamelessly using allegations that Olds was a fellow traveler to derail his nomination. Thus Johnson was a participant in, as well as an observer of, the dynamic by which anticommunism ruled American politics. He knew that anyone who became vulnerable to charges of being "soft on communism" was in deep trouble. Moreover, Johnson came from a generation that believed it was a matter of honor and patriotism to admit no partisan division on matters of foreign policy, and to stand behind America's commitments, whatever they might be. In the South, as the historian Bertram Wyatt Brown has written, the concept of honor reigned supreme, and nothing could be worse than backing down on one's word or failing to act bravely when confronted with a challenge. "If you let a bully come into your front yard one day," Johnson said, "the next day he will be up on your porch and the day after that he will rape your wife in your own bed." In such a view, the concept of "tucking tail and running" was anathema, challenging a person's (and a culture's) most profound sense of identity.

As vice president, Johnson participated in the decisions that extended U.S. military involvement in Vietnam from 850 men in 1961 to 15,000 in 1963. He also witnessed Kennedy's persistent refusal of Pentagon requests for even more troops. He may not have been aware of Kennedy's intention, shared with some friends, to pull out of Vietnam after the 1964 elections, and even had he known of such conversations, the fact remained that all of Kennedy's advisors, and especially the secretaries of defense and state, Robert McNamara and Dean Rusk, vigorously supported making a stand in Vietnam.

Indeed, making a stand was at the heart of Johnson's approach to communism. Henry Cabot Lodge, the American ambassador to Saigon, was heading home to consult with the president the day Kennedy was killed. Johnson told him to continue his trip, and in their discussions in Washington the new president stated simply the foundations of his policy: "I am not going to lose Vietnam. I am not going to be the president who saw Southeast Asia go the way China went . . . I don't think Congress wants us to let the Communists take over South Vietnam." Framing Johnson's position in a more distinctively Texas idiom, national security adviser McGeorge Bundy noted: "Johnson was simply not going to . . . be the man who can't hold the Alamo." In that famous battle, Texas schoolchildren learned, Colonel William Travis had drawn a line in the dirt with his sword, exhorting all his men who were willing to stay and fight to step across the line. The one soldier who chose to leave became an arch-demon in Texas history, an embodiment of cowardice and shame. If Vietnam was a modern version of the Alamo in Johnson's eyes, it would be difficult to persuade him to consider any course other than standing firm.

Yet there was abundant evidence that Johnson entertained severe doubts about the country's Vietnam policy in 1964 and 1965. At one point he compared decisionmaking on Vietnam to a man standing on a piece of newspaper in the middle of the Atlantic: no matter which way he moved, he was bound to sink. Some of the people Johnson respected most saw only disaster ahead. Richard Russell, for example, urged him to "spend whatever it takes to bring to power a government [in Vietnam] that [will] ask us to go home." Johnson's wife said later: "[Lyndon] could see pretty far down the road most of the time, [and] he just didn't think the American public would have the stomach or the desire [to keep fighting]. So early on he wanted to get out, but he couldn't find any gettin' out place." The generals kept telling him to keep bombing, but even they recognized that air power would not win the struggle. In addition to inventing the domino theory, Dwight Eisenhower had cautioned against over-engagement in Vietnam, saying he could "conceive of no greater tragedy than for the United States to become involved in an all-out land war in Indochina."

More and more, Johnson had the same worries about the war. After one conversation with Russell, Johnson told McGeorge Bundy that he had spent a sleepless night. "The more I stayed awake . . . thinking about this thing," he said, "the more it looks like to me we're getting into another Korea . . . I don't think it is worth fighting for and I don't think we can get out . . . It's just the biggest damn mess." Lady Bird wrote in her diary: "Lyndon lives in a cloud of troubles, with few rays of light . . . In talking about the Vietnam situation, Lyndon summed it up quite simply, 'I can't get out. I can't finish with what I have got, so what the hell can I do?'" Irritated by those who claimed that with enough bombing they could see a "light at the end of the tunnel," Johnson sniffed to Moyers: "Light at the end of the tunnel, hell we don't even have a tunnel; we don't even know where the tunnel is."

As the debate on Vietnam unfolded, Johnson found no answers, only additional questions. Contrary to allegations that the inner circles of the Johnson administration never confronted the arguments against escalation, there is abundant evidence that contrarian points of view were vigorously expressed. In tracing the evolution of this debate, the critical question is not so much what was said and by whom, but rather how the framework of the debate shaped the way the options were presented and perceived. In that light, there appears to have been an inexorable momentum toward ever increasing commitments of American manpower and firepower to Vietnam. The steps were incremental, each one apparently having its own justification; and at each stage there were dissenting voices. Yet in the end those opposed to the decisions the administration made—even if with hindsight we see they were correct—never had a chance because their option was always seen as the extreme, not as a responsible middle-ground position.

By the time of the Gulf of Tonkin resolution in the summer of 1964, Johnson had already increased the number of American advisors in Vietnam by 50 percent, from 16,000 to 23,000—while declaring that he "would never send American boys" to fight a war the Asians should fight for themselves. William Bundy, assistant secretary of state for Far Eastern affairs, was ordered to draft a resolution for Congress endorsing the administration's policy in Vietnam. Meanwhile, American patrol boats and destroyers embarked on a series of attacks against North Vietnamese forces. When word came that the North Vietnamese had attacked American ships in the Gulf of Tonkin, the resolution authorizing Johnson "to take all necessary measures to repel any armed attack against the forces of the United States" was passed by the Senate with only two dissenting votes. Although some doubt existed as to whether a real attack had occurred—it could have been freak weather effects on the radar—Johnson portrayed the North Vietnamese action as "aggression on the high seas," and he now had the authority to proceed with the escalation of the war that his advisors had been planning for the past two months. The Tonkin resolution, Johnson said, was "like grandma's nightshirt—it covered everything." Above all, it was the critical first step in a process that soon resulted in irrevocable commitments. At no time did Johnson tell the Congress that the North Vietnamese attack had come in response to covert U.S. military operations; nor did he reveal the ambiguity of the evidence that an attack had actually occurred.

By February 1965 the next crucial stage unfolded. With the South Vietnamese government plummeting toward collapse, administration officials argued that a greater commitment of American troops and planes was essential to bolster the regime (the government in Saigon would change six times in one year, and every time the instability would be used as an argument for increasing, not diminishing, American manpower). Undersecretary of State George Ball made multiple efforts to highlight the disastrous nature of the road American had started to travel. Knowing the futility of the French experience, Ball warned of the danger that history would repeat itself. "Once on the tiger's back," he said, "we cannot be sure of picking the place to dismount." But his was seen as the extreme position. Others argued that Johnson's escalation was a moderate, intermediate step— and so when Vietcong forces attacked an American base at Pleiku, the attack became the occasion for the United States to launch a massive bombing campaign against the North, appropriately nicknamed "Rolling Thunder." The issue was American honor, Johnson said. "They are killing our men while they sleep at night. I can't ask our American soldiers out there to fight with one hand tied behind their backs." When some questioned whether the attack at Pleiku justified such a response, McGeorge Bundy commented, "Pleikus are like streetcars"—there would always be another one coming along, so the immediate issue was whether to use this particular attack to implement a policy long under discussion. Significantly, no public announcement was made that a policy change of significant proportions had occurred.

The final stage in the decisionmaking process came in July 1965, in response to a Pentagon request for a commitment of 175,000–200,000 troops and a call-up of 250,000 reserves. More than 90,000 American troops had already been authorized, supposedly to provide protection for American air bases. In January, six months earlier, Johnson had told Ambassador Maxwell Taylor that he was "now ready to look with great favor" on sending more troops. "I have never felt that this war will be won from the air," he said. Now, McNamara argued, only a massive influx of American forces could buttress another disintegrating South Vietnamese government and prevent total defeat. Once more George Ball weighed in, warning that this would mean the war had become one of the *United States*—not the South Vietnamese—against the Vietcong, would ultimately lead to a commitment of 500,000 troops, and would end up with America becoming the equivalent of French colonialists, fighting a "white man's war" against a third world developing nation. "No one has yet shown that American troops can win a jungle war against an invisible enemy," he said, and it was time to choose carefully "the terrain on which to stand and fight . . . In my view a deep commitment of United States forces in a land war in South Vietnam would be a catastrophic error. If ever there was an occasion for a tactical withdrawal this is it." But, Ball pointed out, "no one has yet looked at the problem [of tactical withdrawal] carefully since we've been unwilling to think in those terms."

As he had over and over again, Johnson constructed the options as two extremes and one middle way. One extreme was unlimited war against Hanoi, with the risk of involving China—the approach Johnson identified with General Curtis LeMay, who wanted to bomb North Vietnam into oblivion and even use nuclear weapons if necessary. The other extreme was to "tuck tail and run," acknowledging defeat (this was not Ball's position, but his case for tactical withdrawal could easily be distorted to mean "tuck tail and run"). The middle way—committing thousands of additional U.S. troops but not as many as McNamara recommended—thus became the apparently "reasonable, moderate" solution. It "avoids clear pitfalls of either of the major alternatives," William Bundy said. "It may not give us quite as much chance of a successful outcome as the major military action . . . [but it] rejects withdrawal or negotiating concessions." In effect, Johnson's decision to enlarge America's armed presence in Vietnam to the 150,000–200,000 range (but without calling up the reserves as McNamara had demanded) constituted the final component of a now total commitment. "It was the end of debate on policy," William Bundy said, "and the beginning of a new debate on tactics . . . In his own favorite phrase, the president had decided to 'put in his stack'."

At each stage of Johnson's evolving policy, important voices of differing perspectives weighed in, making arguments that in retrospect often seem clairvoyant. But the process was structured to foreordain the results. Johnson always positioned himself as taking the middle way—attempting to satisfy those who sought more escalation without infuriating those who saw the direction of his policy as against American self-interest. By pursuing the choices he made, Johnson minimized the immediate risk to his domestic agenda; nor did his approach alarm public opinion. Johnson achieved what one state department official called the "domestication of dissent": those who wished to be allowed to make their case again another day had to play by Johnson's rules. He, in turn, could use the objections they raised as evidence that he had heard all points of view. But the framework undermined the voices of the dissenters. When Johnson referred to Ball as his "devil's advocate" and called Bill Moyers "Mr. Stop the Bombing," he in effect categorized them as deviants and neutralized their arguments. When Johnson settled on a supposedly moderate "middle" course, and used his posture of moderation to forge consensus among his advisors, he played out a very old script. But this time his unwillingness to make the hard choices led to disaster. To paraphrase Barry Goldwater, extremism in pursuit of consensus is no virtue.

Worst of all, in his obsession with pursuing the "middle way," Johnson continually dissembled with the American people and with Congress, never disclosing what had been decided about the war or even that a decision had been made. He failed to announce the major escalation that began with the "Rolling Thunder" bombing campaign in February 1965. When he finally decided in July to dramatically increase the number of American combat troops in Vietnam, his aides urged him to make a full and detailed disclosure of the decision, why he had made it, and what the prognosis was. "There has to be a cogent, convincing case if we are to enjoy sustained public support," Vice President Humphrey told him. Yet Johnson refused to level with the people or the Congress. He ordered that the troop increments be 15,000 soldiers per month, and he never disclosed the total number to be sent to Vietnam. Indeed, Johnson even told a press conference that sending more troops did "not imply any change in policy whatever." It was as if he were back in the Senate making secret deals behind the scenes, thinking he could keep everybody in the dark until success was achieved. But he was no longer in the Senate, and keeping the nation in the dark was probably the worst mistake he could have made.

In all of this Johnson was desperately trying to protect his first love, the Great Society. "I was determined to keep the war from shattering [my dream of domestic transformation]," he later said, "which meant I simply had no choice but to keep my foreign policy in the wings. I knew the Congress as well as I know Lady Bird, and I knew the day it exploded into a major debate on the war, that day would be the beginning of the end of the Great Society." At the same time, he recognized the power of anticommunism in American politics. Even the thought of losing the Great Society, he told Kearns, was "not so terrible as the thought of being responsible for America's losing a war to the Communists. Nothing could possibly be worse than that." And so he tried to do what needed to be done to prevent a communist victory in Vietnam, but hiding his decisions from Congress and the American people to protect the Great Society. Johnson wanted consensus on his terms, with no debate. Tragically, it was precisely his determination not to confront conflict that ensured the failure of both his greatest domestic dreams and his foreign policy. Johnson's complex behind-the-scenes political style, honed to a level of near genius in his years as Senate leader, ultimately failed because it lacked consistency, openness, and integrity.

To a large extent, the same volatility and inconsistency characterized the personal side of Johnson's life. Just as the conflicts of his childhood helped to shape his political life, especially his intense need to be the one figure who could produce consensus and conciliation, they also infused the way he treated friends and intimates and responded to enemies. Johnson was a deeply insecure person who reflected that insecurity at times by reaching out for solace, and at other times by being abusive, intimidating, egocentric, even paranoid. The private and the public Johnson evoked a dialectical tension, the explosiveness of his political persona a mirror image of a darker private side, each informing the other and ultimately helping to illuminate the puzzling contradictions of Lyndon Johnson.

When Johnson was a child, his mother placed heavy demands on him, insisting he excel at violin lessons, schoolwork, and other activities that fit her vision of what he could become. When he failed to fulfill her expectations, she froze him out, withholding her affection to punish him until he redeemed himself. Johnson used this same pattern throughout his life, with colleagues, staff, friends—anyone less powerful than he who displeased him. When Idaho's freshman senator Frank Church voted the "wrong way" on a motion to challenge the filibuster rule, Johnson refused to speak to Church for months, turning his back on him in the Senate cloakroom, intentionally excluding him from drinks in the majority leader's suite when he invited a group of other senators with whom Church was standing. Only after Church took special steps to ingratiate himself with Johnson did Johnson relent; then he showed extra solicitude to reward Church for his new behavior and tie him even more to Johnson's wishes. After Senator Stuart Symington of Missouri, once a Johnson favorite, started getting too much publicity for his role in the Army-McCarthy hearings, overshadowing Johnson, the majority leader shunned him. Commenting on this pattern, Senator Russell Long of Louisiana noted that Johnson "could not have anyone operating outside his camp. When he saw this developing, he would either reconcile them or isolate them."

No one experienced the controlling consequences—good and bad—of Johnson's volatility more than Hubert Humphrey. Entering the Senate the same year as Johnson, Humphrey embodied liberal idealism. He electrified the 1948 Democratic convention, winning support for a minority plank on civil rights by declaring that it was time for the party to "get out of the shadow of states' rights and walk forthrightly into the bright sunshine of human rights." Once in the Senate, Humphrey continued to proclaim his commitment to equal justice, offending the "old bulls" of the Senate not only by speeches they considered intemperate but also by inviting a black staff member to lunch in the Senate dining room at a time when segregation still reigned. Johnson joined other southern senators in isolating Humphrey, turning his back when he entered a room, looking past him in conversations. Then he moved to win Humphrey over, telling him he needed to become something more than a "gramophone for the NAACP," and promising that if he would play ball with Johnson he could advance his own causes. He went so far as to say that Humphrey was the only liberal he would deal with, and that if Humphrey cooperated, he would use Humphrey as a channel through which to reward other liberals with committee assignments and other perquisites.

In effect, Johnson shaped Humphrey into his personal instrument, making any power Humphrey could exercise dependent on his ability to please Johnson. Johnson would freeze him out if he dissented in a way Johnson did not like, then shower him with praise and symbols of influence when he behaved accordingly. For months before the Democratic nominating convention in 1964, most Democrats knew that Humphrey would be the choice for vice president. But Johnson treated him like a criminal suspect in an interrogation room, repeatedly subjecting him to demeaning questions about his background, personal morality, and commitment to fealty to the president. "I want his pecker in my pocket," Johnson told associates. He even made Humphrey sign a pledge to always be a yes man were he to become vice president. Indeed, when Humphrey dared to question Johnson's decision to bomb North Vietnam in 1965, he found himself excluded from government councils for months, until he showed complete subordination once more.

The same controlling behavior characterized Johnson's relationship to his staff. Each day, his aide Horace Busby said, the "first thing every morning, he would make the rounds, stopping at every desk, and beating up on [the staff]." Johnson's unpredictability gave him more, not less, control. To one secretary he would say, "Clean up your fucking desk," and then to another, whose desk was clear, "I hope your mind isn't as empty as your desk." He would yell at staff assistants, once throwing a book at Nellie Connally, wife of the future governor of Texas. Control was the key. "He could be totally charming," Nadine Brammer, a staff member, said, "a lot of fun . . . but there was a rotten side to him . . . It was like a family atmosphere and he was the Big Daddy . . . He ruled with fear—like a heavy duty parent. Fear permeated the whole staff. Lyndon would jump on someone. Just make mincemeat of him. Tongue-lashing people . . . I've seen Walter [Jenkins] shake, just literally shake, when Lyndon was asking him questions. Walter was just stripped of any human dignity." Johnson's longtime aide George Reedy observed: "He seemed to take a special delight at humiliating those who had cast their lot with him. It may be that this was the result of a form of self-loathing in which he concluded that there had to be something wrong with anyone who would associate with him." Whatever the explanation, the pattern pervaded Johnson's interaction with those subordinate to him.

Not surprisingly, some of the same characteristics affected Johnson's relationship with Lady Bird. Throughout much of their lives together, Lyndon treated her like a servant, ordering her impatiently to get food for him and his guests, making fun of the way she looked, the clothes she wore, and the way she styled her hair. "His attitude toward her was utter contempt," one Texas congressman said, while another declared: "Lady Bird was charming, but she was the most beaten down woman I ever saw. You immediately felt sorry for her. Her husband was so mean to her, so publicly humiliating. He would dismiss what she said with a disgusted wave of his arm." Repeatedly, associates of the family commented to Robert Caro: "I don't know how she stood it." Nor was the disregard limited to Lady Bird. The two Johnson daughters, Luci Baines and Lynda Bird, rarely saw their father, and when they did, often failed to receive his attention. "Daddy was the kind of man who believed it was more important to invite Richard Russell . . . over for Sunday breakfast," Lynda recalled, "than to spend time alone with his family." "I wanted a normal life," Luci echoed. "I wanted a father who came home at a reasonable hour and a mother who made cookies. That wasn't what we had."

Johnson flaunted his sexual conquests, seeming not to care whether Lady Bird knew about them or not. "He was always trying to put the make on me," Nadine Brammer recalled. "There was a lot of personal exhibitionism, a lot of hitting on women." Johnson's inner office was known as the "nooky room," where he regularly had sexual liaisons. Johnson once bragged: "Why I had more women by accident than [Kennedy] ever had by design." For years he had an affair with Alice Glass, a stunning woman who was then the mistress (and later the wife) of the publisher of the *Austin American-Statesman*. When that affair ended, Johnson began another with Congresswoman Helen Gahagan Douglas, dubbed "one of the twelve most beautiful women in America," and the wife of the Hollywood actor Melvyn Douglas.

Moreover, Johnson made sure that Alice Glass's sister saw him with Douglas. "Just bragging," Glass's sister said disgustedly, "kissing and telling." The *Time* magazine correspondent Hugh Sidey reported that Johnson even "caressed other women in front of [Lady Bird]," in one instance having his hand under a woman's skirt while driving a car, with Lady Bird in the back seat.

To Johnson, it seemed, sex was one more way of proving his power to himself and showing it off to others. He urinated in front of staff members, male and female. He occasionally displayed his penis—"Jumbo," he called it—asking one man, "Have you ever seen anything as big as this?" Bigness was always a feature of Johnson—in his hovering presence, his grabbing people by the lapels and pulling them toward him, his "in your face" lobbying. And clearly sex—and Johnson's sexual organ—was part of that persona. Once, in a discussion in his office, a reporter asked why the United States was in Vietnam. In response, according to Arthur Goldberg, Johnson's ambassador to the United Nations, "LBJ unzipped his fly, drew out his substantial organ, and declared, 'this is why'."

Despite all this, Lady Bird remained devoted to her husband. She tolerated his affairs—"I would have thought Alice Glass was a bit too plump for Lyndon," she commented—doted on his every request, and placed his happiness and interests above all else. When called upon, she did a superb job of helping with his legislative office, and in the period after his heart attack in 1955 she never left his side. After that episode, Johnson acknowledged a growing dependence on Lady Bird. He did not stop his philandering, but he became grouchy and depressed when she was not around, and gave her more credit than before for all that she did for him. Nevertheless, it is difficult to review Johnson's treatment of Lady Bird, his record of sexual conquests, or his attitudes toward his own sexuality without concluding that an element of egomania was an important part of Lyndon Johnson. His quest for personal power was abnormal, he frequently exceeded all bounds of rational behavior, and he displayed an unquenchable thirst for validation and control.

Given Johnson's obsession with loyalty, subservience, and unanimity from those around him, it is not surprising that he viewed dissent as unacceptable, and attributed it, not to honest differences of opinion, but to subversive, potentially traitorous sources. "Anything less than total agreement burned like salt in his wounds," Robert Caro has written. Fearful that the 1964 convention would be less than a total acclamation of his presidency, Johnson had the FBI wiretap the civil rights forces gathered in Atlantic City to ensure that their protest against the all-white Mississippi delegation could be controlled. He even had a wiretap installed on Hubert Humphrey, the man he was about to designate as his vice president.

When opposition to the Vietnam war began to mount, Johnson first demonized journalists like David Halberstam of the *New York Times* and Peter Arnett of the Associated Press for their stories on the futility of the war effort. "Halberstam . . . is a traitor," he told the journalist Robert Sherrod. "They give Pulitzer prizes to traitors nowadays." But increasingly Johnson saw a larger conspiracy at work. When the Senate foreign relations committee began to hold hearings on the war, Johnson concluded that J. William Fulbright of Arkansas, Wayne Morse of Oregon, and other committee members were "communist dupes" and ordered the FBI to determine whether comments made in the committee reflected communist views. In the face of a growing number of mass demonstrations against the war,

Johnson asked CIA director Richard Helms to ascertain whether the peace movement was being directed by communists; when Helms reported that there was no significant evidence that such was the case, Johnson ordered him to look again. More and more, Johnson alluded in public to a communist plot, insisting in a talk to the nation's governors: "Our country is constantly under threat . . . Communists [are] working every day to divide us, to destroy us . . . It is in the highest counsels of government." He even told a cabinet luncheon that the Soviets were "in constant touch with anti-war senators . . . The Russians think up things for the senators to say." And when the CBS news reporter Morley Safer broadcast a report showing Marines burning down a Vietnamese thatched hut, Johnson exploded to the president of CBS, Frank Stanton: "How could CBS employ a communist like Safer, how could they be so unpatriotic as to put on an enemy film like this?" By 1967 Johnson was telling Bill Moyers that the communists controlled the three major networks and forty other major communication outlets.

In light of the way Johnson responded to criticism of any kind, a number of White House aides began to question the president's mental stability. When Johnson told his aide Richard Goodwin that "he was the target of a gigantic communist conspiracy," Goodwin called Moyers to confide his fear that the president was becoming paranoid. Moyers shared Goodwin's concern, telling him on another occasion that "he was extremely worried, that as he listened to Johnson, he felt weird, almost . . . as [if] he wasn't really talking to a human being at all." Rusk expressed similar sentiments, and when Moyers went to talk to Lady Bird about the issue, he came away "knowing that she herself was more concerned." Johnson "was a tormented man," Moyers told Robert Dallek. "He would just go within himself, just disappear—morose, self-pitying, angry." The president told Moyers he felt as if he was in a Louisiana swamp "that's pulling me down."

Never far below the surface of Johnson's personal obsessions was his antagonism toward, and fear of, Robert F. Kennedy. The two had always detested each other. Kennedy was furious that Johnson had turned down his father's offer to bankroll a Johnson presidential campaign in 1956 if Johnson would choose Jack Kennedy as his vice president. Kennedy was outraged when Johnson forced him to shoot at a deer on a hunting trip at Johnson's ranch, and became even more angry when, after he was knocked down by the recoil of the rifle, Johnson lectured him, "Son, you've got to learn to handle a gun like a man." In 1960 Bobby plotted to withdraw the invitation to Johnson to become Kennedy's running mate, after the invitation had already been accepted. During the Kennedy administration the conflict intensified, with Kennedy using his influence as President Kennedy's alter ego to pressure Johnson on civil rights, even attending the meetings Johnson convened of the president's committee on equal economic opportunity and openly challenging Johnson and his aides. "It was a pretty brutal performance, very sharp," one witness said. "And then finally, after . . . making the vice president look like a fraud, . . . [Kennedy] got up . . . and went out." Johnson turned the tables when he called Kennedy to his office to tell him he would not consider him for the vice presidency in 1964, taped the conversation secretly, and then mocked Kennedy to a group of journalists, making fun of Bobby's unease and "his Adam's apple bobbing up and down." The two could hardly have been more different, nor more determined to get each other.

Johnson's anxiety about Kennedy manifested itself repeatedly.

To the end of the 1964 convention, he feared that Kennedy would sweep the hall in an emotional tidal wave and become the vice presidential nominee. Hence he scheduled Kennedy's speech for after all the nominations had been concluded. When Kennedy started to criticize the Vietnam war, Johnson feared that Kennedy was plotting against him, cultivating sympathizers inside the administration to betray him, and planning to run against him for the presidency in 1968. When the *Washington Star* published a series of articles critical of Johnson's Vietnam policy, Johnson ordered the FBI to investigate whether Kennedy was behind the stories, and whether Kennedy had purchased stock in the newspaper. Johnson started having dreams about Kennedy, telling Richard Goodwin that in one nightmare he was "being chased on all sides by a giant stampede . . . I was being forced over the edge by rioting blacks, demonstrating students, marching welfare mothers, squawking professors and hysterical reporters. And then the final straw. Robert Kennedy had openly announced his intention to reclaim the throne in the memory of his brother. And the American people, swayed by the magic of his name, were dancing in the streets."

There is no way of knowing definitively what if any effect Johnson's tortured relationship with Kennedy had on his decisions on domestic and foreign policy. But veteran observers like Hugh Sidey noted "an increasing worry about the president around town, . . . a fear that his personal eccentricities" might be affecting policies. And Dallek has observed that as criticism of the war intensified, the president saw the debate as "a personal test of his judgment," with Kennedy's opposition to the war adding to Johnson's "determination to see the war through to a proper conclusion." In Dallek's view, "It is not too much of a stretch to conclude that the Johnson personality was inhibiting him from a more realistic and sensible resolution of a war policy that seemed certain to lead to more losses, more domestic divisions, and greater limitations on his capacity to lead at home and abroad." Whatever the reasons, and despite his own deep doubts about the war in Vietnam, Johnson pursued a policy that not only severely compromised his chance to go down in history as someone who transformed the domestic politics of America, but also actually promoted the domestic divisions he had spent his life seeking to avoid.

In a poignant retrospective, Johnson told Doris Kearns one morning in 1970:

> I knew from the start that I was bound to be crucified either way I moved. If I left the woman I really loved—the Great Society—in order to get involved with the bitch of a war on the other side of the world, then I would lose everything at home. All my programs. All my hopes to feed the hungry and shelter the homeless, . . . but if I left that war and let the communists take over South Vietnam, then I would be seen as a coward, and my nation would be seen as an appeaser and we would both find it impossible to accomplish anything for anybody anywhere on the entire globe.

Stuck in that Louisiana swamp he had mentioned to Bill Moyers, Johnson had no way out. By 1968 the public and the administration recognized the futility of further escalation. McNamara had turned against the war, haunted by his personal responsibility for the carnage; and even the council of "wise men" who had ratified each escalation—venerable policy experts such as Dean Acheson—now argued that negotiating for peace was the only possible course. But by that time, it was too late. Johnson had missed his chance.

It was a bitter pill to swallow for someone who had striven for so much. He had wanted to be "the greatest of them all, the whole bunch of them," one observer noted—even to exceed Roosevelt. And in many ways he had done so. "[Johnson's] list of achievements is so long," Tom Wicker wrote in the *New York Times*, "that it reads better than the legislative achievements of most two-term presidents." But in the end he could not have everything at once—social reform, a government that cared for the poor and oppressed, a solid economy, and a foreign policy that triumphed over communism in a war of national liberation. For more than two decades American politics had been guided by the dual goals of what Godfrey Hodgson dubbed the "liberal consensus"—incremental reform at home and containment of communism abroad—but now the contradictions between those two priorities split America into polarized camps and destroyed Lyndon Johnson's presidency.

◆　◆　◆

Ironically, Johnson's greatest achievements and greatest failures flowed from the same dynamic. He desperately sought approval, unanimity, popularity, reconciliation—reflecting his need to escape the conflict of his parents and their disparate demands. Always racked by fear that he would not be respected or loved, Johnson overdid everything—his outreach for affection, his cultivation of legislative support, his pursuit of women, his appetite for power, his maneuvering to get everyone on his side. He had to rule. There could be no dissent, no conflict—because if there were, he would be back in the nightmare of his childhood, torn between irreconcilable opposites.

Two issues, in the end, threatened the consensus, unity, and popular acclaim that Johnson worked so hard to achieve. The first was race. Throughout most of his career he had finessed the issue, retaining unity as his goal and seeking ways to satisfy both southern conservatives and northern liberals by support-ing halfway measures on civil rights. Then after John F. Kennedy was murdered, Johnson was able to harness his own ambitions to Kennedy's legacy and forge a new unity, this time on behalf of a forthright commitment to racial equality and social justice. Kennedy's death did for Johnson what he could not do for him-self—liberated him from the past and allowed him to transcend old divisions. It also cast him in the role of the father figure who brought healing to a wounded nation. "It was as if the disadvan-taged were extensions of himself," Dallek has written—and by helping those in need Johnson could also achieve his own fan-tasy of becoming a national hero, cheered by all and leading the nation to new heights of greatness.

But that same sense of liberation did not occur with Vietnam. Whatever his responsibility for having deepened American in-volvement there, President Kennedy had refused to make Viet-nam his crusade, and had resisted pressure to commit more troops. To a large extent, therefore, it was Johnson who made the primary decisions on Vietnam, notwithstanding the history of support for South Vietnam that he inherited from both Eis-enhower and Kennedy. At this juncture, Johnson's passion for consensus and his penchant for manipulation and behind-the-scenes bargaining prevented him from making decisions that might have preserved his presidency. Reverting to his fundamen-tal political instincts, he always chose an accommodationist "middle way" between sharply divergent choices, and he con-structed the choices so that the option he defined as moderate became the only possibility. Furthermore, Johnson refused to tell either the public or the Congress of the choices he was mak-ing, instead using the secret mechanisms of his congressional days to make policy while keeping the public uninformed.

Holding back information was a way of retaining the appearance of consensus, and of avoiding the debate and conflict that so threatened Johnson's sense of security and domination.

Arguably, the liberation Johnson experienced on race when he became president could have carried over to foreign policy. Clearly he understood the negatives of persisting with a military build-up in Vietnam. Yet he could not bear the prospect of being accused of "losing" Vietnam to communism. Moreover, to have shown the same decisiveness and courage on Vietnam that he had shown on race would have destroyed the personal and political goal he prized more than any other—consensus. "The war," Lady Bird said later, "was . . . a thorn stuck in his throat . . . It wouldn't come up; it wouldn't go down . . . It was pure hell [that he] did not have that reassuring, strong feeling that this is right . . . that he had with . . . civil rights." Yet whenever he started to talk about defending freedom against communism the crowds would cheer, and even if he did not know he was right, he saw no way out of Vietnam.

In his fondest dreams, one correspondent wrote, Johnson saw himself in the "image of a great popular leader something like Franklin Roosevelt, except more so, striding over the land and cupping the people in his hand and molding a national unity that every president dreams about but none is ever able to achieve." Only by pursuing that image could Johnson exorcise the lifelong fears that drove him to such extremes of personal and political behavior. Ultimately, however, in a resolution reminiscent of classical tragedy, Johnson's need to transcend conflict and his pursuit of that hubristic dream brought down upon him—and upon the nation—the very polarization he wished to avoid.

6

RICHARD M. NIXON
Genius and Paranoia

It was the eve of Richard Nixon's decision to invade Cambodia. The president had been writing on his pad of yellow-lined paper all day, contemplating the pros and cons of an action destined to create political cacophony at home, including mass revulsion on the nation's campuses, and dismay abroad. Henry Kissinger, his national security advisor, tried to persuade a *Newsweek* commentator—off the record—that Nixon was like France's Charles de Gaulle, seeking to create an illusion of conquest as a vehicle for strategic withdrawal. In the midst of his deliberations, Nixon suddenly telephoned his chief of staff, H. R. Haldeman, to tell him that the solarium in the White House living quarters would not accommodate the pool table Nixon wanted; the table would have to go elsewhere, he said. "Astonishing," Haldeman wrote, "[devolving] into trivia on the brink of the biggest step he's taken so far." It was pure Nixon—to entertain momentous policy decisions and simultaneously become captive to trivial details.

❖ ❖ ❖

As much as any figure in American political history, Richard Milhous Nixon embodied the theme of paradox. A loner who detested the gregarious give-and-take of political interaction, in 1972 he received the largest electoral mandate of any president in the twentieth century. Consumed with a vision of transforming global power relations, he allowed himself to become bogged down in a petty politics of revenge that destroyed his presidency. A man who spent hours writing notes to himself about the importance of spiritual and moral leadership, he regularly referred to Jews as "kikes" and blacks as "cannibals" while pursuing a politics of cultural hatred. Nixon was elected president on the promise to "bring people together," yet he polarized the nation and in the end nearly destroyed its political system by his deception and lies. While Nixon rose, on occasion, to the stature of a giant striding the world's landscape, he fell at other times into self-loathing and ineffectuality. Ultimately, the brooding introspection that fed his richest dreams of glory also produced the paranoia and hatred that brought him down.

Nixon grew up in a Quaker family with deep roots in Whittier, California. The Quaker tradition dominated the community, including the local college, and the Milhous clan was particularly noted for its closeness and pride. "The Milhouses thought highly of the Milhouses," one relative observed. Hannah Milhous, Nixon's mother, was a particularly strong figure. "Inside this frail, skinny woman," a friend later said, "was steel, pure steel. She was a true Quaker." After a religious conversion at age fifteen, she became devout, praying nightly and asserting through her daily activities the seriousness of her religious commitment. Yet Hannah also had a rebellious streak, reflected in her decision to take a year off from Whittier College, and even more so in her determination at age twenty-three to marry Frank Nixon, a non-Quaker.

From the beginning, the differences between Frank and Hannah Nixon were evident. Many acquaintances believed she had married beneath her. Hannah, said one, was a "cultured, refined, educated person from a rather superior family," while Frank lacked schooling, was loud, and frequently took vocal stands on issues where consensus was unlikely. Indeed, he had come to the Los Angeles area from San Francisco, where he had worked as a motorman, after he protested his working conditions and organized voters to support a candidate for office who promised remedial legislation. A person with a substantial temper, he yelled at his children and occasionally struck them. Although the Milhous clan offered land and some financial support to the Nixons, Frank resisted their control. When Hannah went to visit her family, Frank would wait for her in the car and beep the horn to urge her to hurry. Several times Hannah left her own home to stay with the Milhouses, suggesting a level of recurrent family tension that would inevitably affect a young child.

Richard Nixon was born into this family in 1913, the second of five sons. He would later recall the poverty of his background and how hard his parents had worked to keep things together. It certainly was true that the early years were not ones of economic comfort. Hannah took a job at a packing house, and the boys worked as well. But the family did progress economically. Hannah had brought with her from her family some elegant furniture. By the time Richard was five, his father owned both a car and a tractor. Later there was a second car for the boys to drive to high school. After the family opened its own store, conditions improved further, providing enough economic security that Richard's older bother Harold could be sent to Mount Herman, a prestigious private boarding school in Massachusetts. Not until the 1940s, however, did the family enjoy a substantial economic cushion. It was a hard life compared with Hannah's background, but not the bleak poverty that Nixon subsequently invoked as part of his political persona.

From childhood Richard had a distinctive personality, divided between purposive action and isolated reflection. He was "not someone you wanted to cuddle," one relative said. Impressively bright, he displayed early the excellent memory that would later permit him, without notes, to present perfectly timed speeches. Yet he did not play easily. He was "not as outreaching as many children are," a household worker later recalled. "He lived more within himself." Always seeking privacy, Richard found a vacant corner in the church to make into his study hall, and even on family picnics, one of his younger brothers noted, he "would always go off by himself." When the brothers worked at the family store, Richard preferred to do the chores, such as bookkeeping, that involved solitary effort rather than the jobs that entailed interaction with people. Driven to excel, he was named valedictorian of his grammar school class, and already had plotted a career plan that he said would take him to Whittier College, then to postgraduate work at Columbia and travel to Europe.

As his first step, he joined 57 other local students who entered Whittier College in 1930. With a total freshman class of 139, the "townies" at Whittier constituted a significant presence. Nixon was elected to a number of student offices during college years, and excelled at debating, but his fundamental personality traits persisted. "He was a loner," one classmate said. Not, said another, "a hale fellow well met by a long shot." According to acquaintances, Nixon was "a very tense person" and "did not have any close friends." The pattern of achieving public recognition while remaining isolated and aloof characterized Nixon's experience at Duke Law School as well. After finishing third in his class during his first year at Duke, he fell behind in year two, and in a rash act of short-sighted trickery broke into the dean's office to ascertain his grades. Still, he kept his scholarship, and in his final year he was third in his class and was elected president of the law school association.

In spite of these credentials from a highly regarded law school, and although he interviewed widely in New York, Nixon was not hired by a high-status law firm. Instead, he found himself back in Whittier without prospects, left to rely on his mother to approach a local Quaker lawyer to offer her son a job. Even then, Nixon refused to respond, as though to do so was beneath him. When finally he did consent to go for an interview, a lawyer at the firm said, "he gave the impression that he was there to see whether *he* wanted to work with *us.*" Eventually Nixon took the job, was relatively well treated, and developed political connections that a few years later would help in his first campaign for public office. It remained to be seen whether he could find a career consistent with his talent and his intelligence, given his unattractive personality.

During those same years Nixon engaged in his first serious relationships with women. Throughout college he had dated a classmate, Ola Welch, whom others expected him to marry. But it seemed mostly a courtship of convenience rather than passion. Welch could not recall Nixon's ever saying that he loved her, and although he acted wounded when she told him she was engaged to someone else, there had never been a foundation on which to build a more lasting partnership. "He seemed lonely and so solemn," Welch remembered. "He didn't know how to mix. He was smart and sort of set apart. I think he was unsure of himself deep down."

Back in Whittier after law school, however, Nixon fell in love for the first time, with a trim, independent schoolteacher named Thelma Ryan (who later changed her first name to Patricia). Hard working and self-sufficient, Ryan allowed Nixon to squire her to various events but insisted on going off to Los Angeles every weekend for its more active social life. Yet even as she discouraged intimacy, she met Hannah and Frank, helped Hannah bake pies at the family store, and eventually succumbed to Nixon's wooing. Writing about himself in the third person, as was his wont, Nixon told her that he still "gets the same thrill when you say you'll go someplace with him," concluding: "And when the winds blow and the rains fall and the sun shines through the clouds, as it is now, he still resolves . . . that nothing so fine ever happened to him than falling in love with Thee—my dearest heart." Finally, at age twenty-eight, Patricia Ryan, though still concerned about giving up her independence, accepted Richard Nixon's proposal, and they married in June 1940.

World War II soon disrupted their lives. From being a carefree couple with a combined income of $4,800, they became a nomadic pair, moving as Richard first became an attorney with the office of price administration in Washington, and then joined the navy. As long as she could, Pat followed her husband, securing jobs wherever he moved, but when he shipped off to the South Pacific she settled in San Francisco, enjoying a stimulating, challenging life that restored her sense of independence. "I will have to admit that I am pretty self-reliant," she wrote to him, "and if I didn't love you I would feel very differently. In fact, these many months that you have been away have been full of interest and had I not missed you so much and had I been footloose, could have been extremely happy." But the independence she enjoyed so much would soon disappear. Nixon came back, initially to close out his military career in Maryland (where one associate described the Nixons as "the dullest couple we ever met in the Navy . . . very conservative, very conventional") and then to move back to California, where he had already begun to contemplate a career in politics.

◆　◆　◆

Part of a conservative political area, Whittier boasted at least some leading citizens who combined Quaker religious practice with right-wing Republicanism. Herman Perry, a Quaker and one of Nixon's chief backers, wanted to "put an end to the socialist trend of the New Deal." Nixon was ready, delivering a series of speeches to local audiences declaring that Democrats had "led us far on the road to socialism and communism." Hitching up with Murray Chotiner, a brilliant, shrewd, and ambitious political operative, Nixon soon settled upon a campaign strategy that would become a leitmotif for much of his life over the next fifteen years. Employing half-truths, carefully planted innuendos, and guilt by association against his opponents, Nixon became the guru of the politics of anticommunism, all the while persuading many in his audience that he was more moderate and responsible than others in his party, such as Joseph McCarthy, who were more blatantly demagogic in their approach.

The initial object of Nixon's red-baiting political debut was Jerry Voorhis, a Yale graduate who had written three books on currency reform and was known primarily for his ardent advocacy of New Deal policies. Nixon had already laid the foundation for his campaign by linking the Truman administration to the advance of communism, blaming Democrats not only for being "soft on communism" but for having aided and abetted the communist menace. Now Nixon took advantage of an endorsement of Voorhis by the National Citizens Political Action Committee, a liberal lobbying organization, to claim that in fact Voorhis had been endorsed by the Political Action Committee of the Congress of Industrial Organizations (CIO), a far more left-leaning group alleged by conservatives to be communist-dominated. Asserting repeatedly that Voorhis had accepted support from the CIO PAC, though he knew this to be untrue, Nixon threw the incumbent on the defensive. Striding onto the stage during a joint appearance, Nixon stunned Voorhis by holding out a copy of the endorsement and challenging Voorhis to renounce the communists who had declared their support for him. By the time Voorhis recovered, Nixon had defined his opponent as in bed with the devil and created the major issue of the campaign. "Why are you doing this?" a troubled friend asked Nixon. "Because," Nixon responded, "sometimes you have to do this to be a candidate. I'm gonna win."

Within days, Nixon denounced his opponent as a "lip service American" who voted the communist line and "fronted for un-American elements." Specifically, Nixon's newspaper ads accused the CIO PAC of kowtowing to the interests of the Russians, claimed that Voorhis had taken the same positions as the CIO PAC on 90 percent of all issues, and alleged that Voorhis's support for such issues as soil conservation, abolition of the poll tax, and a federal school lunch program showed how pro-Soviet he was. "REMEMBER," the ad concluded, "Voorhis is a former registered Socialist and his voting record in Congress is more Socialistic and Communistic than Democratic." Voters throughout the district received anonymous phone calls, a voice on the line saying "This is a friend of yours [and] I just wanted you to know that Jerry Voorhis is a communist." In a prototype of Nixon's later campaign, an election day ad declared: "VOTE AGAINST NEW DEAL COMMUNISM. VOTE REPUBLICAN. VOTE AMERICAN." It was all sleight of hand, moving smoothly from identifying the New Deal with communism to suggesting that being a Republican was the same thing as being a patriotic American. Challenged later on his tactics, Nixon averred: "Of course I knew Jerry Voorhis was not a communist . . . [but] I had to win. That's the thing you don't understand. The important thing is to win." Moreover, Nixon had achieved his goal with sufficient shrewdness that many in the national media never grasped the perniciousness of his tactics. Nixon had "politely avoided personal attacks," *Time* magazine declared, even as he "turned a California grass-root campaign . . . into a triumph over high-powered, high-minded Democratic incumbent Jerry Voorhis."

Now a member of the class of 1946 in Congress—where the Republicans gained a total of 89 seats—Nixon moved decisively to cement his triumph and lay the groundwork for even more spectacular advances. He still lacked charm and social ease. With Nixon, the reporter George Reedy said, you had the feeling that you "weren't talking to a human being, but a doll wound up and pulling a string . . . I never had the faintest idea of what the man was like." But Nixon pushed his agenda aggressively, winning a seat on the House Un-American Activities Committee (HUAC) while solidifying his reputation for intelligent conservatism. He voted against all the things he had accused Voorhis of voting for—school lunch funds, soil conservation—while still managing to appear relatively moderate.

Pat Nixon found the new life far less appealing, telling her daughter that she "began to despair that the camaraderie and carefree times of her early married years were a thing of the past." She put up one last fight for a different way of living, candidly telling her husband of her discontent. But with the exception of a fervent love letter and promises of more time at home and more frequent vacations, nothing changed. In fact, events were soon to transpire that would define the remainder of Nixon's political career and would probably end forever Pat's hope for more freedom.

It would not be too much to say that the Alger Hiss case made Richard Nixon's subsequent political success possible. Nixon had been briefed on Hiss's potential importance by Father John Cronin, his behind-the-scenes advisor on all issues of anticommunism. Then Hiss's name became the centerpiece of testimony before the HUAC by Whittaker Chambers, a self-confessed former Communist Party member and now an editor for *Time* magazine. A bizarre personality (he came from a family afflicted by neurosis, sexual scandals, and suicide), Chambers told the committee that he had been close friends with Alger Hiss and his wife as fellow party members, recounting the emotional strain of telling Hiss in 1938 of his decision to leave the party. Within days, Hiss appeared before the committee, of his own volition, to contest the allegations. Hiss, a former assistant secretary of state who had accompanied President Roosevelt at Yalta and was now president of the Carnegie Endowment for International Peace, refuted Chambers's testimony. Confronted with pictures of Chambers, Hiss denied he had ever met the man, and with the polished patina of one who had character references from Felix Frankfurter and Dean Acheson, embarrassed committee members with his total rejection of everything Chambers had said.

At this point Nixon, a freshman member of the committee, made a pivotal intervention that would change both his own life and that of Hiss. While other members of the committee were prepared to dismiss Chambers's allegations, Nixon argued that the investigation should proceed, with a separate subcommittee authorized to pursue the Chambers charges. Nixon had been disturbed by the cocky self-confidence of Hiss's responses, and he recalled that Chambers had used a number of aliases under which Hiss might have known him. There was also an anti-establishment impulse that appeared to move Nixon. Hiss was simply supported by too many members of the eastern elite. Later the chief investigator of HUAC noted: "Nixon had his hat set for Hiss. It was a personal thing. He was no more concerned about whether Hiss was [a communist] than a billy goat." Regardless of his motivation, Nixon prevailed in HUAC's deliberations, and won as well the right to chair the subcommittee to investigate Chambers's accusations. It was a moment of both high drama and enormous political consequence.

Over the next two weeks Nixon and his staff investigators met with Chambers repeatedly, eliciting more detailed information on his contacts with Hiss, including descriptions of the Hiss households, Hiss's love of ornithology, and such details as the fact that Hiss's wife, a Quaker by faith, used the plain language of Quakerism ("thee" and "thou") with her husband. Many of the details were wrong, but some of Chambers's testimony— especially the comment on "plain language," which Nixon's mother used at home—scored with Nixon, who became more and more convinced that Chambers and Hiss had known each other. In the meantime, Nixon cleverly reached out to Republican giants like Thomas Dewey and John Foster Dulles, then chairman of the board of the Carnegie Endowment, keeping them informed about the unfolding drama. As Nixon's biographer Roger Morris observes, during this process, "despite his unsureness and precarious, mercurial judgment, Richard Nixon had kept at it with his habitual intensity and application, subduing his own inner weakness and misgiving . . . The political courage and perseverance were exceptional."

Although the risks remained high, Nixon's intervention looked better and better with the passage of time. Hiss acknowledged in further testimony that he might have known Chambers as George Crosley. He then, inadvertently, disclosed his excitement at having sighted a rare bird near Washington, thereby confirming a detail Chambers had provided. When Hiss admitted that he had let Crosley use his apartment and gave an accurate description of Mrs. Chambers, Nixon declared, "I knew the case had been broken."

Even more explosive developments soon occurred. Although he had previously denied under oath that he had engaged in any espionage or transfer of classified documents, Chambers now asserted that Hiss had used him as a middleman to transmit microfilm of classified government materials to the communists. Moreover, he provided handwritten and typed notes and containers of undeveloped film (dramatically leading investigators to a pumpkin patch where he had hidden the film in a hollowed-out pumpkin) that linked Hiss to the charges. Hiss even seemed to help the accusers by offering evidence that some of the documents had been typed on a typewriter he owned.

Many of these fast-breaking developments occurred during a period when Nixon had promised Pat a long-deferred cruise vacation. Intent on saving his marriage, he agreed to take the vacation as planned. It was "one of the few—and last—instances," Roger Morris writes, "of Nixon allowing family concerns to override political considerations." But not for long. During the first week of the cruise, HUAC staff telegraphed Nixon to return as quickly as possible. Nixon did so, and became the central public figure identified with the allegations against Hiss as a spy who purloined secret government documents and transmitted them to the Soviet Union. He appeared in newsreels showing what came to be called the "pumpkin papers," and he took full credit as the key person who had broken the case. Moreover, Nixon's testimony before a grand jury in New York made the critical difference in a decision, by one vote, to indict Hiss for perjury, and the decision by the same grand jury not to indict Chambers on the same charge.

Although information from Soviet archives would later establish conclusively that Hiss had in fact been a communist spy, for the moment the charges against him remained controversial. The first trial ended in a hung jury. In the second trial, Hiss's supporters accused the prosecution of obfuscating key evidence that the documents might not have been typed on the typewriter Hiss owned. Indeed, in many Americans' minds the degree to which Hiss had helped provide evidence that would eventually be used against him cast doubt on his complicity, since a guilty person would presumably have been more careful not to hurt his own case. Nevertheless, the second jury convicted Hiss, allowing Nixon to declare the verdict "a vindication of the congressional methods of investigation when they are accompanied by adequate staff work and fair procedure."

The Hiss case provided the mantra with which Richard Nixon would, from that moment on, carry his political message to the American people. Almost immediately, Nixon went on the air to allege a conspiracy by two Democratic administrations—Roosevelt's and Truman's—to cover up Hiss's involvement in a communist plot. It was not far from there to the claim that the Democrats were part of that conspiracy in their own right; or even more perniciously, to the assertion that liberals who questioned the tactics of Nixon or other anticommunist crusaders were aiding and abetting a communist cabal. The Hiss case also allowed Nixon to portray himself as the target of an "utterly unprincipled and vicious smear campaign" by those who were discomfited by his victory. It was a crystallizing moment of his political career, helping to shape a politics of righteous polarization in which allegations of impropriety could slide easily into categorical denunciations of a person or a cause.

In his book *Six Crises* Nixon demonstrated the way this process could unfold. Calling Hiss a symbol for "perfectly loyal citizens whose theaters of operation are the nation's mass media and universities," Nixon argued that even though such "liberals" were "not communists," they were "of a mind-set as doctrinaire as those on the extreme right, which makes them singularly vulnerable to the communist popular front appeal under the banner of social justice. In the time of the Hiss case they were 'patsies' for the communist line." Through such arguments Nixon isolated "liberals" as a suspect category, denied he was calling them disloyal, then linked a concern for "social justice" issues, such as income distribution or civil rights, with communism. No longer just an ordinary congressman, Nixon now had both a persona and a mission that left no one neutral toward him. "He has the cruelest face of any man I ever met," House Speaker Sam Rayburn commented. And he was ready to take that hard-edged persona to a new level of political success.

In just four years, using the Hiss case as a springboard to reach new political heights, Richard Nixon went from small-town lawyer to United States senator. His opponent in the California Senate race was Helen Gahagan Douglas, a Democratic congresswoman. Married to the Hollywood actor and director

Melvyn Douglas, she was a movie star, an opera singer, and an ardent, no-holds-barred New Deal liberal. Like Hubert Humphrey later, she hired a black staff member and integrated the House cafeteria, campaigned vigorously for programs to aid poor farmers, opposed supporting right-wing dictatorships just because they were anticommunist, and most important, criticized the HUAC and was one of seventeen members of Congress to vote against contempt citations for the "Hollywood Ten," writers and directors who had refused to testify before the committee. And as if that were not enough, Douglas courageously attacked the mystique of anticommunism in a 1946 speech entitled "My Democratic Credo." "The fear of communism in this country is not rational," she declared. "And that irrational fear of communism is being deliberately used in many quarters to blind us to our real problems . . . I am nauseated and sick to death of the vicious and deliberate ways the word communist has been forged as a weapon and used against those who organize and raise their voices in defense of democratic ideals." Almost by self-definition, Douglas, in that speech, qualified as the quintessential "liberal" Nixon described in *Six Crises:* "of a mindset . . . which makes them singularly vulnerable to the communist popular front appeal under the banner of social justice."

Nixon, meanwhile, having decided to run, defined the themes of his Senate campaign even as he denied he was a candidate. The Democratic party, he claimed, "has been captured and is completely controlled by a group of ruthless, cynical seekers after power who have committed that party to politics and principles that are completely foreign to those of its founders . . . Phony doctrines and ideologies . . . are now being foisted upon the American people." The choice before America, he insisted, was between freedom and "state socialism." And then came the characteristic Nixon slide: "They can call it a planned economy, the Fair Deal or social welfare. It's still the same old socialist baloney any way you slice it." Clearly, Douglas fit into that category of people who supported strong government programs. And she was willing to fight back, calling Nixon to task for the "nice, unadulterated fascism" of his earlier congressional races and saying he was a "pipsqueak" and a "demagogue who will try to win by fear and hysteria." She did not yet know how far Nixon was prepared to go in painting her as "soft on communism."

Nixon began by employing a tactic he had used at the end of his congressional race against Jerry Voorhis. First he singled out the person in Congress most identified with the "Left": Vito Marcantonio, a member of the American Labor Party whom Nixon labeled "the notorious Communist Party-line Congressman from New York." Then his campaign claimed that Douglas had voted with Marcantonio 353 times, intending to imply that she shared all Marcantonio's ideas; and stated further that the *Daily Worker,* a communist newspaper, had called Douglas a hero, implying that such a designation must mean she was a communist ally, a "pink lady."

Most insidiously, the Nixon campaign printed literature blazoning the charge that Douglas shared Marcantonio's positions on 8″ x 14″ pink paper, labeled the "Pink Sheet." At the same time, Nixon was claiming that he had been warned not "to criticize a woman," and promising: "I want to make my position crystal clear. There will be no name-calling, no smears, no misrepresentation in this campaign. We do not need to indulge in such tactics." But he immediately went on to say: "If [Douglas] had her way, the communist conspiracy in the United States would not have been exposed, and Alger Hiss instead of being a convicted perjurer would still be influencing the foreign policy of the United States." Douglas, Nixon concluded, had never voted as a Democrat in Congress, but rather as "a member of a small clique which joins the notorious communist party-liner Vito Marcantonio . . . in voting time after time against measures that are for the security of this country." He later called Douglas "pink right down to her underwear." Even his friend Herb Klein later noted that such tactics were a "smearing distortion."

On election day, Nixon soared to victory, securing nearly 60 percent of the vote. Douglas probably never had a chance. Because of her own principled politics, she not only refused to back down from positions she had taken but placed herself at even more risk by being one of twenty people in Congress to vote against the stridently anticommunist McCarran-Wood bill (which became the Internal Security Act over President Truman's veto). Placed constantly on the defensive, and the object of vicious anti-Semitic slurs such as the demagogic preacher Gerald L. K. Smith's warning against the "movie Jews" taking over California politics, Douglas reeled from attack after attack from the Nixon camp. Given Nixon's skill at portraying other people's politics in ways that painted them into a corner, she furnished, in many respects, the ideal foil for his effort to link people who supported social justice with those who were part of a popular front for communism. Once again, as in the campaign against Voorhis, phone callers the night before the election told voters that Douglas was a communist sympathizer; and once again, Nixon won.

◆ ◆ ◆

Nixon remained in the Senate for only two years before being picked as the perfect running mate for Dwight Eisenhower, the Republican candidate for president in 1952. The party had engaged in a bitter internecine fight over the presidential nomination. Robert Taft, "Mr. Republican," had a devoted following among conservatives. His defeat, in what seemed to many of his supporters a steamroller effort backed by the party's eastern establishment, created a need for a symbolic healing process. How better to achieve unity than by balancing Eisenhower's middle-of-the-road, almost nonpartisan politics with a young, conservative nominee for vice president who was firmly identified with the fight against communism and who, in addition, was from California, the second-largest state in the country? Furthermore, despite Nixon's tactics, Ike and others, such as the *San Francisco Chronicle,* saw him as responsible, not reckless. "The thing that impressed me most about you," Ike told Nixon, "was that you not only got Hiss, but you got him fairly."

The road to the vice presidency highlighted additional qualities of Nixon's political style, as well as magnifying dimensions already familiar from his campaigns in California. While hoping that his nomination, which he had discussed in a meeting with Thomas Dewey in 1951, would become a reality, Nixon carried on a duplicitous campaign, publicly supporting California's favorite son, Governor Earl Warren, while privately organizing for Eisenhower. The entire California delegation was pledged, by oath, to Warren, and Nixon asserted in public that Warren would have a strong chance of being nominated were the convention to be deadlocked. When Nixon joined the California train in Denver on its way to the convention in Chicago, he went to Warren and reaffirmed his loyalty.

As soon as Nixon left Warren, however, he worked the delegates on the train on behalf of Eisenhower, urging them to jump ship to Ike either on the first ballot or on the second. His aide Murray Chotiner had been pursuing the same end, ostensibly as a Warren staffer. Some called the tactics "the great train rob-

bery," and Warren, when he learned what had happened, ex-
claimed, "How do you account for him doing a thing like this?"
Warren wrote to Eisenhower declaring "We have a traitor in our
delegation . . . Nixon," and asking Ike to have the "infiltration"
ended. By the time the balloting actually started, Ike was in
charge, partly because Warren, true to his principles, released his
delegates to vote their consciences on a key procedural issue that
favored Ike; but Nixon had shown a deceptive and dishonest side
of his political persona, one that would come back to haunt
him. Indeed, a law clerk for Warren after he became chief justice of the United States Supreme Court recalled his talking of
Nixon in ways "that would ordinarily be reserved for someone
who has proved to engage in serious violations of criminal law
and ethical conduct."

The other milestone in the campaign was the "funding" scandal that culminated in Nixon's famous "Checkers" speech. Early
in the fall, reports surfaced in California that wealthy Nixon
backers had organized a private fund to provide for political expenditures not covered by their candidate's federal allowance for
service to constituents. Although since Nixon's time such pools
of money have become common, at the time the fund aroused
significant controversy, not only because Nixon had not revealed
its existence to Eisenhower, but also because it suggested the
possibility that Nixon's votes and policies were being controlled
by rich Californians with vested interests. As the scandal intensified, Ike demanded full disclosure and pointedly failed to support Nixon. More and more leaders of the Eisenhower campaign,
and increasing numbers of newspapers, demanded that Nixon
resign from the ticket.

Nixon's first response was to wrap himself in the role of victim
and invoke his triumph in the Hiss case. "You folks know the

work that I did investigating the communists in the United States," he told one audience. "Ever since I have done that work, the communists and left-wingers have been fighting me with every smear that they [could] . . . I was warned that if I continued to attack the communists and crooks in this government that they would continue to smear me . . . They started it yesterday . . . They tried to say I was taking money." In short, the entire controversy reflected nothing about Nixon's own ethics or integrity; rather it was another communist plot, directly related to his success in exposing the communist conspiracy. He promised: "The more they smear, the more I'm going to expose the communists and the crooks and those that defend them until they throw them all out of Washington."

Nixon's second counter also involved playing the self-righteous victim. He could have put his wife on the public payroll, he said, as some Democrats had done, but he refused to bilk the taxpayers that way. Instead, his wife worked for nothing. This approach provided the major theme of Nixon's speech to the nation about the scandal, his effort to retain his place on the ticket by taking his case to the people. "Every time you get before an audience, you win them," Chotiner told Nixon. Now Nixon went before the largest audience in television history and took the decision out of Eisenhower's hands by making his own family and himself the issue. Disclosing details of his family's economic circumstances previously unheard of in politics, Nixon talked with pride about his poor background, and his wife Pat's "respectable Republican cloth coat," not a mink, but a plain cloth coat. Speaking without a text, but after days of compiling notes on a yellow pad and committing them to memory, Nixon was in total control, weaving together vivid and sympathetic portraits of his family, his personal courage, and his devotion to his children.

In one paragraph of the second half of his speech, taking a

page out of FDR's famous defense of his dog Fala in the 1944 campaign, Nixon told the story of a gift that had come to his children, a cocker spaniel they had named Checkers. The children loved the dog, he said, and "regardless of what [people] say about it, we're gonna keep it." By analogy, all the gifts he had received from the fund were in the same category—innocuous testimony to the support his friends wished to provide him. And if they wanted him to stay on the Republican ticket, he told the TV audience, they should let the Republican National Committee know. The network switchboards lit up. People were crying. And Eisenhower knew he had met his match. The next night, when the two candidates finally met up in Wheeling, West Virginia, Ike bounced up the steps to Nixon's plane, clapped him on the back, and said, "You're my boy."

A third feature of the Nixon campaign was the degree to which he continued to tar his political foes with language suggesting not only their lack of patriotism but also their weakness and effeminacy. Once more, as in the Hiss case, the state department provided his foil. The Democratic candidate for president, Adlai Stevenson, he charged, was a "tired relic of a whole series of deals, of dubious State Department training, and of leftist leaning." Truman, Acheson, and now Stevenson, Nixon declared, were guilty of "coddling atheistic communism." Appearing to call into question Stevenson's masculinity, Nixon referred to him as "sidesaddle Adlai." "Like all sidesaddle riders," Nixon said, "[Adlai's] feet hang well out to the left," and no matter how many "clever quips" Stevenson served up to "send the State Department cocktail set into gales of giggles," the fact remained that Stevenson was a "graduate of Dean Acheson's spineless school of diplomacy which cost the free world six hundred million former allies in the past seven years of Trumanism."

All this led Robert Donovan, a veteran political reporter for the *New York Herald Tribune,* to conclude that Nixon was a "hard, narrow, ambitious man, cheerless and partisan to the point of repugnance." Whatever Nixon's success in persuading some newspapers and politicians that he was responsible rather than reckless, moderate rather than extreme, his 1952 campaign, like the 1946 and 1950 campaigns before it, suggested some core qualities that were hardly estimable. He said different things to different people; he was an expert at using guilt by association. Perhaps above all, he demonstrated his own insistence on seeing the world in binary terms, with himself as victim and others as evil attackers. There was a personal edge to every contest, a desire for revenge against all who opposed him. Whittaker Chambers vividly recalled Nixon one day, at the height of the Hiss case, "saying in his quietly savage way . . . 'If the American people understood the real character of Alger Hiss, they would boil him in oil.'" Wherever Nixon's hatred came from, it was personal as well as political, "all of a part," Roger Morris has written, "with the pose and self-justification he had struck from his first months in Washington, the conviction that whatever he did, however he did it, was to be explained and if necessary excused by his enemies." However clever and talented Nixon might be, there could be no toleration of ambiguity, only a mission to overcome and crush the enemy.

Nevertheless, Richard Nixon was now the vice president of the United States. Just six years after his first campaign for Congress as a virtually unknown returning veteran, he had risen to the second-highest office in the land. The funding scandal had created permanent strain between Eisenhower and Nixon, the latter feeling he had been betrayed by Ike and his team, and Eisenhower suspecting that Nixon had never told the whole truth about the fund and in addition had outmaneuvered him. As one reporter later noted, "the association of the two . . . was lastingly tainted; neither would ever wholly trust the other again." Nixon always resented the fact that he was never invited to the president's private residence in the White House and never became one of the boon companions Ike turned to for social pleasure, fishing, golf, and entertainment. Eisenhower, in turn, marveled at how few friends Nixon had, how closed he was to others. (Ike's assistant Ann Whitman had a ready explanation for the contrast: "The difference is obvious—the President is a man of integrity and sincere in his every action . . . But the Vice-President sometimes seems like a man who is acting like a nice man rather than being one.") Still, the two coexisted politically and personally, Nixon ready to take over when Ike suffered a severe heart attack in 1955, Eisenhower choosing, in the end, to keep Nixon as his running mate in 1956 in spite of a substantial movement to replace him with former Minnesota governor Harold Stassen.

Within the Eisenhower White House, Nixon made his most notable contributions in three areas. First, he continued to be Ike's political hatchet man, blasting Democrats for being "soft on communism" and calling them graduates of "Dean Acheson's Cowardly College of Communist Containment." As a fundraiser and front-line advocate, Nixon carried out the hard and dirty work of daily politics, winning substantial gratitude from Republican party functionaries, even as he left Ike to bask in his own carefully cultivated image as a benign, paternal president of all the people.

Second, Nixon became an aggressive spokesman for the country as a whole, traveling abroad as the nation's emissary to Europe, Africa, and Latin America. During his trip to Venezuela, mobs—chanting "Little Rock, Little Rock," in a hostile reference to America's festering racial crisis—pelted Nixon's car with rocks and tomatoes; yet the episode created a public impression that he was a hero, soldiering on courageously despite attacks from radicals on the left. His reputation as an anticommunist gladiator was further strengthened when, in Moscow for the opening of a U.S. trade exhibition, he engaged in the famous "Kitchen debate" with Soviet premier Nikita Khrushchev, extolling the virtues of American capitalism and promoting the appliances so dear to American consumers.

It was in the third area of notable activity that Nixon provided his most interesting contribution to the politics of the 1950s— one that spoke to an abiding tension in his life between some of the values of his Quaker upbringing and the pressures of political accommodation. The issue was race. Nixon knew discrimination constituted America's Achilles' heel in the global competition with communism. "Every act of . . . prejudice in the United States," he declared in 1954, "hurts America just as much as an espionage agent who turns over a weapon to a foreign country." Nixon had fought for the rights of a black student at Whittier when he was in college there, and had opposed policies that created second-class treatment for blacks, Asians, and Latinos. Now, in the Eisenhower administration, he fought alongside Herbert Brownell, Ike's attorney general, to advocate for civil rights within the government. While Eisenhower refused to comment on the Supreme Court's 1954 decision in *Brown v. Board of Education* that racial segregation in public schools was unconstitutional, Nixon supported the decision. Furthermore, he played a major role in securing administration backing for Brownell's effort in 1957 to enact the first civil rights legislation since Reconstruction, a measure that proposed to give the federal government major new authority to intervene on behalf of school desegregation, black voting rights, and equal access to public accommodations like hotels and theaters.

Nixon was even ready to lead an effort to overturn the primary weapon used by the South in resisting civil rights legislation—the filibuster. Rule 22 of the Senate permitted unlimited debate on any issue, with a two-thirds vote of all senators required for cloture to be invoked and debate terminated. Since a two-thirds majority was virtually impossible to achieve, southern senators could count on talking to death any bill they saw as threatening their interests. Now Nixon was prepared, in his role as presiding officer of the Senate, to rule in the opening session in 1957 that a majority vote would be sufficient to reconsider, and potentially overturn, Rule 22. It was a bold stance. And Nixon would have succeeded if the Senate majority leader, Lyndon B. Johnson, had not been even more clever and, exercising his right to be recognized first in any Senate discussion, succeeded in tabling the proposal to eliminate Rule 22. Still, Nixon had shown courage and persistence on a critically important issue. In this situation, and through his work with black leaders both in America and on his trip to Africa, he built a substantial base of black support for his own potential candidacy for the presidency.

That candidacy culminated in the excruciatingly close Kennedy-Nixon race of 1960. Fewer than 150,000 votes separated the two nominees, each a veteran of the congressional class of 1946. The election was memorable for many reasons: the first televised debates between presidential candidates; the two youngest nominees in history; the substantial difference in style between the contenders, Kennedy with his chopping hand, crisp nasal Boston accent, and repeated claim "we can do better," Nixon with his dark "five o'clock shadow," his recollections of his poor family (such as the story of his brother's disappointment "the day the pony died"), his efforts to portray himself as "the voice of experience" who had played a major role in Eisenhower administration policymaking.

The biggest deficiency Nixon had to overcome was the fact that, for the first time in more than a decade, he was not the person on the attack. Instead, it was Kennedy saying "we can do better," lambasting the administration for falling behind the Soviet Union economically and militarily, and charging that Republicans were not being aggressive enough in trying to topple Fidel Castro's regime in Cuba. By contrast, Nixon was playing the elder statesman, defending the status quo, trying to bolster his own image as leader. Eisenhower sharply undercut that image when asked at a news conference to name an issue on which Nixon had made a major difference in his administration. "Let me think about it for a week," Ike replied.

Meanwhile, on civil rights, the one issue where he actually had made a difference, Nixon waffled. When Martin Luther King Jr. was arrested and thrown into a Georgia jail, with many of his allies believing he would never come out alive, John F. Kennedy called Mrs. King to offer his sympathy, and Robert Kennedy called the judge in the case. Nixon, however, did nothing, resisting the advice of some campaign aides to intervene aggressively. The result was that Nixon, who had earlier received the endorsement of Martin Luther King Sr., partly because King did not trust a Catholic in the White House, lost his chance to take a majority of the black vote. King's father switched his endorsement, and the black vote went to Kennedy and, in all likelihood, constituted the critical difference in the final electoral tally. Embittered, Nixon retreated to California, where he ran for gover-

nor in 1962. After losing there as well, he lashed out at the press
and all his enemies, saying to reporters in another portrayal of
himself as a victim: "You won't have Nixon to kick around anymore."

◆ ◆ ◆

Yet just six years later Nixon was back, seeking not only redemption from the shame of his defeat but permanent triumph over
the press, his political foes, and anyone else who opposed him.
During the years between his California defeat and his nomination in 1968, Nixon had moved to New York City, become
wealthy through his partnership in a corporate law firm, and resumed appearing at local Republican fundraising and campaign
functions, where he could cultivate the following necessary for a
second chance at the presidency. Throughout this period he self-
consciously crafted a different image for himself, abjuring the
sharp-edged assaults of his past politicking, creating instead the
vision of a "new" Nixon, a statesman who would both bring expertise to foreign affairs and promote harmony and coherence at
home. Promising a secret plan to end the Vietnam war as well as
a program of domestic reform, he took as his motto a sign held
by a young teenager in Ohio that read: "Bring us together."

Celebrating his election, Nixon declared: "That will be the
great objective of this administration at the outset, to bring the
American people together. To be an open administration, open
to new ideas, open to men and women of both parties, open to
the critics as well as those who support us. We want to bridge
the generation gap. We want to bridge the gap between the races.
We want to bring America together." The reality was that Nixon
had also waged a campaign based on polarization—trumpeting

issues of law and order, consciously exploiting the issue of race by opposing busing and forced desegregation, denouncing student protestors. The question was which approach would characterize the new administration once it took office.

The answer was both: even as Nixon enunciated lofty ideals for his administration, he simultaneously practiced a politics of what Patrick Buchanan called "positive polarization," hoping to forge a new Republican majority based on the "silent majority's" (in Nixon's phrase) abhorrence of civil disobedience, black radicalism, and antiwar demonstrations. The tack that most reflected his positive vision came from his close association with Daniel Patrick Moynihan, a Harvard-educated Irish Catholic intellectual who convinced Nixon he could become an American Disraeli, the conservative as reformer. Plying Nixon with books on the great Tory prime minister who had promoted reform in the 1870s—as Bismarck had in Germany—Moynihan succeeded in winning the president's backing for a family assistance program that would provide a guaranteed annual income for the poorest Americans. Nixon also undertook new initiatives in the realms of environmental protection, consumer rights, and tax reform, telling Moynihan, in an echo of what Moynihan had told him, "You know . . . it is the Tory men with liberal policies who have enlarged democracy."

At the same time, however, Nixon avidly pursued the "Southern strategy" that had been at the heart of his presidential campaign. The political commentator Kevin Phillips had called for an "emerging Republican majority" based on solid support in the South and the rim states of the southwest and the west coast. The secret of American politics, Phillips advised, was knowing "who hates who." John Mitchell, Nixon's attorney general and chief political operative, urged the president to pursue policies that would win over the working-class, white racist constituency of Alabama governor (and presidential candidate) George Wallace. Accordingly, Nixon persisted in recommending "freedom of choice" as his policy toward desegregation of schools, thereby placing the burden of change on individual families, while seeking to weaken enforcement of the Supreme Court's desegregation rulings. In his first year as president, administration officials supported policies of *delay* on school desegregation in five school districts in South Carolina and thirty-three in Mississippi. In a clever articulation of his approach, he told a press conference: "There are two extreme groups [on this civil rights issue]. There are those who want instant integration and those who want segregation forever. I believe we need to have a middle course between those two extremes." What he had done was to define obedience to the law as one extreme and nullification of the law as another, thereby solidly aligning himself with those southerners who since 1954 had been calling integrationists "extremists."

Equally important for his "Southern strategy," Nixon appointed conservative southern judges to federal courts, beginning with the Supreme Court. Under Chief Justice Earl Warren, the Court had handed down landmark rulings in the areas of civil rights and civil liberties: affirming the right of every arrested person to counsel, declaring that one person/one vote should be the foundation for apportioning legislative representation, and significantly expanding the definition of free speech. Nixon sought to reverse what conservatives saw as the imposition of alien values by an effete eastern elite. He started by nominating the conservative Warren Burger as Warren's successor. When Abe Fortas vacated a seat on the Court that had been, for the most part, held by a Jewish American for the previous half-century, Nixon redeemed his promise to the South by nominating Clement Haynesworth of South Carolina, a longtime associate of Strom Thurmond, to replace Fortas. But Haynesworth was too much of a sop to southerners. Twice he had sided with segregationists in critical civil rights cases, and once he had taken the side of the textile industry in a bitter labor case. Northern civil rights Republicans as well as liberal Democrats were appalled, and with seventeen Republican senators joining Democrats in voting no, rejected the nomination.

Nixon was furious. On the principle that when thwarted once, the best response is to strike back twice as hard, he proceeded to nominate another southerner, G. Harold Carswell of Florida, who made Haynesworth look like Oliver Wendell Holmes. Once party to a scheme to purchase a public golf course in Tallahassee to prevent it from being desegregated, Carswell had been repeatedly overturned by higher courts that reviewed his decisions. Many of his colleagues on the federal circuit court refused to sign a letter endorsing him; a majority of professors at the University of Florida law school opposed his confirmation; and even supporters ended up condemning him with faint praise. "There are lots of mediocre judges," Republican Senator Roman Hruska observed. "[Mediocre people] are entitled to a little representation, aren't they?" Carswell went down to defeat, with thirteen Republicans voting no this time. Yet, perversely, Nixon had made his point. He would stand by his commitment to the Southern strategy, and even if he lost in the short run, he would win the war.

The final ploy in Nixon's political campaign of divide and conquer was to unleash his vice president, Spiro Agnew, on the electorate. In many ways Agnew was "Nixon's Nixon," serving primarily as an attack dog to carry forward in the most aggressive manner possible Nixon's strategy of polarization. Chosen as the vice presidential nominee primarily because he had loudly chastised black demonstrators when he was governor of Maryland, Agnew had little expertise or talent in the large policy areas presumably central to being qualified for the second-highest office in the land. What he offered instead was a lacerating political style, a powerful speaking voice, and a bare-knuckled speechwriting team able to deliver vicious political salvos in pretentious, polysyllabic language. In a graduation speech at Ohio State Agnew lashed out at the "sniveling, hand-wringing power structure [that] deserves the violent rebellion it encourages." According to his analysis, the eastern elite establishment was calling the shots of the youthful revolution. These individuals, accompanied by their allies in the universities, Agnew charged, were encouraging the spread of "a spirit of national masochism" that was a product of "an effete corps of impudent snobs who characterize themselves as intellectuals." Lest anyone doubt his meaning, he declared that "small cadres of professional protestors," acting on behalf of this effete elite, were "attempting to jeopardize the peace efforts of the President of the United States." And if in challenging those actions, he said, "we *polarize* the American people, I say it is time for a positive polarization . . . It is time to rip away the rhetoric and to divide on authentic lines."

Nothing could have been clearer. However strongly he professed to wish to "bring the American people together," Nixon's real strategy was to galvanize the "silent majority." Focusing on issues of law and order, patriotism, family values, and the decadence of spoiled and affluent antiwar protestors, Nixon would take the battle to his enemies, provoke them to be even more outrageous than they already were, and then use them as a foil to rally "middle Americans" to the banner of the new "Republican majority." If Nixon succeeded, he would reshape the Republican party with a base among the Catholic working class, southern whites, and sunbelt suburbanites, who would be united by their shared antagonism toward militant blacks, radical peaceniks, and East Coast and West Coast intellectuals. It was a powerful vision, and one that Nixon had a clear blueprint for bringing to realization—another kind of "togetherness" than that evoked by the teenager from Ohio.

The reality, though, was that Nixon cared little for domestic issues. Repeatedly he told his aides to take domestic policies off his agenda, giving him time to focus on the *important* questions that preoccupied him—those of restructuring the relationships among the world's superpowers. Domestic events could take care of themselves, Nixon informed the presidential chronicler Theodore White; it was in foreign affairs that a president would leave his mark on history. Nixon saw his presidency as an opportunity to be the architect of a new world order—to conceptualize, design, and execute a plan to remake the world as America had known it.

To that end, he established a remarkable modus operandi in the White House. "The idea," notes the journalist and historian Richard Reeves, "was to make the President's world secure from outsiders" so that Nixon could focus on his major objectives. While many Americans envision the White House as a beehive of activity, the president moving from meeting to meeting over a fourteen-hour day, the reality of the Nixon White House was that the president spent hours in isolation, alone with his thoughts, mapping out his blueprint for changing the world in endless notes jotted on his ever-present yellow pad. Nixon detested cabinet meetings, wanted little to do with most of the people he had chosen to run the government's various departments, and in particular instructed aides to keep people like Spiro Agnew, his vice president, or George Romney, his secretary of housing and urban affairs, away from him. From early in his administration he largely related to the world through only three men: John Ehrlichman, who became the White House domestic counselor, H. R. Haldeman, White House chief of staff, and Henry Kissinger, national security advisor. Spending as much time deflecting others from the president and preserving their own exclusive access as they did carrying out their official functions, these three became the equivalent of a national junta, weaving webs of secrecy around the man with whom they had entered into a political conspiracy to hoard power.

Nixon's relationship with Henry Kissinger typified this pattern. The two men had much in common. "Loners and outsiders in their own professions," the historian George Herring has written, they shared a "penchant for secrecy and intrigue ... and a flair for the unexpected move." Kissinger had earned his way into Nixon's inner circle in 1968 by secretly sharing with the Nixon camp intelligence he had gleaned from the Paris peace talks about an imminent breakthrough in Vietnamese negotiations. So eager was Kissinger for a powerful role in the next administration that he offered his services to both national candidates, Humphrey and Nixon. His disclosure about the peace talks permitted Nixon to use backchannel contacts with the South Vietnamese government to persuade them to reject the breakthrough, thus preventing a major stride toward peace just before the 1968 election that might have led to a Democratic victory. "Kissinger had proven his mettle by tipping us," Nixon's campaign advisor Richard Allen noted. "It took some balls to give us those tips ... it was inevitable that Kissinger would have to be part of our administration."

Recognizing a kindred spirit, Kissinger embraced Nixon's

scheme for plotting tectonic shifts in the global power structure, starting with Vietnam but extending far beyond that small
country into the superpower worlds of China and Russia. The
two worked ceaselessly to gather all power over military and diplomatic initiatives totally unto themselves. Secretary of State
William Rogers and Secretary of Defense Melvin Laird, the two
most powerful cabinet officers, were specifically excluded from
all critical decisionmaking. Rogers was not told until the very
end that Kissinger was carrying out secret negotiations with the
Vietnamese in Paris, or that he engaged in weekly meetings at
the White House with Soviet ambassador Anatoly Dobrynin.
Nor was the secretary of defense made privy to any of the major
military decisions being made regarding Vietnam, Cambodia,
and Laos. The U.S. government became a two-tier operation,
with the Pentagon and state department bureaucracies providing shadow replicas of power and responsibility, while all foreign
powers, as well as many domestic insiders, understood that any
decisions of real substance would be made in Kissinger's office,
with Nixon as his co-conspirator. So extraordinary was this
secretive government process that Secretary of State Rogers
learned of the Nixon initiative toward China only after the president's trip had been arranged. Furthermore, Rogers and his
state department colleagues learned of the Strategic Arms Limitation Treaty with the USSR—which supposedly they themselves
had been negotiating in Helsinki—only an hour before the document was signed in Moscow.

Nixon and Kissinger thoroughly reinforced each other's tendency to suspicion of others and political paranoia. Kissinger,
Nixon told Haldeman, was "like a psychopath" about Rogers,
threatening to resign whenever the secretary of state sought to
play a major policy role. Nixon was equally paranoid about Laird

and the leaks about U.S. military plans that he was convinced the defense secretary had planted with the *Washington Post* and other papers. Nor were the president and his national security advisor beyond plotting against each other, Nixon complaining to Haldeman and Ehrlichman about Kissinger's mental instability, Kissinger cupping his hand over the receiver and telling his staff that Nixon, "our drunken friend," was on the phone slurring his words and complaining about a foreign policy "screw up" in a late-night call. Still, their conspiracies to deceive others and sustain their own control of all critical decisions were so deep and multilayered that Nixon and Kissinger could not afford to let their differences divide them. However perverse and pathological the partnership, the two men could survive in office only as long as it persisted.

The Nixon White House was thus a closed circle of three or four key players, all understanding that the man who had brought them together wanted to work only through them. Nixon would see each of them every day, dictate memos to them, and ask them to transmit his marching orders to the rest of the administration. Coming from a man who already cherished his isolation, this management structure only isolated Nixon further from regular accountability to others. It also guaranteed that the information reaching him would be carefully filtered. Each day the president received a national news summary prepared by his aides. He would mark that up and dispense instructions by memo on how to respond to items of interest. When the time came to prepare a major speech or to hold a press conference, he would clear his schedule for days at a time to sit alone with his yellow pad and prepare, memorizing the lines he would use in response to reporters' questions, outlining the arguments he would make in a speech. If there are two models of leadership, one based on maximizing the input of information from multiple sources, and the other based on a narrow stream of information and maximum time for introspection, Nixon's style was almost a caricature of the second. De Gaulle's description of his own idea of leadership deeply impressed Nixon: "Great men of action have without exception possessed in very high degree the faculty of withdrawing into themselves." And in his memoirs Nixon wrote: "Time is a person's most important possession. How he makes use of it will determine whether he will fail or succeed in whatever he is undertaking."

Nixon often ruminated privately on what he hoped his presidency could achieve. Tucked away in a private two-room suite in the Executive Office Building, or in the Lincoln study in the White House, he would sit in a comfortable chair with his feet on an ottoman, wearing a smoking jacket (always buttoned), yellow pad in hand, jotting down notes. To a remarkable degree, they were the same notes, or at least had a common theme, throughout his time in office. "Compassionate, Bold, New, Courageous," he wrote. "The nation must be better in spirit at the end of the term. Need for joy, serenity, confidence, inspiration." Over and over again, he made notes about the importance of lifting people's spirits, of being a "spiritual leader," a "moral leader": "The primary contribution a President can make is on Spiritual life, not material solutions . . . Need for dignity, Kindness, drive, Youth, Priority, Spiritual Quality." In September 1969 he wrote: "Each day a chance to do something memorable for someone . . . Need to be good to do good . . . Goals: set example, inspire, instill pride." Then three years later, in October 1972: "I have decided my major role is moral leadership. I cannot exercise this adequately unless I speak out more often and more eloquently."

The more hours he brooded alone, the more Nixon sought to increase that isolation. "The problem is time to prepare," he wrote. "I must take the time to prepare and leave technical matters to others." In some year-end notes after 1970, he concluded that "our greatest weakness was in spreading my time too thin," especially on domestic issues. "I consider [these] to be important . . . but don't bother me." Instead, he often asked aides to clear his schedule so he could concentrate on his priorities. In reality, according to Haldeman, Nixon wasted half of his freed-up schedule on trivia: "He spends as much time discussing the problem he has of shortage of time as he does doing the things he says he doesn't have the time to do." Or again: "Another day supposedly cleared, but no work done." Still, the drive for such time was a powerful motivation. Nixon seemed impelled to escape Washington and the White House. Repeatedly he flew off to Key Biscayne or San Clemente (on each of which the government spent millions of dollars), and on 117 different occasions he went to Camp David in the Maryland mountains, where he could hole up in his cabin and brood. Rarely did he share meals with the staff members who accompanied him; he preferred to eat alone.

In Nixon's endless self-reflections and escapes from Washington, there seems a pattern of trying to reconnect with his Quaker roots. So many of his notes to himself evoke a spiritual and moral mission that he has apparently abandoned but wishes to regain. The words "compassion," "joy," "serenity," "spiritual leadership" all suggest a desire to become a better self, to rise to the level of character that his devout mother would have wished for him. It was as if a struggle was taking place between the Machiavellian politician he had become in his quest for fame and power, on the one hand, and the ultimate moral purpose to which such fame and power should be dedicated, on the other. And whatever noble ideals Nixon articulated on his yellow pads, his Machiavellian side seemed to be prevailing.

For example, Nixon responded to immediate problems with a petty vindictiveness that bordered on cruelty. When the mayor of New York, John Lindsay, made a speech criticizing the administration's Vietnam policy, the president ordered John Ehrlichman to stop payment on all special federal programs aiding the residents of New York City. (Ehrlichman ignored the instructions—as the president's aides often did when faced with one of his temper tantrums.) Nixon responded with fury when people questioned his judgment. Press leaks particularly enraged him. At one point he told Haldeman to cut off all communication with the *New York Times* and the *Washington Post*. Both Nixon and Kissinger exploded when a *New York Times* reporter revealed some of their most closely guarded secret military moves in Vietnam. The leaks were "outrageous," Kissinger told Nixon. "We must do something! We must crush these people." Nixon repeatedly ordered wiretaps on White House staff and even, occasionally, on journalists. When a group of senators contemplated closer monitoring of military expenditure, Nixon demanded of Ehrlichman, "E—can't we infiltrate this group?"

Because of his obsession with leaks and potential political opposition, Nixon supported Ehrlichman's decision to hire Jack Caulfield, a former New York police detective, to move into the White House and head up a secret unit to spy on his enemies. One of Caulfield's first assignments was surveillance of Senator Edward M. Kennedy. Nixon also asked a White House aide, Tom Huston, to draft an intelligence plan for disrupting Nixon's domestic opponents through break-ins, wiretaps, and other extralegal means. FBI director J. Edgar Hoover protested, putting the plan temporarily on hold, but it would be implemented a few months later.

All these moves revealed a frightening degree of viciousness, which Nixon often expressed in racial epithets that belied any intent to practice "togetherness" or compassion. He once told Haldeman that blacks were genetically inferior and that it would take generations of interbreeding for them to be able to compete equally with whites. On another occasion, after the United States lost a vote at the United Nations, he said: "The United States is getting kicked around by a bunch of goddamned Africans and cannibals and the rest." Nixon reserved his strongest bigoted diatribes, however, for Jewish people. When the Senate rejected his nomination of Clement Haynesworth to the Supreme Court, the president declared: "It's those dirty rotten New York Jews." After the Pentagon Papers were published, leaked by a former government official, Nixon insisted the leaker must have been someone on Kissinger's staff or just some group of "fucking Jews." Another leak, from a labor department official, Nixon blamed on "that little Jewish cocksucker . . . who screwed us in the Eisenhower Administration." "Washington is full of Jews," he sputtered to Haldeman and White House counsel Charles Colson. "Most Jews are disloyal . . . You can't trust the bastards. They turn on you." Nixon also repeated the hoary stereotype that "Jewish interests" controlled large chain stores and conspired to manipulate the economy. Whether calling Kissinger "my Jew boy," claiming the IRS was full of Jews who wanted to persecute Billy Graham, or referring to a California tax official as "a kike by the name of Rosenberg," he repeatedly displayed a gutter level of ethnic stereotyping that reflected the hate he brought to politics. As Richard Reeves has written, "he had a tribal and genetic sense of people everywhere," thrived on cul-

tural warfare, and organized the world into conspiracies of enemies. Some were Jewish, some were black, some came from Harvard, the *New York Times,* or the state department. But they were
all out to get him, and he would crush them if he could.

◆ ◆ ◆

Meanwhile, Nixon devoted his greatest energies to accomplishing his bold, transforming goals in foreign affairs. During the
presidential campaign he had referred to his "secret" plan to end
the Vietnam war. (When Adlai Stevenson had similarly spoken of
a "secret" plan to end the Korean War in 1952, Nixon had excori-
ated him for not sharing his plans with the public and with the
military.) In fact he had no secret plan as such, but rather a two-
pronged effort: first, to withdraw American forces as rapidly
as possible and turn the prosecution of the war over to the
South Vietnamese, well armed with American munitions—what
became known as Vietnamization; and second, to frighten the
North Vietnamese with threats of what Nixon *might* do in the future. This was Nixon's "madman theory." "I want the North
Vietnamese to believe I've reached the point where I might do
anything to stop the war," he told Haldeman in 1969. "We'll just
slip the word to them that 'for God's sake, you know Nixon is
obsessed about communists. We can't restrain him when he's
angry—and he has his hand on the nuclear button'—and Ho Chi
Minh himself will be in Paris in two days begging for peace."

Much of Nixon's military and diplomatic strategy over the
next four years was designed to give credibility to the madman
theory. In October 1969 he put the Strategic Air Command on
the highest alert possible, with B-52 bombers armed with nuclear weapons always in the air, to signal that even in the absence

of an imminent world crisis, he was thinking in terms of mass destruction and could not be trusted—and hence to give the Soviet Union and China an additional reason to urge Ho to come to the peace table. Without informing the American people, or even the secretaries of defense and state, Nixon and Kissinger also ordered nonstop bombing of North Vietnamese sanctuaries in neutral Cambodia, dropping more than 110,000 tons of bombs during 3,630 flights over the Cambodian countryside. Under Kissinger's orders, the pilots on these missions created false flight logs so that the military chain of command would be unaware of the secret bombing. Nixon also developed extensive plans for an even more massive military attack, code-named Operation Duck Hook, that would involve mining North Vietnamese harbors, bombing dikes to flood North Vietnam, and sending air attacks to Hanoi. At this time, according to some White House aides, he may also have contemplated using nuclear weapons. "The Old Man is going to drop the bomb before the year is out," Haldeman told Colson. Laird and Rogers, who did know about Operation Duck Hook, vociferously opposed it for fear of the impact it would have on domestic politics, and for the moment the plan was shelved, only to be resurrected three years later when Nixon again sought to inflict "savage, punishing blows" on the North Vietnamese to force them to make peace.

(Although Laird and Rogers prevailed temporarily on Operation Duck Hook, they were less successful in fighting Nixon on other issues, and on occasion found themselves in situations where they felt they had to defy the president's orders. When the North Koreans shot down an American spy plane—by accident, U.S. intelligence forces later confirmed—Kissinger wanted an overwhelming response, including the possible use of nuclear weapons. Without telling Nixon, Laird simply suspended the spy

flights, and the crisis dissipated. Later, when Palestinians hi-
jacked five airliners, Nixon ordered bombing attacks on Palestin-
ian bases in Jordan and Lebanon, and Laird ignored the order,
claiming that bad weather kept the planes grounded.)

In their most controversial military move in Vietnam, Kissinger and Nixon determined that only a full-scale invasion of
Cambodia by U.S. and South Vietnamese forces could unsettle
the status quo sufficiently to force the North Vietnamese to
the negotiating table. Claiming that the invasion would identify and destroy North Vietnamese headquarters in Cambodia,
Nixon went on national television in the spring of 1970 to declare the assault crucial to ending the war. Once again, Laird and
Rogers were opposed, with an outraged Rogers fuming, "Unite
the country! This will make the students puke." For Nixon, however, it was the moment he had been waiting for. Watching the
movie *Patton* repeatedly in the weeks surrounding the attack
(and pacing the office with his hands behind his back, as the
actor George Scott, playing Patton, does in the movie), Nixon
ordered Haldeman: "Cut the crap on my schedule. I'm taking
over here. Troop withdrawal was a boy's job. Cambodia is a
man's job."

Laird and Rogers were once again right. No North Vietnamese headquarters were found in Cambodia, the invasion accomplished little militarily, and domestic opposition reached a new
crescendo, with a million and a half demonstrators taking to the
streets. Congress had not been consulted. Two of Kissinger's
chief staff members resigned in protest ("You can't do that," Al
Haig told one. "You just had an order from your commander-in-
chief and you can't refuse." "Fuck you Al," the aide responded, "I
just have."). The nation appeared to be on the brink of civil
strife. National Guard troops shot and killed four peaceful pro-

testors at Kent State University in Ohio, and police killed two other protesting students a few days later at Jackson State University in Mississippi. "This is a dangerous situation," the editors of *Business Week* declared on May 11. "It threatens the whole economic and social structure of the nation." When antiwar protestors rallied in Washington, a sleepless Nixon went to the Lincoln Memorial to talk with them, telling one woman who was reading a Bible that she reminded him of his mother. "She was a saint," he said. Nixon's staff started to fear for his mental health. It was "the weirdest day yet," Haldeman wrote. "I am concerned about [the president's] condition . . . He has had very little sleep for a long time and his judgment, temper, and mood suffer badly as a result . . . He's still riding on the crisis wave, but the letdown is near at hand and will be huge."

Although neither the bombing and invasion of Cambodia nor the invasion of Laos that followed in 1971 came close to accomplishing Kissinger and Nixon's goals, they did provide cover for a systematic withdrawal of American forces from Vietnam—reducing the number of U.S. troops from 550,000 in 1968 to 85,000 in 1972—and for a new round of secret peace negotiations. Once again without the knowledge or participation of the secretary of state, Kissinger, acting on Nixon's behalf, inaugurated a series of conversations with the North Vietnamese at a secluded villa outside Paris. Weekend after weekend, Kissinger would—in complete secrecy—fly off to Paris. He came close to finalizing an agreement with Le Duc Tho, his North Vietnamese counterpart, specifying that American troops would withdraw, all prisoners of war would be released, and a de facto coalition government would take over in South Vietnam. But then the negotiations foundered on the issue of what legitimacy the regime of South Vietnam's president, General Nguyen Van Thieu, would retain.

Nixon finally launched Operation Duck Hook, now renamed Linebacker, with American planes engaging in unprecedented air attacks on the North and mining Haiphong Harbor. "The bastards have never been bombed like they are going to be bombed this time," Nixon declared. Once more negotiations appeared ready to succeed, but this time General Thieu refused to cooperate, and the peace talks broke off. One last time, Nixon resorted to overwhelming force, unleashing the heaviest attack ever on North Vietnam in December 1972. Having won re-election by an overwhelming majority, Nixon believed he had carte blanche to do whatever he wished. He told his generals: "I don't want any more of this crap about . . . we can't hit this target or that one. This is your chance to use military power to win this war." Critics argued that the president was acting "like a madman," waging war "by tantrum," and trying to bomb North Vietnam into oblivion. But this time the madman theory seemed to work; negotiations resumed in Paris, and a week later a final settlement was achieved, nearly identical to the one that had been negotiated three months earlier. Nixon's "secret" plan to end the war had finally come to fruition—over a four-year period that witnessed the deaths of 21,000 American troops, 107,000 South Vietnamese soldiers, and half a million North Vietnamese forces, plus untold numbers of Vietnamese civilians.

Many Americans were able to accept the bizarre unfolding of Nixon's strategy for Southeast Asia because they were awed by the brilliance with which Nixon and Kissinger executed their major vision for a bold new world: recognition and rapprochement with the People's Republic of China. No one had been more identified with hostility toward Communist China than Richard Nixon. From his days on the HUAC through his vice presidential tirades against Dean Acheson's "cowardly college of Communist containment," Nixon had stood in the front ranks of those who supported the regime of Chiang Kai-shek in Taiwan. He had adamantly refused to contemplate recognizing the communist government in Beijing. But while running for president in 1968 Nixon had told Theodore White that achieving a breakthrough with the communist Chinese was one of his greatest dreams, and now he set out with Kissinger to make that dream a reality.

Once again using backchannel communications, Nixon initiated conversations with the Chinese in Warsaw and private contacts with the Pakistani president, who had his own contacts with Beijing, to suggest to the Chinese that he was ready to move, boldly and with imagination, to reverse more than two decades of total hostility. As contacts intensified in 1970 and 1971, Nixon sent subtle signals publicly to the Chinese, telling a *Time* reporter that he longed to go to China before he died. In a toast to the Romanian president, who was visiting Washington, Nixon used for the first time the proper title of the country, the People's Republic of China, rather than his customary term, "Red China." China played its part in the *pas de deux* by inviting a U.S. Ping-Pong team to Beijing. Two months later Kissinger journeyed to South Asia to consult with Indian and Pakistani officials. As his aides announced to the press that Kissinger had been taken ill with a stomach ailment, Kissinger flew off to Beijing to meet with the Chinese premier, Chou En-lai. Over two days of secret discussion, Kissinger worked out the terms of a dramatic new era in world politics: American troops would withdraw from Taiwan, Nixon would visit China, Beijing would pledge to support peace negotiations with the Vietnamese, and the United States would acknowledge that there was only one China. Secretary of State Rogers knew nothing of the mission until after Kissinger had left Pakistan for China.

Determined to make his trip to China the most masterly public moment of his life, Nixon plotted out elaborate plans for the visit in his retreats at Camp David and the White House. He urged Kissinger to play up the parallels between Chou and himself—their poor background, their triumph over adversity, their brilliance as intellectuals, their willingness to take risks, their ability to speak without notes, their commitment to long-range visions, and above all, their boldness, subtlety, and strength. Reading over the more than five hundred pages of notes Kissinger had compiled on his conversations with Chou, Nixon focused on the drama of meeting with China's communist party chairman and leader, Mao Tse-tung, and encouraged the media to provide heavy television coverage of his trips to the Great Wall, the Imperial Palace, and other legendary sites. In a tour de force with Mao and Chou, Nixon spoke for more than ninety minutes—without notes—articulating his view of a world in which China and America would be partners in Asia, even as they worked toward increasing trade, mutual investment, and political cooperation. It was a "pageant," one reporter said, and Nixon carried it off with panache, startling both the world and his own country with the drama of ending twenty-five years of bitter hostility. The arch-anticommunist had launched a new era of reconciliation.

As if the China drama were not enough, Nixon moved decisively toward an equally important breakthrough with the Soviet Union. Kissinger's secret discussions with Ambassador Dobrynin created momentum for more formalized agreements. Recognizing that China and the USSR viewed each other as mortal enemies, Kissinger and Nixon played the two against each other to advance U.S. national interests. Indeed, the Soviet Union was sufficiently desperate for a summit conference between Brezhnev and Nixon that it did not cancel the conference even though the U.S. military initiative in Operation Duck

Hook resulted in the sinking of a Soviet ship and the loss of a number of Soviet lives. Nixon responded to this determination to proceed by agreeing to a new Strategic Arms Limitation Treaty. As usual, Kissinger negotiated the treaty, while Rogers and the state department's own arms limitations team remained in the dark. Nixon even told Haldeman to order Rogers not to talk to the press about the treaty. Mortified, Rogers said he had been made a "laughingstock" and offered to resign. Perhaps most symptomatic of White House dynamics was Nixon's memo to his own staff about the breakthrough: "The deadlock [in negotiations] was broken by an initiative taken by the President on his own . . . The President is personally assuming responsibility for achieving the goal of an agreement this year . . . this is by far the most important foreign policy achievement since the end of World War II."

Nixon had used his distinctly personal style of drawing up blueprints for global reorganization to good effect with Russia and China. The days spent doodling on yellow legal pads had paid off. The secretive techniques of Kissinger's backchannel operations had made possible events that otherwise might have been prevented by bureaucratic resistance. As Nixon told Mao, perhaps only a strong conservative could have acted in such a progressive way with China. Any Democratic president who had attempted the same breakthrough could have counted on being denounced by Nixon as "soft on communism." But Nixon had succeeded in doing the unthinkable. John Osborne, a columnist for the liberal *New Republic*, commented: "The observer must pause at times and succumb to the wonder that this man, this seeming model of mediocrity, should be the first President of the United States to do what he has done this year . . . in Peking and now in Moscow."

Yet the price had been high. Hundreds of thousands of lives

had been lost in Vietnam, most of them needlessly. On numerous occasions, White House actions had risked the possibility of international disaster. So intent was Nixon on excluding duly appointed leaders from the decisionmaking process that he created a virtual shadow government, and more than once only the refusal of appointed officials to execute his orders prevented catastrophe. Nixon proved so deeply suspicious even of his allies that the entire White House operation became a nest of lies, each one designed to consolidate more and more power in fewer and fewer hands. Nixon might have used the madman theory to make his point with the North Vietnamese and Russians; but the same tendency to use intrigue and backchannel instruments to protect the presidency from its critics would eventually bring about his downfall.

◆　◆　◆

Nixon premised his bid for re-election on the politics of polarization, not togetherness. He believed that by attacking antiwar radicals he could rally the "silent majority" to his side and reshape the Republican party. "There is a small group in this country," he told an audience in 1970, "that shouts obscenities, . . . that throws rocks, . . . a group of people that always tear America down; a group of people that hate this country . . . The way to answer them [is] . . . for the Great Silent Majority to speak out." That same year, secretly, Nixon's campaign raised more than $20 million (and had it laundered through Mexican banks before a new campaign finance law came into effect) to mobilize those who opposed antiwar protestors and who detested "liberals" who supported gay rights, feminism, and abortion. More than $350,000 of the money went to the Committee to Re-Elect the President (CREEP) to be used to finance a series of "dirty tricks" against Democratic candidates. Among other things, the funds were used to hire a Republican spy who got a job as a driver for Ed Muskie, the Maine senator who was contending for the Democratic presidential nomination, and to pay for the operations of Donald Segretti, who circulated scurrilous ethnic attacks on Democratic candidates and anonymous letters accusing Democrats of sexual indiscretions. In the meantime, Nixon's aides, headed by Attorney General John Mitchell (who would soon resign from the justice department to run the president's re-election campaign), resurrected Tom Huston's plan to use electronic surveillance, wiretaps, break-ins, and informers to disrupt Democratic campaigns.

Nothing was to be left to chance. When Senator George McGovern of South Dakota won the Democratic nomination, Nixon saw a golden opportunity to cement a new majority. He used McGovern's support for a huge cut in defense spending, and for substantial new benefits for minorities and welfare recipients, to bring together conservative Catholics, white blue-collar workers, the South, and suburbia. McGovern endorsed legalization of marijuana, school busing to achieve desegregation, and quotas of delegates for minorities at the Democratic convention—all positions that allowed Nixon to portray him as a member of the radical fringe. Nixon, meanwhile, positioned himself at the center of a phalanx of "middle Americans" devoted to traditional values, patriotism, and peace and prosperity. So intent were Nixon and his aides on securing total victory that they were not satisfied with conducting a strong campaign and letting the election take its course. "When you've got a fellow [like McGovern]," Nixon said, "who is under attack like this, and who has fallen on his ass a few times, what you do is kick him again. I mean you have got to keep whacking, whacking, whacking." And so the Nixon team pursued a campaign of subversion against Democrats that broke laws, entangled the White House in a web of lies, and eventually ruined careers, including Richard Nixon's.

The utter collapse of any relationship between means and ends may well have begun with Nixon's paranoia about press leaks. First came the *New York Times* correspondent William Beecher's stories about the secret bombing of Cambodia, then Daniel Ellsberg's leaking of a secret defense department study of U.S. decisionmaking about Vietnam—which came to be known as the Pentagon Papers—to the press. Unless Nixon stopped the leaks, Kissinger warned him, people would think he was a "weakling." Nixon was enraged, and as he talked to Ehrlichman and Haldeman about the leaks, he got even more furious. "One day we will get them," he said. "We'll get them on the ground where we want them. And we'll stick our heels in, step on them hard, and twist—right—get them on the floor and step on them, crush them, show them no mercy." G. Gordon Liddy, a former FBI agent, had come up with a plan to spend as much as $1 million on electronic eavesdropping, kidnapping of dissident leaders, and breaking into Democratic headquarters. Now a watered-down version of Liddy's scheme appealed to Nixon as a way to plug leaks. In June 1971 the president talked about breaking into the Brookings Institution to get confidential material on Ellsberg, who had an office there. He told his aides to talk to E. Howard Hunt, a former CIA operative, about carrying out the mission. "I want the break-in," Nixon declared to Haldeman. "You're to break into the place, rifle the files and bring them out . . . Just go in and take them." And on another occasion: "John [Mitchell] is always worried about is it technically correct? Do you think, for Christ's sake, that the *New York Times* is worried

about all the legal niceties? Those sons of bitches are killing me
. . . We're up against an enemy, a conspiracy. They're using any
means. *We are going to use any means.* Is that clear?"

Thus began the "plumbers"—so named because their job was
to plug leaks in the administration—the White House Special Investigations Unit, which included Hunt, Liddy, and other former
intelligence and security officials, formed in 1971 to ferret out
Nixon's political enemies and ensure that the Democrats would
have no chance to win in 1972. The plumbers broke into Ellsberg's psychiatrist's office in search of files that could be used to
humiliate him, plotted disruptions of Democratic candidates'
campaigns, and installed illegal wiretaps on the phones of potentially valuable informants. Operating directly out of the
White House—Hunt was assigned to Chuck Colson's office in
Ehrlichman's unit—the plumbers had virtual free rein to choose
their targets.

One of those targets was the Democratic National Committee
(DNC) headquarters in the Watergate apartment building in
Washington. Nixon had already ordered the Internal Revenue
Service to audit the taxes of DNC chairman Lawrence O'Brien.
Now, with the approval of John Mitchell, the plumbers broke
into the headquarters to steal secret campaign files and to plant
wiretaps on DNC phones. The first break-in went smoothly, but
the wiretaps were installed incorrectly, so the group decided to
return. This time the five intruders, including James McCord,
head of security for CREEP, and some Cuban émigrés, botched
the break-in, taping the locks on doors so obviously that a security guard noticed and called the police. The men were arrested
in the early hours of June 17, 1972. The break-in became part of
the police blotter, and a pair of enterprising young reporters for
the *Washington Post,* Bob Woodward and Carl Bernstein, soon dis-

covered that McCord's notebook had a phone number for E. Howard Hunt in the White House. When the reporters called, they were referred to Colson's office. Thus began the unraveling of the Nixon presidency.

Initially the story attracted only a brief flurry of attention. Although Bernstein and Woodward learned that a cashier's check for $25,000 made out to one of Nixon's regional campaign chairmen had been deposited in the account of one of the Cuban émigrés, and although a frightened CREEP secretary told them that at least three former White House aides—and probably John Mitchell as well—knew all about the break-in plot, the White House managed to contain the story. In August 1972 Nixon announced that John Dean, his White House counsel, had conducted a full investigation of Watergate and found that "no one on the White House staff . . . was involved in this very bizarre incident." A federal grand jury indicted only the five burglars plus Hunt and Liddy, and although Bernstein and Woodward's continued digging caused the *Post* to report in October that Watergate was but a small part of a "massive campaign of political spying and sabotage conducted on behalf of President Nixon's reelection," it was too late for the additional information to have any bearing on the election. With all other aspects of his campaign strategy working brilliantly, Nixon swept to re-election with 61 percent of the popular vote, and only 17 electoral ballots cast against him. It seemed he had triumphed over his enemies.

As soon as the trial of the Watergate seven began, however, the cover-up started to come apart. Judge John Sirica, a tough Republican former prosecutor, sensed from the beginning that the whole story was not being told. Five of the men pleaded guilty; McCord and Liddy were convicted in January 1973. Then, just before sentencing, McCord handed Sirica a letter stating that government officials and defendants had committed perjury repeatedly during the investigation, that political pressure from the highest levels had silenced the defendants, and that a number of other participants in the planning and execution of the Watergate burglary had never been identified. When Nixon heard about the letter he noted in his diary, "this is a bombshell."

The aftershocks soon started to register. Haldeman, Ehrlichman, and Dean resigned in April. Dean, knowing his own role was about to be exposed, began to talk to prosecutors. L. Patrick Gray, acting FBI director, disclosed that he had been ordered to "deep-six" documents central to the case. In May, a select committee of the Senate, chaired by the North Carolina Democrat Sam Ervin, convened hearings that rivaled in impact any held in the Capitol for decades. Ervin and his Republican colleague Howard Baker used skilled cross-examination and sharp wit to burrow into the fundamental question: "What did the president know and when did he know it?" When the White House aide Alexander Butterfield told the committee in July that in 1971 Nixon had installed a taping system in the White House that recorded all his conversations, it became clear that there was an immutable record that could tell the entire country exactly what the president had known and when he had known it.

The picture of life in the Nixon White House revealed by the tapes was not pretty. Within days after the burglary, Nixon had conspired with his chief aides to block the Watergate inquiry. He ordered Haldeman to arrange for Vernon Walters, deputy CIA director, to tell the FBI that a too careful pursuit of their investigation would compromise sensitive CIA operations. In the meantime, Nixon authorized the payment of hush money to the defendants and E. Howard Hunt. Indeed, Mrs. Hunt disbursed more than $200,000 in White House cash to her husband and the other Watergate burglars before she died in a plane crash over Chicago. In her purse, recovered after the crash, were found one hundred new $100 bills.

E. Howard Hunt subsequently demanded more money. On March 21, 1973, Nixon told John Dean, "We could get that . . . I know where it could be gotten," and arranged for Hunt to receive another $75,000 in cash. Once Butterfield revealed the existence of the tapes, Nixon desperately sought to avoid sharing them with either the Ervin committee or the special prosecutor, Harvard law professor Archibald Cox, who had been appointed to investigate the case for the justice department. Nixon first claimed executive privilege, then asked that transcripts be accepted in place of the actual tapes. When Cox refused, Nixon ordered his attorney general, Elliot Richardson, to fire Cox. Richardson resigned instead, as did his deputy William Ruckelshaus. Finally, Solicitor General Robert Bork did fire Cox, and the Saturday Night Massacre, as it was soon dubbed, was over.

By that time the end was in sight. Vice President Spiro Agnew, whom Nixon detested despite his polysyllabic denunciations of the radical left, was forced to resign, having pleaded "no contest" to charges of income tax fraud and having been accused of accepting bribes while governor of Maryland. (Nixon appointed Gerald Ford, the minority leader of the Senate, to be his new vice president.) More and more details came out about Nixon's own questionable financial dealings, including a $500,000 deduction he had claimed on his income taxes for donating his papers to the National Archives. Judge Sirica disclosed in November that there was a mysterious gap, eighteen and a half minutes long, on a critical White House tape; subsequent investigation showed that someone had erased that portion. A federal grand jury, meanwhile, indicted seven White House officials, including

Mitchell, Haldeman, Ehrlichman, and Colson. In its secret findings, the same grand jury suggested that Richard Nixon was an unindicted co-conspirator. As one columnist, discussing whether Nixon had agreed to pay hush money to the defendants, observed: "If Haldeman had lied, the president had lied." In a televised press conference in November 1973, Nixon insisted: "I am not a crook." But all the evidence suggested otherwise. Judge Sirica announced that he would turn over *all* the evidence to a House impeachment committee. With a staff led by a distinguished Republican lawyer, John Doar, the committee proceeded with meticulous care and due process, zeroing in on a request to hear what would come to be called the "smoking gun": the tape of a conversation on June 23, 1973, in which Nixon told Haldeman to get the FBI not to "go further into this case." This tape placed the president at the center of a conspiracy to obstruct justice. The Supreme Court ruled unanimously on July 24, 1974, that the White House must turn over the tapes. Ten days later, in a quivering voice that acknowledged he had made "a few mistakes of judgment," Richard Nixon resigned as president. Gerald Ford, who had replaced Agnew as vice president, told the country in his first remarks as president: "My fellow Americans, our long national nightmare is over."

❖   ❖   ❖

One way to make sense of Nixon's presidency is to go back to his interminable jottings on those yellow legal pads. In splendid isolation at Camp David, or in Key Biscayne, or in his hideaway in the Executive Office Building or the White House, Nixon scrawled plans for a new world order even as his henchmen—

with his approval—committed crimes on his behalf. Remarkably, the legal pads all said fundamentally the same thing, focusing on spiritual leadership, uplift, joy, boldness, morality—the same words over and over again. The scribblings spoke to the best aspects of Nixon's character—his capacity for long-range thinking, his acute consciousness of history, his profound awareness that he had an opportunity to change the shape of global politics. But there is also the sense that he repeated these phrases so often because he needed to remind himself of the good things he might accomplish—things consistent with his Quaker mother's beliefs—to keep from being overwhelmed by the mean, petty side of his political persona, the side that surfaced whenever he considered "the enemy" whom he must overcome, stomp on, and destroy.

There is also, in these meanderings, a tone of depression, as though Nixon is trying to talk himself out of his more morbid and bitter assessments of his situation. Thus, on December 20, 1972—after his re-election and the Watergate break-in, during the final massive bombing of North Vietnam, and before the Watergate scandal—he wrote: "I must get away from the thought of considering the office at any time a burden . . . It is God's great gift to me to have the opportunity to exert leadership, not only for America, but on the world scene. From this day forward, I am going to look upon it that way and rise to the challenge with as much excitement, energy, enthusiasm, and wherever possible real joy, that I can muster." What a sad commentary, as though Nixon meant exactly the opposite of what he wrote—that the office was a burden, and that he greeted his duties not with joy and enthusiasm but with wariness and despondency. Indeed, his closest aides indicated that even at his moments of greatest accomplishment, as after the trip to China, he appeared morose, preoccupied, unhappy.

There seemed to be a war going on within Richard Nixon all the time—between the bold statesman and the vindictive politician, between the man who regarded himself as a spiritual and moral leader and the insecure loner who always thought people were looking down on him or out to get him. The metaphor of war is appropriate: Nixon's life revolved around the battles of politics, with winners and losers, allies and enemies. But given his distrust of those around him, he would always perceive few allies and many enemies. In the end Nixon relied on only two or three people, and yet he found himself plagued with a suspicion that even they could not be trusted.

When Nixon's best side shone, he could be brilliant. Nothing better demonstrated this than the dramatic opening toward China, the deft diplomacy through which he changed the shape of world politics. Such genius was overwhelming in its courage, its imagination, its transformative impact. Yet, ironically, Nixon's genius arose from the same brooding introspection that subverted his potential for real greatness. At the heart of his character were loneliness and suspicion, both rooted in the fear of being unwanted by his friends and derided by his enemies. Even the way he pursued the rapprochement with China reflected the weakness of his strength—keeping Rogers and Laird in the dark, operating in mysterious layers of deception through Kissinger, secret Pakistani emissaries, symbolic theatrics like the Ping-Pong team. Each move was marked by mistrust of others and contempt for regular processes of decisionmaking.

When loneliness and suspicion monopolized Nixon's political game, they could become self-destructive, even suicidal. If all enemies were demonized, then anything that would contribute to their extermination could be justified. And lest traitors from within obstruct those plans, all but a trusted few would be excluded from any voice in shaping White House policies. A shadow government would be created, with Nixon alone in charge. The strategies to be pursued were those of polarization, divide and conquer, using racism and political dirty tricks to promote the "Southern strategy," while striking out ruthlessly at all those who dissented. It was all of a piece—the same loner mentality that created the China breakthrough also was responsible for the secret bombing, the Cambodian invasion, the denunciation of student radicals and eastern liberal snobs, and the creation of the plumbers unit to get whistle blowers and political opponents. Everything revolved around the "lonely man in the White House" finding, identifying, and caricaturing a political enemy and then destroying that enemy. In the late 1940s, the communist conspiracy and Alger Hiss filled the bill; in the late 1960s, it was radical students, the eastern elite, and disloyal bureaucrats. Only total control would bring Nixon security, and that was a chimera. And so, not surprisingly, after the 1972 election, he retreated to Camp David, told his closest aides that they would be there for weeks, and plotted to reorganize the government, with all cabinet officers being asked to resign, and a new policy manifesto, which all future appointees would be required to sign, stating that the only powers any appointee had must be "expressly delegated by the President," and that all statements must be cleared by the White House. The ultimate goal, in Richard Reeves's words, was "to seize control of the government he believed was filled with time-serving incompetents and secret enemies."

Ultimately, it was this politics of paranoia and polarization that brought Richard Nixon down. *Life* magazine accurately declared: "The Nixon administration remains a small junta, suspicious of the bureaucrats it presides over, ill at ease with Congress, distrustful of those it can't control, at once defensive and sometimes outright arrogant in its behavior . . . The junta's deep sense of being surrounded by enemies has permeated the Washington atmosphere." By the end of his first administration, Nixon had ceased to trust even those who he made his closest confidants. When he was alone with Haldeman, he would ask whether it was time to get rid of Kissinger. When he was alone with Kissinger, he would ask whether it was time to get rid of Haldeman. The deceivers were now plotting against each other. Nixon wondered out loud about Kissinger's paranoia; all of them worried about Nixon's paranoia. So conspiratorial had the White House become that the Joint Chiefs of Staff placed their own spy on Kissinger's staff to let the Pentagon know what was going on in Nixon's and Kissinger's minds. More and more people began to speculate openly about Nixon's sanity. He drank too much, made strange phone calls while inebriated, acted irrationally. The "President is acting very strangely," House Speaker Tip O'Neill confided; and Republican stalwart Barry Goldwater wrote, "I have reason to suspect that all might not be well mentally in the White House." By 1973 the situation had deteriorated so badly that the secretary of defense instructed his top generals that any presidential order to initiate military action should not be executed without the secretary's personal support.

The cycle of being a loner against the world had come full circle. The man who could plot tectonic shifts in the world order, and simultaneously obsess about the location of his pool table, had to be removed from his office—for his own protection, and for the protection of his country.

7

RONALD REAGAN
The Role of a Lifetime

Not since the funeral of John F. Kennedy had an American political figure inspired such an outpouring of emotion. Britain's Margaret Thatcher came to pronounce her benediction on her partner in ending the Cold War; former Soviet premier Mikhail Gorbachev added his gratitude, crediting the man who had dubbed the USSR an "evil empire" with being a peacemaker who had helped save the world from military disaster. Democrats joined Republicans in hailing Reagan as a great unifier who had restored America's self-confidence. Hardly a word of skepticism or doubt was heard, even from pundits ordinarily known for trenchant critical analysis. It was like a standing ovation at the end of a grand performance. Ronald Reagan would have beamed at such unanimity of acclaim.

◆　◆　◆

Few presidents in American history have embodied as much dualism in their personal and political lives as Ronald Reagan. With unprecedented success, he shaped the political contours of a generation, defining a set of economic values, foreign policy objectives, and military priorities that transformed the national agenda. And yet Reagan abhorred legislative detail and was only minimally involved in crafting the laws or implementing the policies designed to achieve his aspirations. According to his biographer Lou Cannon, Reagan was "the most consummate and effective politician I had ever met"; but at the same time he seemed "almost completely ignorant of even civics-book information" about government. A man of enormous charm, self-confidence, and charisma, Reagan nevertheless had almost no personal or emotional relationships with those closest to him, including his children. As with Franklin Roosevelt, millions of Americans responded to Reagan as if he were a friend or a cherished family member, but his inner life, as his former staff member David Gergen wrote, "remained a mystery." Indeed, Edmund Morris, after working for more than a decade on a biography commissioned by the Reagan family, concluded that Reagan was "an airhead." He seemed to have no core personality.

How to make sense of all this? There is no single answer, but the key lies in the way Reagan fused his own persona with a transcendent, superpatriotic view of the meaning of America, and in the process came to personify the values he espoused. He created, then embodied, a triumphalist national identity that soared beyond partisanship.

Ronald Reagan possessed a simple vision of America's glory that he conveyed to the public with extraordinary skill. It was a vision that had little to do with facts, mastery of detail, or sophisticated analysis. Rather, Reagan embraced certain basic values—a faith in capitalism, a belief that too much government was bad—and believed that he himself, embodying these values, could reverse the erosion of America's virtues and lead the nation back to greatness. The secret to Reagan was his sense of the larger good he was destined to serve. In his own mind, he was to be the instrument for restoring America to its destiny. And so, in his words, the voters "rounded up a posse, swore in this old sheriff, and sent us riding into town." This president's role was to rescue America, destroy her enemies, and reestablish the nation's ability to stand tall against all foes. It was a part that Ronald Reagan was ready to play.

◆ ◆ ◆

Ronald Reagan's character was shaped in a family beset by economic uncertainty, interpersonal conflict, and above all, his father's alcoholism. Reagan grew up in a small-town midwestern environment consistent with the simple and idyllic American virtues he came to celebrate. But his own childhood was far from simple. His parents were poor, his father frequently unemployed. The family moved five times before Ronald was ten years old. Worst of all, his parents struggled with each other, divided by conflicts over his father's binge drinking. In his autobiography, *Where's the Rest of Me?*, Reagan describes coming home as a preadolescent and finding his father passed out on the front porch, dead drunk. Children growing up in such an environment, experts on alcoholism say, internalize fear and a sense of responsibility: "They learn to be so sensitive and perceptive to what is happening that they can walk into a room, and without even consciously realizing it, figure out just what the level of tension is, who is fighting with whom, and whether it is safe or dangerous." Reagan's mother, meanwhile, sermonized against the evil of alcohol and instilled a moral sense into her son. But the traits shaped by growing up in the midst of such family tension—a compulsion to run away from disharmony and conflict, to make everything right, and to bring unity rather than division—would remain with Reagan throughout his life.

This quest for transcendent values was one of the things that contributed to Reagan's career choices, all of which had an element of romance, heroism, and identification with the good and the righteous. His first major job was as a lifeguard; in six summers of work he rescued seventy-seven people from drowning. Attending a small, church-related college, he was a popular public figure, and he began to acquire acting skills, most notably in his job as a radio announcer for baseball games, in which he had to make up stories about what was happening on the field, since all he had to work from was a pitch-by-pitch description of the game conveyed by telegraph. On one occasion the telegraph temporarily ceased functioning, and for several minutes Reagan made up out of whole cloth a series of pitches, with the batter fouling them all off.

With his skill at such fantasy creation, Reagan quickly became enamored of acting and decided to pursue a career in Hollywood. There, before long, the handsome young man became a successful movie star, usually cast in semi-romantic, all-American roles. During World War II he made patriotic films on behalf of the U.S. army. After the war he was elected president of the Screen Actors Guild, the craft union of Hollywood actors that represented them in negotiations with producers. Though he never achieved the stature of a John Wayne or a Gregory Peck, Reagan was a solid B-movie actor. In 1940 he married a better-known star, the actress Jane Wyman. When Wyman left him after a few years (she would later say the relationship had been too superficial for her taste), Reagan was crushed. But he quickly recovered, fell in love with Nancy Davis, and with a new self-confidence became more active in Hollywood's political and social life.

That involvement led to the next major transition in Reagan's career, an eight-year tenure with the hugely successful (and politically conservative) General Electric Corporation, which he served primarily as a public relations spokesperson. As a representative of a company with the slogan "Progress is our most important product," Reagan traveled the country trumpeting the virtues of General Electric and celebrating the values of America. Reagan spent more than six hundred days on the road, going to all 135 General Electric plants and addressing more than 250,000 employees. At every stop he gave "The Speech," a patriotic paean to the values of capitalism, the importance of cutting government down to size, and the need to remain ever vigilant against communist subversion. Although in his earlier incarnation as president of the Screen Actors Guild Reagan had been a liberal supporter of Harry Truman, he had by this time forsworn his allegiance to the Democratic party: he testified before the House Un-American Activities Committee about communists in Hollywood, and his views gradually shifted to the right. Although Reagan retained Roosevelt as a hero, he had by the early 1960s moved decisively and enthusiastically into the Republican camp.

Largely because of Reagan's successful career at General Electric and his growing fame as an evangelist for conservative causes, in 1964 the Barry Goldwater campaign invited Reagan to be a speaker in its televised efforts to mobilize political support. In responding to that request, Reagan galvanized the nation. Although he in fact used an only slightly modified version of "The Speech" he had been giving across the country for nearly a decade, he succeeded in communicating patriotic fervor to a mass audience, arousing in them his own enthusiasm for the values of

America's glorious past, and simultaneously transforming them into fans of both his personality and his politics. Before long, almost inevitably, he became a politician in his own right, and in 1966 he ran successfully for the governorship of California, defeating the two-term incumbent, Governor Edmund Brown. The freshness of Reagan's message, the sparkle of his personality, and the persuasiveness of his exhortations rallied people to his banner. Denouncing student protesters at Berkeley, he sent National Guardsmen to suppress demonstrations by radicals; the rigor and sternness of his response made Reagan a hero to Americans concerned with defending traditional values. He was the "citizen politician" who gave credence to the notion that a Mr. America could speak for the values that united all right-thinking citizens. After two successful terms as governor, Reagan challenged and almost defeated the incumbent, Gerald Ford, for the Republican party's presidential nomination in 1976. With that background, Reagan was poised to run against another incumbent, President Jimmy Carter, in 1980.

The match-up was perfect. In his term as president, Carter, a serious, somewhat dour man, had come to symbolize pessimism and a lack of buoyant leadership. Proclaiming that Americans had lost confidence in themselves, he called for a spiritual revival of social conscience and national commitment. Yet the news kept getting worse. Inflation soared into double digits. Unemployment rates did almost the same. Iranian radicals had held American diplomats hostage for more than a year in the U.S. embassy in Tehran. A rescue mission had ended in disaster because of bad weather and helicopter crashes. America, the vaunted superpower, now appeared helpless and weak, with television news programs each night chronicling the latest experience of humiliation.

Into this mix came Reagan, an ebullient celebrant of American power and promise. The contrast could hardly have been greater. While doubt seemed to plague Carter, Reagan was full of patriotic fervor, totally convinced (and convincing) that far from being at the nadir of its strength, America was about to engage in new conquests based upon values as old as the republic itself. Carter's one chance was that Reagan might expose himself in a presidential debate to be a reckless and uninformed extremist. Instead, Reagan excelled, looking every bit the part of a man fully prepared to be president. By election day Carter did not have a chance.

Part of Reagan's success was rooted in his "emotional intelligence," his ability to sense the mood and sentiments of those around him and to speak directly to their concerns. Reagan had "perfect pitch," as David Gergen has commented: "He had a fingertip feel for the mood of the country." Perhaps because of the sensitivity to his environment that he had developed as the child of an alcoholic father, Reagan discouraged confrontation and invited audiences to affirm the values they shared. Like Lyndon Johnson, he was in some ways a quintessentially "other-directed" personality, to use the sociologist David Riesman's phrase—someone exquisitely attuned to other people's moods and wishes. By using his skill at sensing his audience, Reagan was brilliantly successful at getting them to believe his message because he was telling them what they wanted to hear.

Reagan's message, in fact, so much reflected the values that most citizens shared that it was easy to create a bond of commonality. In his years as a salesman and an actor, Reagan had developed a supreme confidence in his ability to perform effectively, which in turn allowed him to be open and welcoming to those different from himself. As Lou Cannon has noted: "He answered questions sensibly and without a hint of guile . . . Everyone seemed to like him . . . He was as pleasant in response to skeptical questioners as he was to friendly ones." Precisely because he was so "other-directed," he never placed his own ego on the line or acted in a defensive manner. Instead, he focused on those who made up his audience, and by tying into their emotional priorities and concerns he established a strong link with them. When the audience was the nation, and the message the core meaning of America, a natural recipe existed for success.

In his earlier careers Reagan had also honed to a fine edge his skill as a raconteur and a humorist. Every question led to a story, most of them anecdotes about his childhood, his radio days, or the movies. When confronted with hard problems, Reagan responded with an analogy, not an analysis. Thus, even the most serious briefing about a complicated foreign policy or economic issue might generate a vignette from a Hollywood film as a response—usually accompanied by humor. His genius was the kind of folk wisdom reflected in entertaining stories that reminded people of their favorite uncle or Will Rogers. Indeed, part of Reagan's ability to make people feel comfortable with him was his knack for making fun of himself, causing people to laugh *with* him as he joked about his age or his memory or his Hollywood roles. At no time was this skill more apparent than when Reagan was shot during his first year in office. As he was about to undergo surgery to remove a bullet lodged next to his heart, Reagan bantered with his doctors, saying, "Please tell me you are all Republicans." And after the surgery was over and he was convalescing with tubes in and out of his body, he wrote on a piece of paper: "All in all, I'd rather be in Philadelphia." It was hard to resist such charm.

For all these reasons, Reagan came as close as anyone could to

being what Gergen called a "natural," the political version of
the perfect baseball player depicted by Bernard Malamud in his
novel *The Natural.* Reagan was always "on," ready to say what
needed to be said to please and satisfy his audience. For Gergen,
he was one of those "rare men like Teddy Roosevelt, Franklin
Roosevelt, who seemed blessed with instincts and intuition that
set them apart as leaders." Like any good actor, Reagan knew
how to rise to the occasion, deliver the lines that fit the moment,
and establish a bond of affinity with his followers.

All this was of a piece with the central metaphor of Reagan's
life—he was an actor ready to perform, always at home on stage.
No one better described the metaphor's aptness than Reagan
himself. When asked before becoming governor of California
what kind of leader he would be, he responded: "I don't know,
I've never played a governor." After he gave his first presidential
speech to the Congress, Reagan was asked how he felt. His response: "You're always in good spirits when you figure you got
by without losing your place or forgetting your lines." And Reagan reflected after eight years in the White House: "Some of my
critics . . . have said that I became president because I was an actor who knew how to give a good speech. I suppose that's not
too far wrong. Because an actor knows two important things—to
be honest in what he's doing and to be in touch with the audience. That's not bad advice for a politician either. My actor's instinct simply told me to speak the truth as I saw it and felt it."

In fact, the "truth" that Reagan spoke so powerfully and effectively consisted of a few basic ideas, all of which went back to
"The Speech" he gave for General Electric. The Reagan credo was
a set of simple but powerful convictions: (a) America was in
trouble because its leaders had become too obsessed with thinking that government had the answers for all problems; (b) big

government was bad—a "monkey" on people's backs—and should be dramatically reduced in size; (c) capitalism was the best economic system in the world and had to be given free rein, especially from government regulation, to achieve its potential; (d) in order to liberate free enterprise, taxes should be slashed; (e) the only exception to the evil of big government was the military, and it was imperative to increase its size and weaponry; and (f) the purpose of a strong economic system and a powerful military was to defeat communism once and for all. Clear and concise, these elements of Reagan's credo became the equivalent of a religious catechism. Like all matters of faith, they could neither be questioned in principle nor become subject to argument based on evidence or perspective. Precisely because they were articles of faith and the faith was shared by so many of his fellow citizens, Reagan could preach them with certainty and pursue their achievement with total confidence.

The downside of the Reagan credo was that while these convictions were sufficient to shape an agenda, achieving that agenda required follow-through, detailed planning, and implementation. Reagan's very strength as someone who could articulate a simple vision became a weakness given the indifference he displayed toward detail, process, and bureaucracy. From the outset of his political career, and throughout his days in Washington, those closest to Reagan knew that he would never become engaged in the nitty-gritty of making decisions or shaping policy. Others would bear that responsibility, and Reagan would delegate his authority to them. He would paint the vision of where he believed America should go in broad brush strokes; others could fill in the rest of the canvas.

This method of operating entailed the danger that the president would be ignorant about issues central to his responsibilities. Too often Reagan seemed indifferent to information. Briefing papers bored him. He consciously rejected engagement with policy debate. The *Washington Post* columnist David Broder wrote: "When someone approaches Reagan bearing information, he flees as if from a leper's touch." And on occasion his ignorance was stunning. At one time he told an audience that intercontinental ballistic missiles (ICBMs) could be called back after they were launched; at another that submarines did not carry nuclear missiles. The key question was whether a person who was a genius at communicating a vision of the country's future could achieve his goals without hands-on mastery of the mechanisms of government.

In part, Reagan's disengagement may have reflected the physical fact that he was hard of hearing. Peggy Noonan, one of his speechwriters, noted: "There was a quizzical look on his face as he listened to what was going on around him, and I realized: he doesn't really hear very much, and his appearance of constant good humor is connected to his deafness. He misses much of what is not said straight to him, and because of that, he keeps a pleasant look on his face as people chat around him." Although Lou Cannon and others have noted that Reagan became an excellent lip-reader, and that in small groups he often did appear to comprehend the message, Noonan's observation may help to explain why Reagan responded to all policy presentations with anecdotes, rarely engaging their specific content. By resorting to stories rather than acknowledging that he had not heard all of what was said, he could appear to be in control. Others, without hearing problems, had employed the same strategy: Roosevelt, for example, had used a similar form of deflection to retain control over conversations with staff members and congressmen. But in Reagan's case the issue was more than simply a hearing problem, and it threatened to lead to losing control.

By temperament, Reagan seemed unwilling to grapple with complexity. A positive way to describe him is to say that he focused on only a few ideas. The negative consequence of this was his reluctance to consider multiple options or variations on those ideas. His daily schedule was light. Having read the newspaper over breakfast, he arrived at his office as late as 9:00, fed the squirrels in the Rose Garden, received a security briefing, and then had "personal time" for an hour before lunch to read and answer mail, writing lengthy personal letters in longhand and keeping up with friends. He then napped, exercised, had a few more meetings, and was back in the family living quarters by 5:00 ready for an evening of entertainment, whether movies or television. When, at one point, his scheduling office put together a jam-packed itinerary to highlight for the media how hard the president worked on an average day, regular White House reporters chortled, commenting that the schedule looked more like Reagan's average month.

Perhaps more to the point, Reagan seemed indifferent to complex details. The night before a world economic summit, his chief of staff, James Baker, gave him a carefully boiled-down briefing book that he could read quickly to prepare for his meeting with other world leaders. In the morning Reagan confessed that he had not even opened the briefing book, explaining: "Well, Jim, the *Sound of Music* was on last night." Before his inauguration Reagan spent an hour with the outgoing president, Jimmy Carter, to be briefed on the pressing issues he would inherit. He failed to take a single note—a response inconceivable for any other modern-day president-elect. Although Reagan later impressed his staff with his recollection of the briefing, Carter was appalled.

Others agreed that there was a fundamental flaw in Reagan's approach. According to Lou Cannon, Reagan's "biggest problem

was that he didn't know enough about public policy to participate fully in his presidency—and often didn't realize how much
he didn't know." It was almost as if policies or legislation did not
matter to him. When as governor of California he was asked
about his legislative program, Reagan turned to his aides and
said: "I could take some coaching from the sidelines if anyone
can recall my legislative program." Coming out of a congressional briefing at the White House, one Republican loyalist lamented: "The president is just out of it too much of the time."
Even the conservative columnist George Will, a Reagan disciple,
wondered "how anyone so uninformed could reach the top of
the American political system."

Reagan also appeared singularly indifferent, on a personal
level, to staff, friends, and even family. Although he was generous, charming, and eminently accessible to people who had
never met him, he seemed opaque and impenetrable to those
who knew him well. As his longtime friend Len Nofziger commented: "He's a genuinely nice man, but there's a kind of barrier
between him and the rest of the world, a film you can't get
through. You can't get inside of him." Reagan forgot the names
of close aides, showed little interest in their personal lives, and
in most cases shied away from hearing about their problems—
as if, Cannon observed, "to protect himself, to compensate for
some childhood hurt." "He didn't make you feel needed,"
Gergen wrote. "People left, and didn't hear from him, and there
was no real sense of connection. I think they felt hurt by it." To
be sure, others found that Reagan did, in fact, tune in to their
personal or family problems, but most commented on the other
side.

Reagan's children fell into the same category as his staff assistants and personal aides. His son Michael recalled that his father

had been "completely oblivious" to his children and had not even recognized Michael in his cap and gown when he graduated from boarding school. A second son, Ronald, said his father got "a little bit antsy" if he tried to "get too close and too personal to father." "I never knew who he was," his daughter Patti said. "I could never get through to him." Only his wife Nancy was his confidante and friend. And even she admitted: "Although he loves people, he often seems remote, and doesn't let anybody get too close. There's a wall around him. He lets me come closer than anyone else, but there are times when even I feel that barrier." And in perhaps the most devastating comment, Michael declared: "He can give his heart to the country, but he just finds it difficult to hug his own children." Clearly, giving oneself to family and friends in a committed relationship is qualitatively different from immersing oneself in detailed briefing papers and policy disputes. Nevertheless, Reagan's detachment with regard to both public and family matters suggests a quality of temperament that militated against full-scale engagement in either realm.

Reagan's removal from intimate involvement with issues and people made all the more critical the quality of staff support he received. Reagan had mastered the role of visionary for the country. Yet all too often he knew nothing about the daily realities of administration and policy follow-through. That made him, in effect, a passive president dependent upon others to decide on the specifics of policy implementation, schedule his time, dictate his scripts, and shape his public persona. Reagan never had a meeting with a congressman, a foreign leader, or anyone else without a series of cards on which the remarks he would make to his guests were written. If the topic of conversation wandered from what was scripted on the cards, he appeared helpless, and soon reverted to telling anecdotes about Hollywood. House Speaker Thomas P. O'Neill became so enraged at this dependence on cards that he erupted during a conversation with the president and asked why they could not have a spontaneous give-and-take.

Overseeing the day-to-day details of Reagan's schedule was Reagan's longtime friend Michael Deaver. He chose to act as if the president's days were a movie production with Reagan in the starring role. "He tried to see to it," Lou Cannon has written, "that the script, staging, and lighting of each scene provided Reagan an opportunity to give a smashing performance." Almost always, Reagan responded effectively. Still, some staff members were shocked at the implied condescension of such stage management. When Secretary of State George Shultz walked Reagan through a series of "scenes" that would occur with a foreign leader, one of his assistants observed that Shultz was treating Reagan as someone "who didn't have the intellectual wherewithal to think or act on his own." In fact, that was largely the case. Using the typology of different kinds of intelligence developed by the psychologist Howard Gardner, Cannon has noted that Reagan was brilliant with language and interpersonal intelligence but completely lacked logical and analytical abilities. It thus was imperative that his staff compensate for these deficiencies, maximizing Reagan's opportunities to display the kinds of intelligence he did have, while minimizing his exposure to situations that would require those he lacked.

Fortunately for both the country and Reagan's presidency, during his first term he had a staff well suited to this mission. The key player was James Baker, formerly campaign manager for Vice President George H. W. Bush. A brilliant tactician and an evenhanded analyst, Baker provided the balance needed to ensure that Reagan would not be embarrassed or humiliated by his ignorance about policy details. Baker had been chosen as chief of staff by a quiet cabal led by Nancy Reagan, Michael Deaver, and Stuart Spencer of Reagan's campaign staff. Baker was in charge of political management, communications, and outreach; Ed Meese, formerly Reagan's chief of staff in California, took on responsibility for policy management; while Deaver organized the president's personal schedule. From the beginning it was their show, not Reagan's. "He made no demands," one aide said, "and gave almost no instructions." As Cannon observed the operation, he concluded that the White House staff "saw their task as protecting the Reagan presidency from the clear and present danger of Ronald Reagan."

Not surprisingly, Reagan knew little about the other major players in his administration. He named Alexander Haig as his secretary of state, for example, largely at Richard Nixon's behest. The one evening he spent with Haig, Reagan devoted most of the conversation to reminiscing about an old show business pal, Edgar Bergen. Donald Regan, whom Reagan appointed as secretary of the treasury, came into office having held only an abbreviated phone conversation with the president. "From the first day to the last at Treasury," Regan later wrote, "I was flying by the seat of my pants. The president never told me . . . what he wanted to accomplish in the field of economics." The White House staff even ran cabinet meetings, with Ed Meese setting the agenda and orchestrating the conversation. Reagan rarely asked questions, and simply performed according to the script that had been written out for him.

From the outside, the White House operation appeared smooth and efficient. The president's days were organized to give him a maximum of "personal staff time," otherwise known as time for him to pursue his own interests, and enough well-designed public appearances to reassure the people that he was in charge. It was "a splendid routine," one observer noted, but "often [Reagan] held the reins of power so lightly that he did not appear to hold them at all." And Haig observed: "To me, the White House was as mysterious as a ghost ship; you heard the creak of the rigging and the groan of the timbers and sometimes even glimpsed the crew on deck. But which of the crew had the helm? Was it Meese, was it Baker, was it someone else? It was impossible to know for sure."

The president's staff not only protected him but also crafted a political agenda that made it possible for him to move forward on his bold vision for a changed America, at least during his first term. Without question, Reagan's part in that drama was critical. He articulated the vision, engaged in repeated exhortations to the American people of the basic themes of his GE speech, and ordered his staff to organize the follow-through. Because the staff was so good, the result was one of the most effective political operations that had ever been seen in the White House. Reagan could tell the stories, many of them based upon movies and offering inspiration and emotional reinforcement, while staff people put together the program to implement the vision.

The heart of that vision consisted of Reagan's belief that government should be downsized and taxes should be reduced so private individuals could invest in the economy and let it grow on its own momentum. With David Stockman, a brilliant budget director chosen by James Baker, in charge, the Reagan White House proposed a massive tax cut focused on the wealthiest Americans to encourage saving and investment, deregulation of most major industries to make businesses more competitive, a cutback in social expenditures to help offset the tax cut, and a variety of other programs designed, in Stockman's words, to create a "minimalist government . . . a spare and stingy creature which offered even-handed public justice, but no more." Although some Americans would suffer, Stockman recognized, the programs would strengthen the country in the long run "by abruptly severing the umbilical cords of dependency that ran from Washington to every nook and cranny of the nation."

Although the cuts in funding for social welfare programs were never as severe as Stockman wanted, the Reagan administration clearly signaled its intention to restructure the philosophical foundations of government. Congress sliced more than $25 billion from welfare programs in 1981, and radically cut taxes by $750 billion over five years. Environmental controls on businesses were eviscerated. Interior Secretary James Watt initiated an effort to grant oil and coal developers mineral rights to public lands. Meanwhile, the administration secured congressional approval for its second major objective, a staggering $1.2 trillion increase in defense expenditures over five years. Denouncing the Soviet Union as "an evil empire" committed to a policy of lying and cheating the world, Reagan won a 41 percent increase in defense spending, even as he cut budget resources dramatically through his tax bill. By ratcheting up America's defense expenditures and weapons systems, Reagan demonstrated his determination to stare down the Soviet Union and his belief that the Soviets would not be able, economically or militarily, to respond in kind.

In reality, the two priorities of Reagan's first term were totally at odds with each other. It was impossible to balance the budget by simultaneously slashing taxes and geometrically increasing military spending. David Stockman, in an interview he gave William Greider for the *Atlantic Monthly* in the fall of 1981, virtually admitted that the administration's economic policies were self-contradictory. "You mean it really is voodoo economics after all?" asked Reagan's chief of staff James Baker. For a time it appeared as though the country might turn against Reagan's policies. Unemployment shot up, inflation continued to grow, and the deficit exploded. Yet by the third year of Reagan's first term, the economy turned around. Everything was on the rebound. The recession ended, prosperity returned, at least for the middle and upper classes, housing construction soared, and consumer spending skyrocketed. Although Stockman had admitted in 1981 that "none of us really understands what's going on with all these numbers," supply-side economics now seemed to be kicking in. Although the long-term economic consequences of a ballooning deficit would eventually come back to haunt the country, in the short term, at least, the bad news had gone away. Reagan suddenly appeared to be a prophet whose vision had been redeemed. The political commentator Elizabeth Drew noted in the *New Yorker:* "Reagan is a political phenomenon—a man who by force of personality and marvelous stage management superimposes himself over his own mistakes."

By the time the 1984 election approached, Reagan seemed unbeatable. Although he spent about one-quarter of his time at his ranch in California, and another eighth of his time at the presidential retreat at Camp David, Maryland, the public seemed oblivious to the relatively limited amount of time he devoted to presidential business. Instead, they felt reassured by the eloquence of his statements on behalf of the Reagan credo. Congresswoman Patricia Schroeder at one point called Reagan the "Teflon president," because even bad things failed to stick to him.

Nothing illustrated Schroeder's point better than a series of foreign policy events in the fall of 1983. Soviet fighter planes shot down a Korean airliner over Russia, killing more than two hundred civilians, including a number of Americans. Reagan used the occasion to condemn the Soviets, labeling them "inhumane, barbarous, and uncivilized," even though U.S. intelligence indicated that the episode had been unintentional and the Soviets had not known this was a passenger airliner. In October of the same year a terrorist attack in Beirut, Lebanon, murdered 241 marines—a disaster that a blue ribbon investigation later blamed on politicians in Washington who had not listened carefully enough to the Pentagon's recommendations. Yet here, too, Reagan escaped criticism. Within days of the Beirut disaster, he sent 10,000 American paratroopers into the small island nation of Grenada, whose president had been assassinated, arguing that the troops were needed to protect American medical students ostensibly threatened by a communist dictatorship.

Reagan might have been criticized for any of these situations, and especially for the loss of hundreds of marines, but instead he mesmerized the nation with a brilliant televised speech in which he conflated the catastrophe in Beirut with the liberation of Grenada and made each an example of American patriotism. In an extraordinary peroration to his address, Reagan, visibly moved, described a badly wounded marine who had written the marine motto, *semper fi* (*semper fidelis,* "always faithful"), on a pad when the commandant of the marine corps visited him in the hospital. One more time, Reagan the Hollywood star had used a performance to identify his own leadership with the courageous soldiers fighting under his command. Notwithstanding the fact that Reagan's own policymakers were largely responsible for the Beirut disaster, the next day his popularity rating rose 15 points.

In the face of such success, the 1984 Democratic presidential candidate, Walter Mondale, barely stood a chance. Although Mondale was well qualified for the presidency, ridiculed Reagan's tax program as the old Herbert Hoover "trickle-down" theory, and portrayed Reagan's rhetoric as excessive and reckless, the president appeared invulnerable to criticism. "America is back," Reagan proclaimed, and he took a good share of the credit with most people agreeing that he deserved it. In contrast to 1980, when America had boycotted the Moscow Olympics, Americans swept the gold medals at Los Angeles in 1984. Patriotism seemed to be everywhere. "Just about every place you look," said one Reagan television ad, which showed a man painting a white picket fence, "things are looking up, life is better—and people have a sense of pride they never thought they would feel again."

At the heart of Reagan's appeal was the degree to which he seemed to be *like* most of his countrymen. He was the average "guy in the bar," Tip O'Neill said, someone you could drink with, share a story with. Reagan himself commented: "Would you laugh if I told you that I think, maybe, [the American people] see themselves and think that I am one of them? I've never been able to detach myself or think that I, somehow, am apart from them." As one journalist noted, Reagan never lost that quality of next-door neighborliness. "He never became part of the system . . . [he was] a cultural democrat . . . a citizen cast up from among politicians." Largely because Reagan so effectively used his public statements to identify with the American people and their values, he had become, in Elizabeth Drew's words, "the personification of America . . . [so that] to suggest that anything is wrong with him is to run down the country." With such political chemistry, even the most brilliant Mondale speech was doomed to failure. As a prominent Democrat said: "You couldn't touch Reagan without hurting yourself."

In one of the most decisive elections in American history, Reagan swept to victory, losing only one state, Mondale's home state of Minnesota. His candidacy generated support from 57 percent of women, 61 percent of the elderly, 66 percent of Roman Catholics, and more than a third of American Jews. Even families from trade union backgrounds split 50–50. That night, *Newsweek* magazine said, "Ronald Wilson Reagan became Mr. America." The turnabout had been dramatic. In 1980, polls had indicated that 75 percent of Americans did not feel confident that the future would be better than the past; now more than half affirmed their confidence in the future. Reagan had declared during the campaign, "Let's take our cue from our [Olympic] athletes . . . let's go for growth, let's go for the gold." And the people had responded. They felt better, and Reagan's personality was a major reason. His staff had succeeded in its fundamental goal—to highlight the good and obscure the bad about the Reagan presidency.

After this election victory by near acclamation, however, ominous portents began to appear. One was a seemingly innocent shakeup in the White House staff. All three of the major figures who had facilitated Reagan's success during his first term were now ready to leave. Part of the reason was that Reagan paid little attention to them and showed inadequate appreciation for their work. Another was the constant tension between the staff and Nancy Reagan, particularly over her desire to protect her husband from virtually every kind of pressure. She even consulted an astrologer, who mandated changes in Reagan's schedule to be sure his activities were aligned with the stars. Now, in a critical switch apparently never discussed in detail with the president, James Baker and Donald Regan exchanged positions, Regan coming to the White House as chief of staff and Baker assuming the post of secretary of the treasury. The president was completely passive in the face of these major transitions. In Lou Cannon's words, "For Reagan, it was merely another shift of casts and directors."

But the results proved disastrous. While Baker was consummately skilled in protecting Reagan from himself and from the humiliating errors that could embarrass him, Regan had none of Baker's skills. A loner like the president, yet without any strong relationship with his boss, Regan was the wrong man for the job. Baker had been attuned to those around him and had sought consensus. Regan was authoritarian. Baker was always cautious; Regan took chances. Baker always put the president first; Regan was more egotistical. As a result, more and more, people saw the bad side of Reagan, with his worst traits accentuated. He became, Cannon wrote, a "remote and disengaged monarch," with no one to pore over every detail to make sure he looked and sounded presidential. A whole new team had taken over, from the national security staff all the way through the White House scheduling office. Suddenly the production faltered and the performance became erratic.

One of the first errors Regan made was to schedule a ceremony in Bitburg, Germany, where the president would lay a wreath at a military cemetery in honor of Germany's war dead. What Regan did not realize was that officers of Hitler's Waffen SS were buried there, including many who had taken part in the massacre of Jews. Even when he discovered that fact, he did not protect Reagan from the decision or attempt to reverse it. The president had always been so good at symbolic events, using them to highlight his fundamental faith in American values; yet now he was about to pay homage to people who had helped perpetrate the Holocaust. In some ways, the visit to Bitburg was simply a passing mistake. Yet it pointed to a more serious unraveling of control in the administration, a failure to present Reagan in a one hundred percent positive light.

The breakdown of staff confidence and control continued. Members of the national security staff, with Regan's tacit support, manipulated Reagan into sanctioning two unwise moves: an exchange of arms for hostages with Iran, and illegal support for the Contras in Nicaragua, anti-Marxist guerrillas fighting the duly constituted regime of Daniel Ortega. What came to be known as the Iran-Contra affair was a humiliating policy disaster for the administration. It illuminated all the worst consequences of Reagan's inability to master the details of policy, while illustrating how close a bad staff could bring a presidency to self-destruction.

The Iran-Contra affair represented the convergence of two passions of Ronald Reagan and his administration. The first was his commitment to eliminate communism in the western hemisphere. Devoted to liberating Nicaragua from Marxist rule, Reagan gave rhetorical support to the Contra "freedom fighters." At the same time, he was intent on rescuing the hostages that Iran and its allies had seized as part of their jihad against the West. Reagan had come into office buoyed by the release of 52 Americans who had been taken captive at the U.S. embassy in Tehran more than a year earlier. But he was determined to finish the liberation of hostages, and his personal dedication to that goal—almost an obsession—became very much connected to a heroic and romantic vision of rescue that went back to his lifeguard and Hollywood days. Now the two passions of deposing the Sandinistas and freeing the hostages suddenly became joined.

Inevitably, the details of policy in both areas became far murkier than Reagan's simple passions might suggest. Thus, for example, some national security staffers suggested that the United

States provide arms to Iran via Israel, in return for which Iran would help secure the release of Americans held hostage by a pro-Iranian faction in Lebanon. Although the United States would not directly supply the arms, it would resupply Israel, thereby violating Reagan's (and the government's) long-standing policy against trading arms for hostages. Evidently Reagan never understood that he was betraying his own policy and rhetoric; he authorized his national security advisor, Robert McFarlane, to engage in the initial exchange in the fall of 1985. Another of Reagan's national security advisors, Admiral John Poindexter, went even further, securing Reagan's signature on a "presidential finding" that allowed the circumvention of policy as necessary to the "national security." Poindexter's success in doing so is a particularly vivid illustration of inattentiveness on Reagan's part, since Secretary of Defense Caspar Weinberger and Secretary of State George Shultz had argued adamantly against any exchange, and believed they had won their case. As Weinberger later said, they thought this baby "had been strangled in its cradle." But in fact Reagan, who often sided with the last person he spoke with on an issue, had been persuaded to side with his national security council (NSC) aides.

The circumvention of policy deepened when NSC staff members sought to use the Iranian arms exchange to raise funds to support the Nicaraguan rebels. Even though Congress, in the 1984 Boland amendment, had explicitly forbidden any aid to the Contras by the U.S. government, Colonel Oliver North and his cohorts at the NSC now proposed that the United States overcharge the Iranian government for the weapons being sent, and divert the profits to the "freedom fighters" in Nicaragua. In short, not only was the government explicitly contradicting its own policy of no arms for hostages; it was now participating in a conspiracy to violate U.S. law.

By now, enough people were aware of these transactions that it was only a matter of time before the press tracked down the truth and published it. Within weeks, all the attempts to disguise the Iran-Contra affair had been exposed, and the administration found itself in the humiliating position of being caught in an act of massive duplicity. The most devastating indictment came from a blue ribbon commission headed by a former Texas senator, John Tower, and including a former secretary of state, Edwin Muskie, and a former NSC advisor, Brent Scowcroft. What startled the commission was the degree to which Reagan was forgetful, uninvolved, and unaware of his administration's policies and their consequences. As one reporter noted, some commission members saw the president as "a man who sometimes inhabited a fantasy island." Witnesses told them that the release of hostages was Reagan's number-one preoccupation—"and yet he can't remember anything about it, my God!" In a clear example of understatement, one commission member concluded: "The system of [decisionmaking at the White House] did not compensate adequately for the management style of the president." More to the point was Republican senator William Cohen's observation that it would be a "waste of time" to ask Reagan what had happened because "with Ronald Reagan, no one is there. The sad fact is that we don't have a president." A harsh judgment by any standard, particularly for a man who had done so much to strengthen America in the world—but one that accurately identified the Achilles' heel of his presidency.

In the end, Reagan himself was not charged with explicit responsibility, largely because no one could trace the exact sequence of events by which he had approved the illegal policies. He had written in his diary on January 17, 1986: "I agreed to sell TOWs [missiles] to Iran." But he had no recollection of how that agreement had come about.

The Tower commission concluded that Donald Regan "must bear primary responsibility for the chaos that descended upon the White House when [the Iran-Contra] disclosures did occur." He had been involved in all the meetings, had failed to foresee the consequences, and had done almost nothing to protect the president from humiliation. Worse, Reagan's NSC staff brazenly defended their right to operate outside the control of laws or institutions. Poindexter, North, and McFarland, the Tower commission concluded, had operated "largely outside the orbit of the U.S. government." Poindexter even told Congress that he had the right to pursue these actions without going to Reagan since he knew what the president wanted, and after all, the people had chosen the president. Nor was that the limit of the misuse of power that was taking place. It turned out that North, together with the CIA director, William Casey, wished to create an intelligence unit operating outside the CIA with funds and orders that had *no* authorization from Congress or the president. It was a terrifying prospect. "What we see [here]," one reporter wrote, "is a combination of right-wing fervor, militaristic nationalism, and religiosity . . . reminiscent of the stirrings of authoritarianism in Europe."

By the middle of 1987 the entire Reagan operation seemed to be coming apart. The massive deficit continued to grow, with Reagan seemingly unaware that it was his military budgets and his tax cuts that had created the problem. The shortfall in 1986 was $283 billion, more than three times what it had been just four years earlier. Reagan eventually went on television to confess his responsibility for Iran-Contra: "A few months ago I told the American people I did not trade arms for hostages. My heart and my best intentions still tell me that's true, but the facts and the evidence tell me it is not . . . There are reasons why it happened, but no excuses. It was a mistake." But that admission did not keep his reputation from crumbling. His approval rating plummeted from 67 percent to 46 percent. The reality was that Reagan could not remember whether he had approved all the details of the Iran-Contra deal. It was also probably true that no one on his staff told him it was illegal and unconstitutional to do what the government did. The tragedy was twofold: first, that the staff was sufficiently reckless and irresponsible that it permitted Reagan to get into such a position; and second, that the president himself, by virtue of his "management style," was so uninvolved in oversight of policy that it was conceivable he could have said yes to anything.

It appeared that the protective cocoon that had always surrounded the Reagan White House was gone, leaving fully exposed the organizational weakness at the heart of the administration. "No sadder tale could be spun in this holiday season," David Broder wrote at Christmas time, "than the unraveling of yet another presidency." When Poindexter told Congress that he had lied, James Reston wrote: "You shouldn't be surprised. This administration has been living a life of pretense, cheating and borrowing for over six years." Even staunch Republicans agreed. One party leader noted: "We have as weak a cast of political characters as anyone in the western world, [and] this government still has fourteen months to go." There was almost no good news to counter the bad, and the White House seemed besieged and overwhelmed. As the *New Yorker*'s Elizabeth Drew commented: "It is hard to see how [things] could change sufficiently to give us a presidency that is not—and does not put the country—in danger."

Then, almost as in a surprise Hollywood ending, a decisive breakthrough allowed Reagan to end his presidency in triumph.

Having fired Donald Regan after the Iran-Contra affair, Reagan
and his wife turned to Howard Baker, former Senate republican
leader, to rescue the White House staff from its chaos and inef-
ficiency. Baker, like James Baker before him, understood the importance of protecting the president, highlighting his best side,
and not exposing his vulnerabilities to the public. At the same
time, Reagan began to focus once again on some of the visionary
goals he had long articulated. Together, these events allowed his
administration to conclude with a round of summit talks with
Soviet leader Mikhail Gorbachev, a dramatic treaty reducing the
number of intermediate-range nuclear missiles, and the widely
hailed beginning of a new era of détente between the United
States and the Soviet Union.

Appropriately enough, the vision for this near miracle seems
to have had its origins in Reagan's penchant for using Hollywood movies as an inspiration for policy. He frequently confused personal experience with film. Thus, for example, he loved
to tell an emotional story about a tail gunner on a bomber who
was badly wounded, unable to bail out, and about to crash all by
himself as his plane went into the sea, until the pilot came back
and said, "Never mind, son, we'll ride it down together." He told
the story as though it had happened in reality, with the pilot receiving a posthumous congressional medal of honor. In fact,
this anecdote came from a movie starring Dana Andrews and a
story in *Reader's Digest*. Another film that inspired Reagan was a
science fiction thriller called *The Day the Earth Stood Still*, in
which an invasion of aliens from other planets created the kind
of mortal threat that brought universal peace to the world by
uniting former enemies into a common defense. That idea gradually evolved into Reagan's proposal for a strategic defense initiative (SDI), otherwise known as "star wars," wherein Ameri-

cans would create the technology for destroying all offensive missiles aimed at any power, thereby saving the world from mutual assured destruction in atomic warfare. Although Reagan's "star wars" proposal was opposed by the joint chiefs of staff and had only marginal scientific validity, he put it forward as a major initiative. The Soviets were terrified at the idea, since, if successful, it would make the United States invulnerable and take away the credibility of the Soviet deterrent. In addition, it constituted a violation of the anti–ballistic missile treaty of 1972. Nevertheless, Reagan saw the SDI as the means by which the United States could forge a deal with the Soviets to ban all nuclear weapons. It was a utopian notion, but one totally consistent with Reagan's penchant for thinking in terms of transcendent goals.

At the beginning of the Reagan presidency, there seemed no possibility of détente with the Soviet Union. The Soviets had just invaded Afghanistan, the United States had embarked on clandestine efforts to support anti-Soviet guerrillas both in Afghanistan and in Latin America, and the president was committed to a rhetoric that defined Russia as "an evil empire." Nor was the Soviet leadership particularly imaginative or responsive to any possibilities of détente. A series of Soviet apparachiks—Brezhnev, Andropov, and Chernenko—displayed little flexibility, seemingly committed to a stagnant policy of hunkering down for a long winter's night of Cold War with little chance of any thaw.

But then Chernenko died, and a new, young leader named Mikhail Gorbachev came into office demonstrating an openness that heralded a new age. "This is a man that we can do business with," British Prime Minister Margaret Thatcher told Reagan, and soon it became clear why. Gorbachev sought to democratize the Soviet Union, create more entrepreneurship in its economy, and move toward meeting some of the country's infrastructure needs by limiting defense spending. He hoped to revitalize the Soviet society and economic system by encouraging freedom and decentralization. Having experienced the internal disintegration of Soviet power, most clearly demonstrated by the Solidarity movement's insurgency in Poland, Gorbachev recognized that trying to match Reagan's dramatic increases in U.S. defense spending would drive his country into bankruptcy, and so chose instead the path of disarmament and peace.

After an initial period of hesitation, Reagan seized the moment, combining his "star wars" initiative with a call for radical disarmament in both the Soviet Union and the United States. With Nancy Reagan's encouragement and the support of America's allies in Europe, Reagan met with Gorbachev in Reykjavik, Iceland, in the fall of 1986. The two men had an intense and extended personal discussion, actually contemplating the abolition of all nuclear weapons—a concept that, while consistent with Reagan's science fiction movie, appalled his diplomatic and military aides. In the end, Gorbachev was unwilling to trade acceptance of SDI for such an agreement, but a start had been made.

In a series of additional summits that culminated in Moscow in April 1988, Reagan and Gorbachev moved steadily toward an agreement that would substantially reduce the arms race, even if it did not lead to the destruction of all nuclear weapons. Reagan had been right in thinking that the Soviets would not be able to match America's increases in defense spending without ruining their economy. In effect, Reagan had raised the ante so high that Russia could not stay in the game. But it was also Gorbachev's willingness to take huge risks and make dramatic changes in the direction of Soviet society that made the agreement possible.

"We are going to do something terrible to you Americans," one Soviet leader announced. "We are going to deprive you of an enemy." Within two years, in fact, that prediction would become reality as the Soviet empire came apart, the Berlin Wall was torn down, and Eastern Europe became democratic. Both leaders deserved credit. As Strobe Talbot, an American expert on the Soviet Union, noted, Reagan "was a romantic, a radical, a nuclear abolitionist." Always a visionary, he had persisted in seeking his goal of world peace and had now come close to realizing one of his fantasies. But none of this would have happened without the courage Gorbachev displayed in launching the Soviet Union on a radical new path.

◆ ◆ ◆

How then to make sense of this bundle of paradoxes? A brilliant politician who always connected with his audiences—and a bungler who did not even know that nuclear missiles could not be recalled once launched. A charismatic visionary—and an ineffectual manager who reacted to detail as though it were a poisonous snake. A person who seemed like the "guy in the bar," a man Americans could identify with and feel close to—and someone who occasionally forgot the names of his cabinet members and had almost no emotional relationship with his children.

One answer, clearly, was the importance of those who ran his life: his staff, his wife, his closest friends. As David Gergen observed, there were in fact three presidencies: that of James Baker, that of Donald Regan, and that of Howard Baker. The first and the last chiefs of staff knew how to protect the president and show his best side to the public. Donald Regan, more egocentric and authoritarian, did not. Reagan triumphed when people like

Michael Deaver and James Baker, in close alliance with Nancy Reagan, limited his public role to scenarios in which he had a superior message to convey, and one that was close to his heart. His presidency failed when people like Oliver North, John Poindexter, and Regan put their own priorities ahead of his, and took advantage of his organizational shortcomings to advance their own agendas.

In the end, it came down to the roles Reagan played, how they were scripted, and the degree to which they allowed him to do what he did best—perform the part he passionately cared about, the leader who embodied America's ideal self and noblest dreams. Theorists of role-play in sociology talk about the degree to which individuals become the part they are acting, identify with it, internalize it. In most cases, there is another self—detached from the part being played—that goes in and out of multiple roles. But sometimes the role and the person become one. That description seems appropriate to Ronald Reagan. He not only delivered the lines written for him with consummate skill; he was the role he played.

If the psychologists are correct and Reagan was profoundly affected by growing up in a divided household with an alcoholic father, it makes sense that he would seek to avoid conflict and try to bring people together. It also makes sense that one way he escaped domestic turmoil was to retreat to a world of romantic heroism, of utopian dreams. That is why he was so good at making up the play-by-play of baseball games, or at acting the dramatic parts he was assigned. He became the person he was playing, caught up in the fantasy. To pay attention to detail, to engage emotionally with people, to become entangled in human conflict—all these introduced complexity, pain, lack of clarity. Besides, that was someone else's part.

In contrast, when Reagan could play a role in which he identified with transcendent values—patriotism, love of God, sacrifice,
anticommunism, the American creed—he could rise above conflict and achieve a level of affirmation, confidence, and popularity that no one could challenge. His dedication to that role helps
explain why he was so successful when his scriptwriters and directors (the White House staff) highlighted him in the right
parts. At the same time, his refusal to play the role of detail-ori-
ented manager explains why his presidency was at its worst when
his staff put themselves and their own agendas first. In those instances, his shortcomings endangered the entire country.

Precisely because Reagan was most comfortable when playing
a role, he was passive, aloof, and unaware when no direction was
given or when he confronted new and strained circumstances. As
Elizabeth Drew noted, Reagan treated "knowledge as if it was
dangerous to his convictions," but given a stage to play on where
he could express his convictions, he was a consummate success.
"The whole thing was P.R.," one White House aide noted. "This
was a P.R. outfit that became president and took over the country." This is what came out in the memoirs his colleagues wrote
about him. The critic and writer Frances FitzGerald found the
portrayal of Reagan in those memoirs appalling: "a president
almost devoid of curiosity, reflectiveness, energy or purpose, a
man full of his own preconceptions, yet easily manipulated and
fooled by others." Only when he played the part of hero and res-
cuer did he triumph.

It was on his final trip to Russia that Reagan spoke most revealingly about this dynamic. Talking to a group of artists, he
declared that acting had helped him greatly in "the work I do
now . . . the most important thing is to have the vision. The next
is to grasp and hold it . . . to grasp and hold a vision, to fix it in

your senses, that is the very essence, I believe, of successful leadership." In the role he was then playing—the leader of the Western superpower who had achieved a diplomatic breakthrough that would make the world a safer place—he had "gotten inside a character, a place, and a moment." As he told reporters on the way back from Moscow, the trip had been like a "Cecil B. DeMille production," and as president, he had "dropped into a grand historical moment." It was, he said, the role of a lifetime.

8

THE CLINTONS
A Flawed Co-Presidency

In one of the most revealing sections of his memoir, *My Life,* Bill Clinton writes: "I detest selfishness, but see it in the mirror every day." When a child, he recalls, "most of the time I was happy, but I could never be sure I was as good as I wanted to be." Seeking to explain these conflicts, Clinton observes: "A lot of people who grow up in difficult circumstances subconsciously blame themselves . . . I think this problem arises from leading parallel lives, an external life that takes its natural course, and an internal life where the secrets are hidden. When I was a child, my outside life was filled with friends and fun, learning and doing. My internal life was full of uncertainty, anger, and a dread of ever-looming violence. No one can live parallel lives with complete success." Clinton thus gives us insight into the pattern of his remarkable career, and into one of the dilemmas of his partnership with his wife.

❖ ❖ ❖

They were, from one perspective, the dream team of the modern political era. She was a feminist, he a deeply committed advocate of civil rights; they hoped to work in tandem—and on equal terms—to shape the world they lived in. Bill Clinton, an aide noted, was "one of the smartest men ever elected president." Hillary Rodham Clinton possessed a razor-sharp mind capable of comprehending complicated data about a problem and then envisioning a solution. Yet each also was capable of acting to sabotage the success they both wanted. Almost totally dependent on each other, they formed a political partnership that held the potential of bringing to the White House a political co-presidency that only Eleanor and Franklin Roosevelt had ever come close to reaching before. Yet almost because they were so dependent on each other, they failed to realize that potential. Neither Bill nor Hillary Clinton could have reached the White House without the other; yet neither could achieve the objectives they shared because each did so much harm to the other.

In one clairvoyant moment after a political defeat in Arkansas, Bill Clinton spoke to a university class on the great political figures he had read about. He concluded that those most worthy of study represented a combination of "darkness and light." In this moment of self-reflection, Clinton penetrated to the heart of his own political persona. As the *New York Times* reporter Todd Purdum wrote, Clinton was "one of the biggest, most talented, articulate, intelligent, open [and] colorful characters ever to inhabit the Oval Office"; yet he was also an "undisciplined, fumbling, obtuse, defensive, [and] self-justifying rogue."

Hillary was equally complicated. An egalitarian democrat morally and politically committed to helping those least able to help themselves, she often acted in an authoritarian and domineering manner, apparently oblivious to the political sensitivities of those around her. In the end, it was Bill Clinton whose flaws brought down what could have been a triumphant presidency. But at every step of the way, Hillary Clinton was a contributing and enabling partner. No two figures in American history embodied so perfectly the possibility of husband-and-wife leadership in politics, and no two demonstrated such a tragic tendency to undermine their own dreams.

◆ ◆ ◆

Bill Clinton was born in a small town in Arkansas to Virginia Blythe, who a couple of years earlier had married Bill Blythe. Virginia was a strong, bold, some would say brazen woman. She had dramatic arching eyebrows, smoked heavily, and wore her dyed black hair with a white streak down the middle. She enjoyed flirting with men and loved to play the horses at the racetrack. She had found Bill Blythe charming and interesting, not knowing that he had already been married and divorced three times, had fathered at least two children, and had been found guilty of "extreme cruelty and gross neglect of duty" regarding one of his former wives. According to one of Bill Clinton's biographers: "Everything about Blythe was contradictory and mysterious. He constantly reinvented himself, starting over every day, the familiar stranger and ultimate traveling salesman, surviving off charm and affability." Although nine months before the baby's birth Bill Blythe was in Italy—raising some suspicion that he was not the biological father—the description of him as a charmer who constantly reinvented himself almost sounds like a genetic prototype of Bill Clinton, and in photographs the two bear a strong resemblance. Blythe was killed in an automobile accident two months before his namesake's birth.

A year after young Bill's birth his mother went to New Orleans for specialized training in nursing, leaving him in his grandmother's care. According to Clinton's biographer David Maraniss, Virginia and her mother warred for the boy's attention and devotion. His grandmother Edith was known for her volunteer work as a nurse in the black community and for the ease of her connection to African Americans. His grandfather owned a grocery store, and many of his customers were black. He "treated them like he did everybody else," Clinton later noted, "and no matter how strapped he was, he never denied them groceries on credit." Clinton was "the only white boy in that neighborhood who played with black kids," one African-American neighbor later recalled. It was a partnership with black Americans that Clinton would retain for the rest of his life.

Shortly after finishing her training as nurse anesthetist, Virginia married again, this time to Roger Clinton, a car dealer, who like Virginia loved to drink and bet on horses. In this instance, as in her first marriage, she was unaware that her new husband had been married before, or that he had been accused of beating his wife. Although her son Bill, nearly four years old, did not attend the ceremony (nor did his grandmother), he soon started calling Roger "Daddy" and took his last name. He also became involved in protecting his mother from Roger's temper tantrums and abuse. By the age of eleven he was swearing out affidavits testifying to his stepfather's cruelty and seeking police intervention. As a young adolescent, the story goes, Clinton came upon his stepfather in a drunken state and said "Daddy you must stand up to hear what I have to say. And if you can't then I'll help you." He then told Roger Clinton, "Don't you ever lay a hand on my mother again." And according to family lore, Roger never did.

In the view of many, Clinton displayed in later life the consequences of being the child of an alcoholic father who abused his mother. Maraniss believes that Bill Clinton perfectly fit the model of the Family Hero, portrayed in books on alcoholism as the eldest son in an alcoholic family: "As protector, the Family Hero . . . assumes adult responsibilities and provides an anchor of coherence to siblings and parents, leading to an attitude that things are always better, the family safer, when this person is in charge. As redeemer [of the family name], the Family Hero . . . is dispatched into the world to excel and to return with praise and rewards that will make the entire [family] unit feel worthy." It was a script tantalizing in its prophetic promise.

Much of Clinton's personality seems to have been shaped by the experience of protecting his mother. He devoted himself to her, and he sought, through his own popularity and success, to make things whole. The children of alcoholics, or of parents who are constantly fighting, will do almost anything make to things right. Almost compulsively—and in some ways reminiscent of Lyndon Johnson—Clinton pursued that goal, ingratiating himself with all those he met, avoiding conflict wherever possible, even if to do so he had to lie or dissemble. By becoming the Family Hero, the person who would personify the highest aspirations of the family, Clinton could redeem what had been lost. He would make himself so popular, develop so many friendships, please so many people that all the sordid and painful parts of his past could be overcome. In pursuit of this goal the young Bill Clinton learned to read a situation, understand what mattered to the participants, calculate the best way to approach them, and then win them to his side.

He even professed to have reconciled with his stepfather and become a devoted stepson until Roger Sr. died. After that time, he later told a White House aide, "I immersed myself and my friends in my work. But I think some of that was trying to compensate for my mother and some of it was trying to do it for my father . . . I always felt like maybe I could live the life that he never was able to live. It was like living for two people." Reflecting on the same issue in his autobiography, Clinton elaborated: "If I did it well enough, somehow [I believed] I could make up for the life he should have had."

The theme of twoness runs through Clinton's life. "I liked most of what I learned about myself but not all of it," he said of his early adolescence. "And some of what came into my head and life scared the living hell out of me, including anger at Daddy, the first stirrings of sexual feelings toward girls, and doubts about my religious convictions." Beginning at that time, Clinton started to think of himself as living "parallel lives"—a public one in which he could ascend to levels of achievement that redeemed his and his family's deficiencies, and a private one based on the secrets he carried within him. Clinton's secrets were "rooted in Daddy's alcoholism and abuse." But they extended to the other parts of his life as well. "Secrets can be an awful burden to bear," he wrote in his autobiography, "especially if some sense of shame is attached to them . . . It became a struggle for me to find the right balance between secrets of internal richness and those of hidden fears and shame." Striving to succeed and to be recognized as a good person was a way to suppress and handle the secrets of his other life.

Clinton was already pursuing patterns of behavior that would help him achieve his goals. Early on he ingratiated himself with his teachers and other adults. At a statewide conference of the American Legion Boys Nation, Clinton was determined to be designated a leader. Getting to know everyone at the encampment, he applied all his political skills to win support for his candidacy as a Boys Nation senator, one of those to be sent to

Washington, D.C., for the national conference. Although some would later claim that these skills were artificial, and "a little too slick for some people," they worked beautifully at the Little Rock Boys Nation assembly. Shortly thereafter, Bill Clinton journeyed to the nation's capital, where one sunny day he and the other Boys Nation senators went to the Rose Garden to meet President John F. Kennedy. Maneuvering his way to the front of the line, Clinton got himself photographed with the president in a picture that would become a motif of his life. As Maraniss notes: "Along with an overwhelming feeling that in Washington he had seen the career he longed for, Bill Clinton brought home a captured moment, bonding his joyous present with his imagined future, a photograph he had been bound and determined to get—the picture that his mother wanted."

Clinton then set out to make his mark on the wider world. A brilliant student, he was accepted at Georgetown University, where he could pursue his interest in politics and international affairs. Going to Georgetown elevated Clinton to a stage far grander and more cosmopolitan than any he could have found in Fayetteville, Arkansas, the home of the state university. Clinton had already demonstrated his worldliness at the Boys Nation National Conference, where he had been one of the few southern delegates to embrace an activist civil rights stance. Now he used his southern background to help solidify an identity both rooted in his region and committed to an agenda far beyond it. At Georgetown he charmed his classmates, used his "down home" past to win attention as well as plaudits for his liberalism, and expanded his network to those very different from himself. So effective was he in the classroom, as well as in the corridors of politics, that one of his philosophy teachers compared him to a Jesuit, "so serious, political, and empathetic" was he. Taking up where he had left off in Arkansas, Clinton quickly sought out a myriad of colleagues, solicited their support for a campaign to become freshman class president, and before long was one of the most widely recognized and popular students on campus. It was a role he would repeat throughout college, except in his junior year when, in the turmoil of the 1960s, he was perceived as a mainstream and "machine" candidate, too smooth for the politics of 1967, even at a conservative institution like Georgetown.

Clinton had always practiced his charms equally on women and men, putting his arms around them, hugging them, suggesting by his intensity that he was interested only in them. But given his good looks, his height, and his charm, he attracted women in particular. At Georgetown he began a lengthy romance with Denise Hyland, a tall, self-contained woman from New Jersey. With her, as with all his friends, both women and men, Clinton enjoyed long discussions about their own futures and the problems of the nation. "Maybe," he wrote to Hyland, "I am beginning to realize that I am almost grown and will soon have to choose that one final motive in life which I hope will put a little asterisk by my name in the billion pages of the book of life." Yet even when he seemed to pour out his heart to friends, he kept a part of himself distant and unknown. Despite a three-year relationship with Hyland, he never confided in her that Roger Clinton was an alcoholic or that he himself had had to protect his mother from Roger's abuse.

The romance with Hyland ended before Clinton's senior year, and he began to play the field. One of his friends noted: "Then he became a free agent, and young ladies figured it out, and it was, 'holy shit, Bill Clinton is free and available and looking forward to having a good time.'" By that time Clinton had spent a

summer working for Senator J. William Fulbright, was more sophisticated in his taste, and thrived on being the center of attention for a growing number of young women. Carolyn Yeldell, a
friend from childhood, became romantically involved with Clinton in his last year at Georgetown, often visiting him, although
she was never sure what his intentions were. In fact he had another girlfriend—maybe more than one. Later, when Yeldell knew
more about his penchant for multiple relationships, she asked
herself whether she should marry such a man. The answer came
quickly: "No, he'll never be faithful."

By the end of his senior year, Clinton had scored one of the ultimate triumphs for an ambitious college student in America—
he was named a Rhodes Scholar, one of the elite group of intellectually precocious students who were chosen each year to go to
Oxford University for graduate work. Although never trained
as an athlete like most Rhodes scholars (his skill was in debating), Clinton impressed the interviewers. Calling his mother, he
broke the news by asking how she thought he would look in
English tweeds. Among his fellow Rhodes Scholars were some
who would be part of his network of FOBs (Friends of Bill)
throughout his political career: Robert Reich, later to become
his secretary of labor; Strobe Talbott, subsequently a reporter for
Time magazine and deputy secretary of state; Rick Stearns, a
mover and shaker in the politics of the late 1970s and 1980s; and
Daniel Singer, a prominent intellectual. They went to England
together on the ocean liner *The United States*. As Singer noted,
Clinton was among the most gregarious of the group, seeking
out "everybody that he thought was informative or valuable."
Politics, the war in Vietnam, future world leadership—all of these
figured prominently in the electric conversations that took place
on the way across the Atlantic. Clinton was not the smartest

among them—although a faculty member once said he had a "sharp analytical mind and an impressive power to master and synthesize complex material"—but he stood at the forefront of his cohort by virtue of his energy, his personality, and his magnetism. He was, another faculty member said, "always a character who wanted to do one more thing, go one more place, stay up one more hour, have one more drink. He came across as somebody with a great appetite for life." He was everyone's friend, the social cement that bonded the group together, the person with whom others shared their innermost thoughts, their anxieties and hopes. It was a continuation of his ability to seduce and empower those around him.

No issue raged more during Clinton's first year at Oxford than how he and his American classmates would respond if drafted to fight in Vietnam. All the Rhodes Scholars were called to being drafted, and virtually the entire group opposed the war. Clinton had learned his antiwar politics while working for Senator Fulbright. Paul Parish, one of his Rhodes colleagues, became a conscientious objector, with Clinton helping to write a letter of moral anguish to persuade Parish's draft board to classify him as one of those who on religious principle could avoid military service. Another of Clinton's friends, Frank Aller, suffered deep depression over his need to resist an immoral conflict in a moral fashion. Bill Clinton talked with all these friends, as well as with young women, as he too struggled with how to respond.

Before Clinton left for England, his uncle had used local political connections to have his draft notice deferred while he went to Oxford. Nine months later, he received his induction papers and set out to explore his options. One was to join the Arkansas National Guard, another was to enter the ROTC program at the University of Arkansas. He called Senator Fulbright's office for help. Eventually, back in the United States, he was accepted into a law school ROTC program. Because it was too late to enroll in law school and ROTC that fall, he secured permission from the local commanding officer to go back to Oxford for his second and final year. Then, in late fall, he decided to renounce his arrangement with ROTC and to resubmit his name for the draft. By that time, President Nixon's new lottery system was in place, and when Clinton's number was selected, it was 311—a number that almost guaranteed he would never be called. Thus he had avoided both military service and the need to attend law school in Arkansas and join ROTC.

Beneath these simple facts was a story of both existential anguish and political manipulation. From one perspective, Clinton had played the system with the skill of a virtuoso. He used his connections to secure a deferral, then betrayed the commitment he had made as soon as the odds were in his favor to avoid the draft entirely. His actions could be construed as calculating, opportunistic; he achieved all of his goals without paying any significant price, at least at the time.

From another perspective, however, Clinton was part of a generation of anguished, ambivalent, and passionately concerned antiwar activists who were seeking some honorable way to remain devoted citizens while being true to the principles they believed in. "Nothing could be worse than this torment," Clinton wrote to Rick Stearns in September.

> And if I cannot rid myself of it, I will just have to go into the service and begin to root out the cause . . . I have been [in Arkansas] all summer in a place where everyone else's children seemed to be in the military, most of them in Vietnam . . . I have this thing hanging over me like a pall . . . I

am running away from something for the first time in my
life . . . One of the worst side effects of this whole thing is
the way it's ravaged my own image of myself, taking my
mind off the higher things, restricting my ability to become involved in good causes with other people—I honestly
feel so screwed up tight that I'm incapable, I think, of giving myself, of really loving.

The letter Clinton wrote to the commanding officer about his
decision to renounce the ROTC contract—which was made public during the presidential campaign of 1992—lends some support to each interpretation of Clinton's actions. He was both
struggling with an issue of personal honor and engaging in calculated deceit and manipulation. With candor, he wrote to the
ROTC colonel that his "decision not to be a resister" and to accept the draft had one reason and one reason only: "to maintain
my political viability within the system. For years I have worked
to prepare myself for a political life characterized by both practical political ability and concern for rapid social progress." But he
also declared that he was now abandoning the ROTC arrangement because it was the right thing to do. "I began to think I
had deceived you," he wrote, by not acknowledging the degree to
which he was opposed to the war. In a self-justifying mode,
Clinton wanted the colonel to believe that he was now ready to
accept the possibility of being drafted in order to live up to his
moral principles. And so Clinton had it both ways.

The trickiness in Clinton's self-presentation was understand-
able since he needed to think of himself as moral, and as making
honorable choices. But it also reflected the way in which he hid
parts of his life from those close to him—his "secrets"—as in hiding the existence of multiple girlfriends to make each one believe

she occupied his exclusive attention. There was a degree of self-absorption about Clinton that bordered on narcissism. He took advantage of the intimate contacts he had with so many people, using those relationships for his own purposes. He was a friend, with an open door and a ready ear; but at the same time he manipulated those ties of attachment to feed his own ego. Not so coincidentally, when Clinton finished his term at Oxford he traveled across Europe, calling people he had not seen for years, attaching himself to others he was just meeting for the first time, using them to provide his physical sustenance while fulfilling his deep emotional need for reinforcement and connectedness. He had a wonderful capacity to be empathetic, gregarious, focused on learning about and relating to countless people. But it was a virtue that could also be a vice.

After completing his second year at Oxford, Clinton returned to the United States and enrolled at Yale Law School. Getting a law degree at Yale was a far better career move than getting one at the University of Arkansas. Yale was perhaps the only law school in the country that provided total freedom for its students to engage in intellectual, social, and political activities independent of the law school curriculum. Class attendance was not required. Independent thinking was. The best minds and most passionate activists with interest in the law gathered in this environment to nurture, stimulate, and compete with one another. Bill Clinton rarely went to class. Indeed, during his second year he helped manage George McGovern's presidential campaign in Texas for more than two months before returning to his studies.

At Yale, as at Georgetown and Oxford, Clinton was a magnetic figure around whom a cluster of brilliant individuals soon formed a constellation. His Oxford classmate Robert Reich was there. So was Steve Cohen, an antiwar activist. Almost immediately Clinton became involved in Joseph Duffey's campaign for the United States Senate; in the campaign he met Tony Podesta, another confidant who would remain with him through his political career. Yale provided multiple opportunities to taste, savor, and cultivate people and causes. Of the countless charismatic personalities Clinton encountered there, the one who would most affect his life was his classmate Hillary Rodham.

If Bill Clinton embodied the almost Horatio Alger myth of moving from a disturbed family and lower-middle-class background in the American south to a storied career of academic and political success, Hillary Rodham personified middle-class midwestern stability. Hillary grew up in an upper-middle-class suburb of Chicago. The most remarkable feature of her family was the courage and personality of her mother, who had overcome a childhood of emotional neglect to become in her own maternal role a model of nurturance. There were no Jews or blacks in Hillary's hometown, and little social conflict. Bright, studious, and involved with her peers, she had a very typical childhood in a milieu noted for its complacency, conformity, and conservatism. Not surprisingly, given her family's politics, she was a "Goldwater girl" in 1964.

The one exception to this rather bland upbringing was a Methodist Youth Fellowship (MYF) group that she joined at her church. MYF groups throughout the country became a seedbed for social activism in the early 1960s, causing many young women to question some of their social values and become engaged in the struggles of blacks for civil rights, women for sexual equality, and students against the war in Vietnam. Hillary Rodham's MYF group was led by an associate minister, Don Jones, who became a lifelong friend to Hillary. Jones wanted to put spark into the young people to whom he was ministering. He opened their eyes to the complexities of the world around them. He took them to hear Martin Luther King Jr. preach a sermon, led them to the inner city of Chicago so they could see what life was like in an urban slum, and urged them to broaden their horizons and think about a wider, more challenging, and needier world. That kind of MYF experience produced people like Mary King and Casey Hayden, who became leaders of the Student Nonviolent Coordinating Committee (SNCC) and Students for a Democratic Society (SDS). It also altered, in a definitive way, Hillary Rodham's perspective on life.

By the time Hillary enrolled at Wellesley College in 1965, she had become a more free and independent spirit. Still conservative in her personal mores, she nevertheless reached out to the Boston community, volunteering to work with poor children in the black slums of Roxbury, and by 1966, becoming a strong antiwar activist. As her college boyfriend later observed, Hillary had "grown up and out of the conservative materialistic mindset which is typical of affluent suburbs . . . She was [no longer] interested in making money or being affluent." Like many college students, she tried out a variety of roles. Her commitment to Christian values of equal justice and peace became the core of her new identity. But she also played a number of other roles—the intellectual, the social butterfly, the aspiring career woman.

When she graduated from Wellesley, Rodham was at the top of her class, both politically and intellectually. In many ways she represented the elite of the mainstream of her generation. She was not a radical. She believed in the message of Martin Luther King Jr.; she did not believe in Black Power. And she was more concerned with pragmatic achievement than with ideological slogans. But a leader she clearly was, and because of her prominence she was chosen to give the student graduation speech at Wellesley's commencement. Speaking about the absence of moorings that she and her generation felt, she said: "We are, all of us, exploring a world that none of us understands." Hillary, like her age-mates at Columbia and Harvard and Yale, denounced the prevailing values of "acquisitive and competitive corporate life," including the values of universities that were training new soldiers to enter the corporate army. But what would take the place of those now besmirched values? Hillary did not know, but she declared: "We are searching for more immediate, ecstatic, and penetrating modes of living." Rewarded with a *Life* magazine story (and picture) covering her speech, Hillary headed off to Yale Law School.

There, in her first year, she met Bill Clinton. Singular personalities both, Hillary Rodham and Bill Clinton could not have been more different. Bill, it turned out, was one of the few men not intimidated by Hillary. Rather, he was challenged by the quality of her mind, her moral passion, and her independence. As David Maraniss notes: "Rodham's intellect, her reputation, her refusal to be cowed or wowed, seemed to attract him and scare him at the same time." Hillary, in turn, was engulfed by Clinton's charm, intrigued by his political talent, and smitten by his physical and sexual appeal. Eventually, after circling each other warily for a time, they became a couple. By their second year, they were living together in a New Haven apartment, Rodham spending her spare time doing legal work on the rights of children and helping to provide counsel to the poor, Clinton involved in a variety of political activities, the two together talking intensely about the burning issues of their time.

It was a period of extraordinary volatility. In the fall of 1971 Clinton's close friend from Oxford, Frank Aller, committed suicide. Having resolved, for the moment, his decision to resist the draft, Aller returned to his home in Oregon, only to contemplate the even deeper terrors that lay beneath his torment over the war in Vietnam. Clinton, devastated, wondered openly for the first time whether working within the system for political change and success made any sense. As his friend Greg Craig later recalled: "It was a tough time for him, an angry, hostile period of his life, it was consistent with what a lot of us felt."

Nor were things easy between Bill and Hillary. They fought often, arguing about issues of personal style, political choice, philosophy, and temperament. At least in part, their conflicts reflected the profound differences in their personalities. As one friend said, Hillary would not "take any of Bill's soft stories, his southern boy stuff. She would just puncture it, even while showing a real affection. She'd say, 'spit it out, Clinton.'" While he was a bit scattered in his interests, she was focused. In many respects, he was more feminine—in the traditional meaning of the word—with his sensitivity to others, his empathy, his outreach. By contrast, she was more traditionally masculine, direct in her questions, singular in her intensity and in her determination to get to the roots of a problem.

Yet they were a team, even working as partners in the moot court trials that were a highlight of Yale's law school culture. One friend said: "What lingers in the minds of most of those who watched . . . is the way the partnership of Clinton and Rodham operated. Clinton was soft and engaging, eager to charm the judge and jury and make the witnesses feel comfortable, pouting when a ruling went the other way. Rodham was clear and all business." Another noted: "It was like Ms. Inside and Mr. Outside . . . Hillary was very sharp and Chicago[-like] and Bill was very *To Kill a Mockingbird.*" Hillary did not mind if she offended someone as she strove for her goals; Bill wanted to make everyone feel good about him and what he was doing. The two did not get along, but they could not be apart. It was attraction and anger, both almost always present, each lurking just beneath the surface.

By the time he graduated, Bill Clinton was ready to return to Arkansas and begin his quest for political glory. He got his hair cut, changed his clothes, and put on the patina of a candidate. "Let me know when you are running for president, Bill," one of his classmates said. "I'll help you." Clinton had served on the staff of J. William Fulbright in the Senate, had worked on Joe Duffey's campaign for the U.S. Senate in Connecticut, and had helped manage George McGovern's presidential campaign in Texas. Now he was ready to bring to bear all that he had learned. There are two stories about the conditions under which he journeyed back to Arkansas. As he told it, people from the University of Arkansas law school came to him and offered him a job, asking if he would help them. The truth was that he had been tenaciously pursuing the job for months. It was not the first or the last time Clinton's version of what transpired conflicted with reality.

As a teacher, Clinton could exercise his talents for identifying with students, generating discussion among them, and bonding with their aspirations and concerns. He preferred a Socratic to a lecture system, and placed a premium on getting students to express their own perspectives, which he then engaged. Nowhere was this more successful than in his relationship with African-American students. As one black student said: "In the south . . . whites would say one thing, but their deeds and words were often different. So here comes a person where, no matter what your relationship with him was, he was not prejudiced . . . that's why we called him wonder boy. It was a miracle the way he was. He could have shunned black students politically . . . Northwest Arkansas was a white enclave. [But] Wonder Boy Bill did not waiver in respect to his conduct with African Americans."

With blacks as well as whites, Clinton honed his skill at connecting with people and mobilizing them into a phalanx of potential campaign supporters. What a later White House aide said of him was already vividly present in his interaction with his peers: "He is the most seductive and persuasive person I have ever met." Immediately connecting with politicians in the Arkansas Democratic party, Clinton started visiting around the state, meeting potential voters. Wherever he went, he made physical contact with those he talked to—almost like Lyndon Johnson. He held their arms as he gazed into their eyes, gave them total attention, never looked behind to see who else was present, and walked away from every gathering with a new cluster of loyal supporters. By 1974 he was ready to make his move, announcing a campaign for Congress against the local incumbent, a Republican devotee of Richard Nixon. Using all his skills, and making his opponent's support of Nixon on Watergate a critical issue, Clinton scoured the state, put together a winning coalition in the Democratic primary, and prepared for the November election.

In the meantime, Hillary Rodham went to work for the Watergate prosecutor, John Doar, in Washington, toiling seven days a week and fourteen hours a day preparing the brief that would lead to a vote on Richard Nixon's impeachment. Single-mindedly focused on her work, she nevertheless retained a fascination and love for Bill Clinton. By now she was aware of his interest in women more generally, having learned, at least indirectly, about his multiple flirtations while running the McGovern campaign in Texas. She was now fairly certain that he had more than one girlfriend in Arkansas, as well as his relationship with her. As before in her time with Clinton, stability seemed a foreign idea. Clinton's mother did not like Hillary. Clinton's brother did not think she was attractive enough for him. Yet, Bill said to a friend about Hillary, "I'm going for brains and ability rather than glamour." Hillary, in turn, continued to be drawn back to Clinton. "When he was coming to town," a Washington friend said, "her face would change. It would light up. It was un-Hillary-esque."

In the summer of 1974 Hillary was ready to make a decision. Although the Watergate investigation was still in process, she determined to move to Arkansas. Setting up an interview at the University of Arkansas Law School, where she could join Bill as a faculty member, she bowled over her future colleagues by her command of legal material. Once offered the job, she quickly moved to accept, in the interim sending her father and brother to help Bill in his congressional campaign—and also to make sure Bill did not proceed too far with his other girlfriend. Clinton, meanwhile, repeated what had become his customary pattern of persisting with one relationship even as he professed commitment to another. Whenever Hillary came to his campaign headquarters, staff members would squire his other girlfriend out the back door, until finally Hillary succeeded in getting her competition removed from the campaign, inserting herself instead as a central figure in all decisionmaking. Not surprisingly, Hillary Rodham and Bill Clinton as often as not ended up in open conflict. "They had the biggest damn fights," one campaign assistant said, "shouting and swearing." "All we ever do is argue," Clinton told his old friend Carolyn Yeldell.

In the end, Clinton came close, but did not win the congressional election. A key element in the close contest was whether Clinton would agree to buy votes in a pivotal area. Hillary said no, and she prevailed. The area in question was decisive to Clinton's final loss. In the aftermath, Clinton and Rodham returned to the University of Arkansas to teach, and Clinton to prepare for his next race, a statewide run to become Arkansas attorney general. In the meantime, Hillary had made the decision to spend her life with Bill Clinton, and he had decided that, no matter how much they might squabble, she was the woman he wanted as his lifetime partner. On October 11, 1975, they were married. Not surprisingly, they did not take a honeymoon, nor even plan a trip. Rather they continued their careers as law school professors, while Clinton mobilized his supporters for what became his successful race for attorney general in the fall of 1976. He was thirty years old.

The next twelve years were a blur of political activity, defining, as well as anticipating, the contours of Clinton's later political life. All along, everyone who knew Clinton knew that the office of attorney general was simply a way station. The key question was to where. By 1978 Clinton made a pivotal choice not to run for the U.S. Senate against Governor David Pryor, but to go for the governorship of Arkansas instead. Clinton had used his two-year term as attorney general to reach out to consumer groups, constituencies concerned about equity and safety, and those ready for a neopopulist champion. He and Hillary also made a real estate investment in a development scheme called Whitewater sponsored by James McDougal. Clinton continued his playboy ways, while Hillary invested in the livestock commodities market, stretching a $1,000 initial investment to a $99,000 profit in one year's time. When Clinton ran for governor, the issue of his draft deferment arose, but he denied he had ever received a deferment and the critical paper trail documenting the deferment remained hidden.

When he was inaugurated as Arkansas's governor in 1978 at the age of thirty-two, Clinton was the youngest person ever to hold the office in America. For many of his Yale, Oxford, and Georgetown friends—who gathered in Little Rock from around the country—it was as if their generation had been vindicated. Steve Cohen, one of many activists who attended the inauguration, declared: "I feel two emotions that I have not experienced in a long time—pride and hope." In a brilliant inaugural address, Clinton outlined themes he would return to repeatedly over the next two decades—opportunity, responsibility, and community. America was about all three, he insisted, each one tied to the others. It was the job of government to ensure that all citizens could participate in a competition based upon equal opportunity, yet with every person having responsibility for his or her success or failure, and all united together—whatever their backgrounds—in a community of concern and caring.

There then commenced a decade of political volatility that, from the perspective of the early twenty-first century, seems almost a rehearsal for the Clinton years in the White House. Despite all the hope engendered by his inaugural address and its promise of a new era of politics, Clinton's gubernatorial administration was badly disorganized. There was no focus, no clear legislative agenda, no clarion set of missions or goals. The governor's office had no single chief of staff. Instead, three people shared control. All of them were young; his management team was dubbed "the children's crusade." His legislative efforts foundered, constituency groups turned against him, and suddenly, after two years in office, he was the youngest ex-governor in the country. At the age of thirty-four, as Maraniss notes, Clinton fit "the ironic description of the quintessential Rhodes scholar: someone with a great future behind him." The man everyone had thought would be president seemed like a has-been.

At precisely that moment, Clinton started to earn the sobriquet "the comeback kid." Although he took a job as an attorney in Little Rock, in fact he did little else but put in place the foundation for a new campaign. Aided by a pollster, Richard Morris, he identified the themes that he needed to articulate to win back the confidence of the people of Arkansas. Dick Morris, while a student at Columbia, had organized young people on the West Side of Manhattan in the late 1960s to create a powerful political machine; Morris and his henchmen were called the "young Mafia" by West Side veterans. Morris seemed to know instinctively which issues would appeal to important blocs of voters. He also recommended that Clinton apologize to the people of Arkansas for the errors he had made: "You have to recognize your sins, confess to them, and promise to sin no more . . . you can't be self-justified. You have to say 'I'm very sorry, ashamed, I know I did wrong and I'll never do it again.'" Clinton had a difficult time bringing himself to make such an apology. In that period, he told two national correspondents that, despite all the evidence to the contrary, "there *is* no campaign." But eventually he followed Morris's advice, ran for reelection, and proved that with persistence, tenacity, and skill, he could regain the top position.

Back in the governor's office, he tried to avoid the mistakes of his first term. Gathering an older and more seasoned staff, he made an effort to narrow his goals and stay focused. In particular, he chose to become known as the "education governor" and created an Education Standards Committee. To chair the committee, he appointed his wife, Hillary Rodham Clinton (she had taken Clinton's last name during the reelection campaign because many people in Arkansas made an issue of her retaining her maiden name). He declared: "This guarantees that I will have a person who is closer to me than anyone else overseeing a project that is more important to me than anything else." Under Rodham Clinton's direction, the education committee held more than seventy meetings and provided a report to the state legislature that led to the enactment of an education-reform package that gave Clinton the political label he had been seeking.

Yet for every positive sign of an effective partnership between Bill and Hillary, there were negatives as well. The two argued frequently, often in public, sometimes screaming at each other. Bill continued to pursue other women. State troopers described the governor as promiscuous on his travels, and later talked about having been assigned to solicit women on his behalf. He seemed to have no guiding principles, no core sense of self that would lead to discipline, focus, and control. Clinton's philandering fit his penchant for leading parallel lives, fueling that side of himself that he tried to hold secret, but which contradicted the image of stewardship and idealism he otherwise projected.

Perhaps the closest Clinton came to confronting his lack of a moral compass occurred when his brother Roger was arrested for trafficking in drugs. There ensued a series of family therapy sessions with Clinton, his brother, and their mother. During those encounters, Virginia Clinton acknowledged her need to repress and deny the pain and ugliness of her own life, including her husband's alcoholism and abuse. Bill Clinton acknowledged his own inability to tell the truth about his stepfather. He said on a later occasion: "We learned a lot about how you do a lot of damage to yourself if you are living with an alcoholic and you sort of deny that behavior and deflect it all. You pay a big price for that." It was as if, for the first time, he recognized in front of others the power of secrets in his life, and grappled with the contradictions and oppositional instincts that prompted him to sabotage his own success. He also acknowledged the link between his experience with his father and his avoidance of conflict about personal issues, including with the people he cared about most. Betsy Wright, a close political and personal friend, noted that at that time "he did a lot of introspection that I'd never seen him do like that before . . . Most notable was why he was always trying to please people. He was fascinated by it, and it rang so true. It was kind of like he was being introduced to something that he wished he had known a long time ago."

In the confessional mode he sometimes used with friends, Clinton told Carolyn Yeldell Staley (now married) about his new self-awareness. "I think," he said, "that we are all addicted to something. Some people are addicted to drugs. Some to power. Some to food. Some to sex. We're all addicted to something." In Staley's view, Clinton was finally realizing that "he had places of real weakness. He was trying to sort all that out in his life." In that context, he turned more and more to his Baptist faith for salvation and healing. He met with his minister once a week, sought spiritual counseling, and reached out to religion as the anchor that had been missing in his life.

All of these issues came to a head in 1988 as Clinton confronted the next major decision in his life, whether or not to run for president. His instincts told him to proceed. He had been governor for eight years, elected four times. He had made his mark as the "education governor." Twice he had spoken at Democratic national conventions, and now he was chair of the National Governors' Association. As Robert Reich pointed out in a Rhodes Scholars' newsletter, Clinton had a 72 percent approval rating. What better time to run for president. Using the myriad connections he had developed, Clinton embarked on exploratory visits to Iowa and New Hampshire. He was leaning heavily toward announcing his candidacy.

But 1988 was a difficult campaign year. Gary Hart, the person who had recruited Clinton to run the McGovern campaign in Texas in 1972, was forced to drop out of the Democratic race because of a scandal involving his womanizing. The parallels to Clinton's own experience were powerful. Betsy Wright, the Texas woman he had turned to for political advice ever since the McGovern campaign, confronted him about his sexual escapades. She went through a list of women and asked him to tell her the truth about his past. As a result, Dick Morris noted, Clinton had a "tremendous terror of the race because of the personal scandals."

Another factor in his decision was the Clintons' eight-year-old daughter, Chelsea. Clinton loved to spend time with her, to read to her, to be the kind of father that he himself had never had. The night before he was to announce whether or not he would run, Clinton was ruminating about the decision when Chelsea asked him where they would go on their summer vacation. When her father responded that he might not be able to take a vacation because he might run for the presidency, Chelsea said, "Well, Mom and I will go without you." Her comment crystallized for Clinton the fact that if he ran, his relationship with his daughter would never be the same, and the next four years of her life would be largely lost to him.

So he decided not to run, and instead to put "his house in order." "I need some family time," he said. "I need some personal time. Politicians are people, too . . . That part of my life needs renewal . . . I've seen a lot of kids grow up under these pressures and a long, long time ago I made a promise to myself that if I were ever lucky enough to have a child, she would never grow up wondering who her father was." It appeared as though Clinton had learned something from the travails of the 1980s—perhaps even the importance of making the priorities of his family a touchstone for his decisions. But like most of the lessons of his years as governor, this one was not destined to last.

◆　◆　◆

In classic Bill Clinton roller-coaster fashion, his journey to the presidential nomination in 1992 began with a plummeting descent. Having taken himself out of the contest in 1988, he was asked to make the nominating speech for Michael Dukakis at the Democratic Convention in New York. It was the third time in three conventions he had been asked to address the nation's Democrats, but this time his speech was a dismal failure. Droning on for more than half an hour, he exploded people's sense that here was "someone to watch." The *Washington Post* TV critic Tom Shales dubbed the speech "The Numb and Restless," while on the *Tonight Show* Johnny Carson joked that the nation's surgeon general had approved Bill Clinton as a new sleeping pill. Once again, however, Clinton pulled himself together and came back, proving to Johnny Carson—by playing his saxophone on national television—that he was far from soporific. Running for reelection in Arkansas, he bolstered his reputation as one of the nation's most dynamic state governors, and as keynote speaker at the new Democratic Leadership Council, he riveted his audience. "Our burden," he told the delegates, "is to give the people a new choice rooted in old values. A new choice that is simple, offers opportunity, demands responsibility, gives citizens more say, . . . all because we recognize that we are a community."

With centrist politics and a dynamic image as his chief weapons, Clinton entered the fray for the presidential nomination in 1992. It was a crowded field. The Massachusetts senator Paul Tsongas spoke for those who wanted to "grow the economy" by supporting capitalism. Jerry Brown, the anti-establishment governor of California, sought to give politics back to the people. Outside the Democratic party, Ross Perot, a Texas billionaire, used his resources and his access to talk shows to push his message of government reform. Perot gambled that Americans were tired of big government, looking for honesty, and ready to respond to someone who, like a car mechanic, could look under the hood of government, tell them what was wrong, and provide an answer.

Nevertheless, Clinton thrived in the Democratic pack, using his charm, his dynamism, and his moderate politics to reach out to voters in Iowa and New Hampshire. Sensitive to the womanizing issue, he discussed his marriage at a breakfast with Washington reporters and presumably addressed the concern adequately. "Like nearly anybody who has been together for twenty years," he said, "our relationship has not been perfect or free of difficulties, but we feel good about where we are and we believe in our obligation to each other, and we intend to be together thirty or forty years from now, whether I run for president or not." Clinton appeared to be cruising on high-octane fuel. After he announced for president, he spent hours greeting people in the Arkansas capitol, and then ended the evening singing with his oldest friends, leading the group in intoning the moving song about murdered heroes "Abraham, Martin, and John," and concluding with "Amazing grace, how sweet the sound, that saved a wretch like me . . ."

And then came a crisis. A woman named Gennifer Flowers, interviewed by a tabloid newspaper, the *National Star,* boasted of having tapes to prove she had had a twelve-year relationship with Clinton. All the fears that Betsy Wright and Dick Morris had talked to Clinton about four years earlier suddenly came back. Suddenly Clinton's poll numbers fell to single digits in New Hampshire. But once again, he came back. This time, he and Hillary appeared on national television, on the CBS show *60 Minutes*. There they went public with what Clinton had already told the reporters, confessing that they had had serious marital problems in the past, but saying they had worked them out. "I think the American people—at least people who have been married a long time—know what [that] means," Clinton said. "Listen to what I've said . . . I've acknowledged causing pain in my marriage. I have said things to you tonight . . . that no American politician ever has [said]. I think most Americans [will] . . . know what we're saying; they'll get it and they'll feel that we have been more than candid."

Supporting her husband completely, Hillary Clinton insisted that she was "not sitting here—some little woman standing by my man, like Tammy Wynette. I'm sitting here because I love him, and I respect him, and I honor what he's been through and what we've been through together. And you know, if that's not enough for people, then, heck, don't vote for him." Amazingly, the Clintons that night took the air out of the sex scandal balloon. The plummeting poll figures started going back up. Clinton recovered his pace and dynamism in New Hampshire. On primary day, he achieved a strong second-place showing. Having again earned the label "the comeback kid," Clinton, with a superb campaign staff, wrapped up the nomination by late spring, defeating most of his competitors in head-to-head primaries. He was now the Democratic candidate for president.

The election campaign of 1992 was one of the strangest of

post–World War II history. Once again, as with Strom Thurmond's candidacy in 1948 and George Wallace's candidacy in 1968, a third-party candidate—this time Ross Perot—played a major role. For a time Clinton was running third behind the Republican incumbent, President George H. W. Bush, and Perot. But Clinton was ideally suited, as a centrist Democrat, to win back the Democrats who had voted for Ronald Reagan; and he had the intelligence to make the nation's rising unemployment and slowed economic growth his major theme: "It's the economy, stupid." Repeatedly, he emphasized his commitment to helping the middle class, those who had been ignored by the Reagan revolution, which, Clinton said, had benefited only the richest one percent of the population. Focusing on his themes of opportunity, responsibility, and community, Clinton insisted that the hardworking middle class must finally be rewarded with a fair taxation system and a move away from the politics of special interest groups and toward a government of all the people. Brilliantly, Clinton tried to reassemble the Roosevelt coalition—labor, minorities, urban America, white ethnics, women—addressing the needs of each of its constituencies, while focusing above all on the values and concerns that united members of those diverse groups.

In 1992 Clinton had no greater help than that provided by the Republican party itself. Although President Bush had a popularity rating of 91 percent after the Persian Gulf War, he allowed his base of support to disintegrate by largely ignoring the economy as it went into decline. Moreover, in contrast to Clinton's appeal to community and the middle class, Bush allowed right-wing Republicans to dominate the party's convention, with the television evangelist Pat Robertson raging against feminism, homosexuality, and any other perspective that did not fit his definition of one hundred percent Americanism. Bush lacked a clearly defined vision, and he even failed to provide a positive reason why people should vote for him. "I still can't tell you what he stands for," a Republican staff member said, "and I've worked for him for ten years." Although Bush lashed out at Clinton's "character," raising the issues of his draft deferment, his opposition to the Vietnam war, and a trip he had taken to Moscow—which Bush insinuated was a sign of a lack of patriotism—Clinton easily survived the assault. He kept his focus on the mainstream values that he had come to represent. Although he won the presidency with only 43 percent of the vote, it was, he said, "a victory for the people who work hard and play by the rules . . . a victory for the people who are ready to compete and win in the global economy but who need a government that offers a hand, not a handout."

Just as Clinton's inauguration as governor of Arkansas led many of his Oxford and Yale friends to herald the triumph of a new generation, his election to the presidency augured the triumph of a new politics. Clinton was young, energetic, married to an independent woman who was a distinguished politician and activist in her own right—a team more powerful than any since Eleanor and Franklin Roosevelt occupied the White House. It was, Clinton said, "two for the price of one," a "co-presidency." Many members of the public were enchanted. One magazine noted: "What excites most people about Clinton is precisely the degree to which he speaks to their hunger for meaning and purpose, their half-conscious and often inchoate desire to transcend the selfishness and a meaninglessness of a materialistic and narcissistic society." This sentence could have come straight from Hillary Rodham's Wellesley commencement address. Indeed, in many respects, the 1992 election recalled the better side of the

1960s, with Clinton embodying the noble aspirations and activism of the president whose hand he had shaken as a sixteen-year-old member of Boys Nation. *Time* magazine put it this way: "For years Americans have been in a kind of vague mourning for something they sensed they had lost somewhere—what was best in the country, a distinctive American endowment of youth and energy amid ideals and luck: the sacred American stuff." And now Clinton seemed the answer. His victory, *Time* declared, "places him in a position to preside over one of the periodic reinventions of the country—those moments when Americans dig themselves out of their deepest problems by re-imagining themselves."

As Clinton prepared to take office, many who had come of age in the 1960s shared the impression that Clinton was, as one writer said, "our generation's second chance." Clinton himself nurtured such romantic aspirations. "Today," he told the nation at his inaugural address, "we celebrate the mystery of American renewal . . . In the depth of winter, we force the spring . . . This is our time. Let us embrace it." The challenge facing the new president—and the first lady—was to redeem the vision he had articulated, escape the mistakes of the past, and put in place a new politics.

❖   ❖   ❖

Almost immediately the euphoric expectations generated by victory dissolved in disarray. "They really weren't ready to govern," Senator Daniel Patrick Moynihan said. Despite an exhilarating series of workshops on the economy and other pressing national issues that Clinton convened in the two months before his inauguration, he entered office with no work plan, no focused agenda, no vision about how to use his first hundred days. Instead, according to a presidential aide, he "slipped on one banana peel after another." It was like his first term as Arkansas governor all over again.

The problems were legion. Clinton had to withdraw the nominations of his first two candidates for attorney general because FBI background checks revealed embarrassing lapses such as failure to pay social security taxes for a domestic worker. Instead of launching his first major initiative on the economy as expected, Clinton found himself trapped in a discussion about the viability of admitting gays into the military. Just three months after he took office the justice department, after a long siege, attacked the compound of a religious sect known as the Branch Davidians, leaving eighty-nine people, including many women and children, dead. The press seized on these missteps, making Clinton look like a bumbling idiot. Subsequently he was forced to withdraw the nomination of an old law school friend, Lani Guinier, because of her views on how to guarantee minority representation, and a scandal arose in the White House travel office over efforts to replace staff members who had served under multiple administrations. It seemed everything was falling apart.

Without question, part of the responsibility rested with a skeptical, angry, and alienated press corps. The Clintons closed off reporters' access to the west wing of the White House. Consequently, instead of the honeymoon usually granted to a new president, Clinton encountered frosty anger. The *Washington Post*, in particular, seemed offended by the Clintons. At an early dinner party at the home of the *Post*'s publisher, Katharine Graham, Clinton suggested that those who looked only to the "in" group in Washington for solutions were making a mistake, and implicitly criticized the elitism of the capital. Sally Quinn, a *Post* columnist, responded in print: "Washington has its own totems and taboos. It would serve the newcomers well to learn them and abide by them." Over the next few months the *Post* published scathing condemnations of the Clintons. "People who have been here and who have obtained a certain social or political position," Quinn wrote, "do not want to be 'dissed.' They want the new team to respect them. Because these trivial rituals were not fulfilled, many people were virtually gleeful when Clinton went into free fall in the polls. You reap what you sow was the attitude."

But in addition to a hostile press and a series of miscues, the rocky start reflected Clinton's failure to put together a coherent plan with a well-qualified and disciplined staff. Instead of following Ronald Reagan's example of bringing into his administration people associated with former political opponents—Reagan chose James Baker, formerly George H. W. Bush's campaign manager, as chief of staff—Clinton rejected such excellent potential appointees as Jimmy Carter's former domestic counselor Stuart Eizenstat. Too often he relied on an "Arkansas Mafia," or on people primarily known for their close association with Hillary. Just as in Arkansas, people could not get appointments with Clinton, and chaos reigned more often than order. Republicans, meanwhile, refused to provide any aid, proceeding on the ground rule that no one should ever give Clinton a vote in Congress.

By the summer of 1993, Clinton was desperate. Every day, it seemed, he erupted in anger at his staff. Convinced he needed an old hand to create discipline, he turned to David Gergen, who previously had served three Republican presidents: Richard Nixon, Gerald Ford, and Ronald Reagan.

There were occasional bright moments. In August, after finally zeroing in on the economy as his primary concern, Clinton persuaded the House and Senate to approve his major economic initiatives. He had determined that the best way to reverse the nation's economic decline was by reducing the federal government's budget deficit. Although doing this required tax increases, Clinton wisely limited these to the top five percent of the population and provided income tax credits for the poor. Revealingly, approval came on a straight party-line vote, Clinton winning support in the House by a vote of 218–216, and in the Senate by a vote of 51–50, with the vice president, Al Gore, casting the decisive vote. Nevertheless, Clinton's deficit-reduction package set in place the foundations for an unprecedented growth spurt in the American economy, and a shift from a $200 billion budget deficit in 1992 to a $200 billion surplus in 2000.

For a brief period, other positive achievements led to renewed optimism in the Clinton administration. With substantial Republican support (since originally it had been a Republican idea) and bold leadership from Clinton, Congress ratified the North American Free Trade Agreement (NAFTA). Clinton also secured the first gun control legislation ever passed—the Brady Bill, named after James Brady, the White House press secretary who was badly wounded during the attempted assassination of President Reagan in 1981—placing restrictions on the purchase of handguns. Other legislation included the creation of a national service corps (Americorps) to encourage young people to volunteer to work to help the most disadvantaged citizens in the country, and a voter registration bill that made it significantly easier for people to gain access to the right to vote. The president's initiative to create a national health insurance program also appeared to be moving forward.

Then the Clintons' investment in James McDougal's Whitewater scheme became a public issue, one that would haunt the president through the rest of his time in office and create a backdrop for the defeat of his major legislative initiatives. McDougal, a behind-the-scenes operator in Arkansas, had acquired an unsavory reputation for his land development and banking projects, some of which broke the law and attracted the attention of prosecutors. Clinton thought he had put the controversy over Whitewater behind him. As early as 1992, the FBI had reported that no evidence existed that Bill and Hillary Clinton had knowledge of, or engaged in, illegal activities in Whitewater. As throughout the next eight years, every official report on Whitewater exonerated the Clintons from wrongdoing.

But the Whitewater scandal was really about the entire Clinton administration, his persona, his style, the Clintons' ambitions for changing America. Something about Bill and Hillary Clinton infuriated their opposition, so that many Republicans became their bitter enemies, magnifying every allegation about Whitewater into national headlines promoting the idea that Bill and Hillary Clinton had committed a crime and were engaged in a major cover-up to conceal their guilt. A network of right-wing columnists and foundations, funded by Clinton haters, worked to dig up evidence that the Clintons had broken the law in the Whitewater venture, with polemical editorials appearing in the *Wall Street Journal*, the talk show host Rush Limbaugh alleging massive conspiracies to conceal evidence, and even respectable journalists at the *New York Times* and the *Washington Post* devoting more newsprint to the Whitewater story than to any other issue.

In December 1993, everything started to come apart. Vincent Foster, a White House legal counsel who had been Hillary Clinton's law partner in Little Rock, drove to a park in suburban

Virginia and shot himself. In a suicide note, Foster bemoaned the degree to which "getting people" had become the fashion in Washington's political culture. In particular, Foster was distraught about the *Wall Street Journal's* editorial allegations about his supposed role in the Whitewater cover-up. Then in January 1994, an article in the conservative magazine *American Spectator* alleged that Bill Clinton, when he was governor of Arkansas, had used state troopers to procure women for him. The article mentioned a "Paula" who, it claimed, had been taken to Clinton's room in a hotel. Soon a woman named Paula Jones, who had been a state government employee in Arkansas, sued Clinton for sexual harassment, alleging that he had asked her to perform oral sex. By March the talk show host Rush Limbaugh was claiming, on the air, that Vincent Foster had been murdered on property owned by Hillary Clinton and that his body had then been moved to the park where it was found. Between November 1993 and February 1994, sixty-one articles about Whitewater appeared in the *Washington Post*, including sixteen on the front page. There was a feeding frenzy in Washington with no one to put a halt to it. Only Barry Goldwater stood up and said the Republican party was going too far. In the face of such an onslaught, Clinton, reeling from his mother's recent death and sapped, for the moment, of the instinct to fight, agreed in January 1994 to the appointment of an independent prosecutor to look into the entire Whitewater scandal. Clinton's attorney general, Janet Reno, chose Robert Fiske, a distinguished Republican lawyer, to lead the effort.

The surge of scandal-mongering about Whitewater coincided with a steady downward slope for Clinton's health-care proposals. Clinton had hoped that his legacy would be a program guaranteeing health insurance to every American. One of very few industrialized societies without some form of national health insurance, the United States had always shied away from such a plan because foes castigated the idea as socialized medicine. But now the Cold War was over, and with nearly forty million Americans lacking health-care coverage, it was a burning issue—one that for the first time seemed to have a chance at passage. Clinton had made the issue a central focus of his presidential campaign, and he understood that if he could secure enactment of health-care legislation, it would be the most dramatic piece of social legislation since the New Deal. If passed, national health insurance would potentially solidify public support of the Democratic party for a generation.

Significantly, Clinton chose the same strategy on health care that he had used for education reform in Arkansas: he put Hillary Rodham Clinton in charge of the task force that would develop the bill. In many ways Hillary seemed perfect for the role. She was her husband's closest political confidante and ally. As he later told reporters, he named her to the post because "she cared enough about it, had enough talent, and had enough understanding that if anybody had a chance to do it, she had the best chance." Using the same procedures she had employed in Arkansas, Hillary Clinton—with her co-leader Ira Magaziner—conducted hearings across the country to gather information about the health-care problem. The task force consulted more than six hundred experts on thirty-four different issues.

Yet certain aspects of the process that had been chosen undermined the project from the very beginning. For one thing, the task force did not follow the usual practice of extensive consultation with congressional leaders; instead, it largely ignored Congress, thus alienating the very people who would vote on its proposals. Second, because the first lady was in charge, it became impossible for the president to keep himself at a distance from the task force's deliberations, to act independently to find compromises, or to say no to any of its recommendations. Perhaps worst of all, the task force conducted its deliberations in secret and refused to share its insights with the public.

The prospects for Clinton's initiative seemed bright after he went before a joint session of Congress in September 1993 to convey his vision of health-care reform. It was a brilliant speech. Clinton focused upon issues of quality of care, simplicity, security, and the importance of healing one of the nation's major social ills. One Republican senator called the speech "the most comprehensive, brilliantly presented analytical dissection of everything that is wrong with the present health system." Haynes Johnson and David Broder, *Washington Post* journalists, later described the speech as one of the great moments of Clinton's presidency. In the days immediately afterward, public opinion polls showed approval for the health-care initiative exceeding disapproval by thirty-two points. Had the president been able to act immediately, gain the support of congressional leaders, and present a simplified bill to the Senate and the House, the chances of success would have been excellent.

But none of that was to happen. It took three more months for Hillary Clinton's task force to complete its work. There continued to be no consultation with House or Senate leadership. Nor did Hillary Clinton mobilize pivotal members of the administration such as Donna Shalala, secretary of health and human services, or Lloyd Bentsen, secretary of the treasury, who was one of the most knowledgeable people in the country about the health-care issue. Instead, the task force proceeded as if oblivious to the political realities. One congressional leader said about Ira Magaziner: "I wish he had some dirt under his fingernails."

In the end, the task force presented a bill that was 1,354 pages long, that was exceedingly complicated, and that stood almost no chance of being passed. Republican senator Robert Bennett of Utah called it "incredibly bloated, complex, unresponsive, [and] incomprehensible." Even the American Association of Retired People—logically one of the bill's most ardent supporters—complained about "the complexity of this [plan] and the ability for people to feel comfortable with something that is so complicated."

Seizing on this weakness, Newt Gingrich, the Georgia congressman who was speaker of the House of Representatives, and other Republican leaders declared all-out war on the Clinton plan. Recognizing that if it passed, it could well ensure a generation of Democratic electoral victories, Republicans were determined to defeat it. A series of powerful television commercials, featuring "Harry and Louise" sitting at their kitchen table, condemned the plan as bloating the government bureaucracy and doing nothing to help health care. Rush Limbaugh said on the radio that health care was really about Whitewater, and attacked the entire Clinton family for its connection to both issues. Rarely had American politics fallen to such a level of scurrilous demagoguery.

At the very end, Senator Daniel Patrick Moynihan of New York, together with the Rhode Island Republican John Chaffee and others, came forward with a compromise proposal that had one final chance of success. Joined by people in the administration like Shalala and Bentsen, they asked that the White House agree to a moderate package that would at least put the nation on the road toward universal health care. But the administration said no, and as a result the boldest political initiative of Bill Clinton's presidency never even came to a vote. In the meantime, more than a million additional people each year were losing health insurance.

To a significant degree, the problems confronted by the Clintons in both Whitewater and health care reflected the peculiar dynamics of their own interrelationship. As Clinton had told the nation repeatedly, in electing him they would have "two for one." What he failed to convey was the degree to which this "co-presidency" created not only cooperation but also conflict, not simply partnership but also paralyzing division, not simply concerted action but also deeply rooted disagreement.

The negative side of the relationship was visible in the way White House staffing decisions were made. Hillary Clinton was the only first lady who had ever occupied a suite in the west wing of the White House. That decision reflected not only the wishes of the Clintons but also the organizational structure they favored. Mack McLarty, the ostensible chief of staff, told David Gergen: "In this White House we usually have three people in that top [organizational] box: the president, the vice president, and the first lady. All three of them sign off on big decisions. You'll just have to get used to it." In short, the White House was organized so that there were three co-equals in charge—just as in Arkansas in Clinton's first gubernatorial term. That meant that each had a veto over all matters, and that anyone who disagreed with an administration decision might be able to lobby any of the three to reverse the decision. The structure was an invitation to paralysis, not partnership.

In addition, the rivalry—and the arguments—that had been part of the relationship of Bill and Hillary from the beginning continued to flare. David Gergen recounts one episode, in a strategy session of the top people working on domestic matters, when Hillary Clinton berated her husband and his staff.

When Bill defended his people, she berated him further. "One felt party to a massive violation of their privacy," Gergen said. "Later on, one of the participants told me that this happened frequently. In the middle of a conversation, she would launch a deadly missile straight at his heart and just before it hit, the missile would explode, the shrapnel hitting the staff . . . Those conversations were demoralizing, deepened the divisions between the Bill and Hillary camps, and made one tiptoe around the principals." As long as the two Clintons worked together cooperatively and held the relationship in balance, Gergen concluded, they helped each other and facilitated the administration's mission. But once they lost that balance, bad things happened.

Gergen also recounts one of the clearest examples of the destructive side of the relationship. Early in his time in the White House, the managing editor of the *Washington Post* asked Gergen to help get documents related to Whitewater released to the press, indicating that the Clintons' reluctance to release the documents was arousing suspicions about their motives. In Gergen's view, the Clintons would lose nothing by turning over the documentation, particularly if they had nothing to hide, as was suggested by various FBI and government reports. Although he recognized that releasing the documents might produce some negative stories, in the long run it would enhance the Clintons' reputation with the press, and—if the materials indicated innocence—help in exonerating them.

There is little question that Gergen was right. But when he pressed his case, he met resistance. Although he scheduled a meeting with the Clintons to debate the issue, it was canceled at the last minute because Hillary Clinton decided they should not comply with the *Post*'s request. Supposedly her lawyers had said the same. When Gergen persisted and talked to Bill Clinton himself, the president indicated his willingness to release the documents. But he refused to act without the first lady's agreement, and instructed Gergen to persuade her. Hillary refused to give Gergen an appointment, and two weeks later the White House wrote a letter to the *Washington Post* denying its request. At that point, according to Gergen, the *Post* became convinced that the Clintons were suppressing evidence. Almost immediately, a long series of stories began to appear in the *Post*—and eventually elsewhere—investigating Whitewater.

It was these stories, along with the scandal around Vincent Foster's suicide, that led to the appointment of an independent counsel. In Gergen's view, had the Clintons released the documents when they were requested, the office of independent counsel would never have become involved, there would never have been a grand jury, and ultimately never an impeachment. From Gergen's perspective, Hillary had "listened too eagerly to the lawyers and to her own instincts as a litigator, instincts that told her never to give an edge to the other side. [But] Whitewater was always more a political than a legal problem." In the end, though, Gergen blames the president himself: "Why didn't he go to his wife and persuade her that it was in their mutual best interest to take a different path? Why didn't he take charge? These questions ran headlong into something fundamental about Clinton."

The health-care failure provided another example of Bill Clinton's inability to operate effectively in the partnership with Hillary. By putting her in charge, he made it difficult if not impossible for supporters of the principle of universal health care to voice any criticism of the process being followed. Hillary Clinton showed little tolerance for skeptical perspectives. When Laura Tyson, a member of the council of economic advisors, posed critical questions about the economics of the plan, she was peremptorily put down by Hillary. The president refused to intervene. Others, observing the political chemistry of the situation, were discouraged from dissenting. Clinton allowed his loyalty to Hillary to cloud his political judgment. Most important, when prominent senators made a final effort to secure support for a compromise proposal, the president refused, in large part because his wife did not wish to see a change in her plan. The president was unwilling to challenge her, particularly at a time when—with the Paula Jones story in the press—he was anxious to avoid any further conflict with the first lady. Gergen recalled: "Like a bouncing golden retriever who has pooped on the living room rug, he curled up and looked baleful for days . . . I sensed that he was in no mood—and no position—to challenge her on anything . . . We were heading into the most important months of the health care fight with a president who was tiptoeing around the person in charge . . . Apparently, he was in no position to challenge her or to assert himself in a way that would have been better for them both." The dynamics of the marital relationship helped frustrate possible success in the political relationship. Gergen later speculated: "Might Clinton have passed a bipartisan [health-care] reform if the shadow of his past had not hung over his relationship with his wife?"

One way to make sense of the Clintons' co-presidency is to see it as flawed precisely to the degree that Bill Clinton failed to integrate his "parallel lives" and discipline the "secret," unacceptable side of his persona. By his philandering, Bill ceded a power to Hillary that immobilized him when circumstances called for decisions that ran counter to her will. His guilt gave Hillary a weapon that, whether she was conscious of it or not, she could use to get her own way. This sick pattern, more than anything else, undermined the positive potential of their partnership and instead rendered it dysfunctional at critical points in their lives.

The renewed scandals over Whitewater and Paula Jones, as well as the demise of Clinton's number-one domestic priority, set in motion a period of retribution and renunciation similar to—but far more virulent than—that which had followed Clinton's first term as governor of Arkansas. Had Clinton been a prime minister in Great Britain, his term of office would have been over, so thoroughgoing was the repudiation of his leadership by the nation. Taking advantage of the party discipline and hard-line conservatism that had characterized Republicans in Congress throughout Clinton's presidency, Newt Gingrich mobilized a massive campaign calling for a new "contract with America" that would repeal many of the gains of the Great Society. In the 1994 congressional elections, the Republican party gained nine Senate seats, eleven governorships, and fifty-two House seats. Now Clinton's opponents were comfortably in control of the Congress.

One Democratic leader lamented: "The New Deal era is over . . . The nails are in the coffin . . . New Deal liberalism . . . is dead and buried." As if pronouncing a final epitaph to Clinton's political career, another Democrat noted: "The Republicans enjoyed a double triumph [in 1994], killing reform and then watching jurors—the American people—find the president guilty. It was the political equivalent of the perfect crime." Even the most prominent Democrats were ready to pronounce Clinton politically dead. "The president is done," one declared. "He's finished. He's like that old . . . cartoon where the guy has just had his head sliced off in a fencing match. He just hasn't noticed it yet."

But Clinton had been pronounced dead before, and those

writing his obituary forgot his capacity for political resurrection. He had demonstrated that capacity in Arkansas in his reelection bid for governor, in 1988 after a disastrous nomination speech for Dukakis, and in New Hampshire after the Gennifer Flowers scandal. Now, clearly bruised and in disarray, Clinton nevertheless mobilized his troops, called in Dick Morris to provide the same kind of shrewd political advice he had offered in Arkansas, and prepared himself for one more appearance as "the comeback kid."

Clinton's chief ally, in many respects, was Gingrich himself. Overreaching significantly, Gingrich sought to organize an ideological war against the Democratic party. He miscalculated the degree to which the American people had voted for a revolution as opposed to expressing their disapproval of a president. The *New York Times* columnist Russell Baker compared Gingrich to Dr. Jack Kevorkian, the physician who provided medical assistance to those who wished to end their lives. Gingrich, Baker suggested, was attempting to provide the vehicle for finishing off "the government we have known for sixty years," but the American people were not ready. Robert Reischauer, head of the congressional budget office, had noted: "Our institutions were created to stop things from happening, and they're very good at it." Just as congressmen had stopped Clinton's health-care reform, America's political institutions would stop the Gingrich revolution. In that process, Robert Dole of Kansas, the Senate majority leader, represented a measured counterpoint to the House speaker's radicalism. The American people responded. Just nine months after Gingrich's massive victory in 1994, polls indicated that 58 percent of the American people disapproved of the job Congress was doing under his leadership.

In the meantime, Clinton put together an effective counterattack. It started in April 1995, with his impressive presidential leadership after the terrorist bombing of a federal building in Oklahoma City. Immediately flying to the site of the devastation, Clinton rallied the country in a healing and inspiring way, revealing a quality of leadership in times of national crisis that recalled John Kennedy and Franklin Roosevelt. Simultaneously, Clinton took Dick Morris's advice and began to focus on a series of limited, specific, and effective measures that could respond to people's immediate concerns. In order to address popular fear of rising crime rates, Clinton introduced a crime bill that would put one hundred thousand new police officers on the streets, and he endorsed the strategy of "three strikes and you're out" in issuing criminal sentences. For those who were concerned about the number of Americans receiving welfare, he supported welfare reform, with a jobs program and a two-year limit on the length of time a person could stay on welfare. For those concerned about high taxes, he proposed reductions targeted at the middle class. The deficit continued to shrink, and everything Clinton did seemed to please significant constituencies.

By the end of 1995 Clinton not only had recovered his poise and balance but had swept past the Republicans in the polls. Seizing upon a careless remark by Gingrich about letting Medicare "wither on the vine," Clinton proclaimed his own commitment to the nation's most venerable entitlement program, while pointing out that the Republicans favored a tax cut for the wealthy that would give to the richest five percent of the nation's citizens the same amount that Gingrich was proposing to cut from Medicare. Clinton even co-opted the Republicans' key slogan, telling the country in his State of the Union address in 1996, "The era of big government is over." Having reoccupied the center, secured his authority and symbolic leadership by his response to the Oklahoma City bombing, and put in place a series of incremental reforms on issues of concern to the American people, he was in a position to reclaim political victory in 1996. When the Republicans forced a "shutdown" of the government in a budget dispute with the president, they damaged their own cause, making Clinton look responsible and moderate in contrast to their willingness to sanction radical deeds that did no one any good.

Bill Clinton could not have asked for a more ideal candidate to oppose him in 1996 than Robert Dole. Clinton was young, charming, charismatic, and inspiring. To many, Dole seemed mean-spirited, old-fashioned, and pedestrian. Commenting on Dole's response to Clinton's 1996 State of the Union address, Senator Jesse Helms, a conservative Republican from North Carolina, declared: "That was the worse performance I've ever seen." Although in fact Dole had a sharp sense of humor, a brilliant mind, and a profound commitment to mainstream Republican values, he never overcame the appearance of being from an older generation with a message that was irrelevant to contemporary America.

As the election campaign proceeded, Clinton's margin steadily grew. Whenever Dole attempted to caricature him as a classic liberal, Clinton could point out that he had reduced the deficit, fought crime, created policies like the Family Leave Act, and secured welfare reform. By election day Clinton had recovered almost all the popularity that he had lost in the previous two years. One more time, this extraordinary example of political talent and resilience had fooled the experts, coming back from a precipitous decline to a new height of popularity.

But Clinton's penchant for taking the country on a roller-coaster ride had not yet played itself out. It seemed that whenever Bill Clinton was at his strongest he felt compelled to give in to his weakness—the secret side of his parallel lives—as if some nagging instinct prevented him from sustaining a position of power and good fortune. Thus during his combat with Gingrich over the shutdown of the government, at a time when Clinton was in his strongest position politically, he gave in once more to his weakness for sexual dalliances. This time the woman was a twenty-three-year-old intern named Monica Lewinsky. For about a year, off and on, there were repeated instances of oral sex, including one that left a semen stain from Clinton on Lewinsky's dress. After Clinton ended the affair, Lewinsky started to share her recollections of the relationship with Linda Tripp, a staunch Republican who hated Clinton, and who, without Lewinsky's knowledge, began to tape their conversations. By January 1998 Tripp had made those tapes available to the office of the independent counsel, and gradually, piece by piece, the entire world learned of Bill Clinton's latest episode of sexual infidelity.

Although the independent counsel had been assigned to investigate the Whitewater scandal, there was no evidence of wrongdoing in that matter, as David Gergen had predicted. However, a conservative judicial panel appointed a new independent counsel named Kenneth Starr. Starr had an obsession with getting Clinton, and also with sexual impropriety. After he secured the permission of the attorney general to include the Paula Jones matter within his purview, participants in the Jones case—often in collusion with Starr's office—led Starr to the president's connection with Monica Lewinsky. While giving testimony in the Jones case, Clinton was suddenly asked whether he had ever had sex with Lewinsky. He denied having done so, foolishly focusing on the precise legal definition of what constituted "sexual relations." Within a week, the allegation and the denial had become public, with Starr now able to include possible perjury in the Lewinsky matter as part of his bill of indictment.

Clinton engaged in total denial. "There *is* no sexual relationship," he said on television. Interestingly, he chose the present tense, just as he had told journalists in 1981 in Arkansas "There *is* no campaign" for governor. In both cases, his dissembling was evident. Yet his denials persisted. "I never had sex with that woman," he declared. Clinton evidently convinced his aides and family members that his denials were authentic. Indeed, Hillary Clinton went on national television to affirm her faith in her husband and to assert that the allegations were the work of a "right-wing conspiracy" to destroy him.

She was right: there was, in fact, a right-wing conspiracy. The Scaife Foundation poured millions into the *American Spectator*'s "Arkansas Project" seeking to generate evidence against Clinton. Kenneth Starr had close connections to the Paula Jones legal team, and significant numbers of informants and journalists were paid by a network of conservatives intent on securing Clinton's fall. But however widespread his enemies' conspiracy, Clinton had brought his demise upon himself. Not only did he succumb to the temptation to have an illicit sexual relationship with Lewinsky; he then brought humiliation on himself and his presidency by lying about it—including lying under oath.

In the face of the Lewinsky scandal, Republicans—in close collaboration with the independent prosecutor's office—demanded that the House of Representatives initiate impeachment proceedings. Intent on humiliating the president and if possible forcing his removal from office, they put together a grab bag of allegations that had been made against Clinton since the Whitewater imbroglio, now given new gravity by the Lewinsky affair.

The impeachment process itself was simply a mirror image of

the shoddy politics that had gone on for much of the 1990s. In an appearance before a federal grand jury, Clinton finally acknowledged that he had had "a relationship with Ms. Lewinsky that was not appropriate." Still reluctant to apologize for his behavior—just as he had been reluctant to confess to Arkansas voters in 1981 his failures as governor—Clinton seemed intent on displacing the blame onto others, especially the independent prosecutor. Starr and his team, meanwhile, showed their worst side, focusing almost exclusively on sexual details in the absence of any substantive evidence of wrongdoing by the Clintons in Whitewater or other matters such as the scandal concerning the White House travel office. Conservative Republicans, meanwhile, seized control of the impeachment process, resisting the importunings of moderates from both parties to step back. Even when Clinton's popularity remained high and the Democrats picked up congressional seats in the off-year election in 1998, the Republicans persisted.

There was never any real possibility that the United States Senate would convict the president by a two-thirds vote. The Senate acquitted him both of perjury before the grand jury and of obstruction of justice. In the middle of all this, Clinton's popularity continued to rise, and after his State of the Union speech in January 1999, his approval rating reached 80 percent. The whole story was like a bad psychodrama with all the actors losing a sense of proportion or responsibility. A conservative *New York Times* columnist, William Safire, declared: "Our first lady . . . is a congenital liar." The *Washington Post* columnist and socialite Sally Quinn told a *New Yorker* writer: "There's just something about Hillary that pisses people off." And in fact the Clintons did seem to inspire unusual rancor in their opponents. Kenneth Starr was one example. Samuel Dash, a former Watergate prosecutor who was the ethics advisor to Starr's office, reflected: "I saw decisions made on moral grounds that had nothing to do with criminal grounds. They believed that someone was a bad person, a sinful person, who ought to be punished for it. They distorted their judgment. Ken allowed his personal concepts of morality to interfere with the role of a prosecutor." But whatever the motives of those who pushed for impeachment, the reality was that Clinton had brought it upon himself. By his own self-destructive behavior he had harmed his family and many other people, and he had undermined what might have been a brilliantly successful presidency.

Bill Clinton had the capacity to be one of the best presidents of the twentieth century. He presided over an expanding economy in large part fueled by his deficit-reduction package; if he had secured national health insurance, his domestic record would have begun to approach those of Franklin Roosevelt and Lyndon Johnson, though he faced no international crisis comparable to World War II or Vietnam. Clinton was, according to the political writer Joe Klein, "the ultimate post-modern political practitioner . . . a fabulous communicator." Instinctively, Clinton reached out to those around him, creating instant bonds of engagement and loyalty. "He used surpassing gifts of innate empathy," said Todd Purdum of the *New York Times*, "to find a new presidential style of relating to the public, and forge an extraordinary connection with ordinary Americans, especially minorities." It was partly for that reason that the novelist Toni Morrison called Clinton "our first black president"; from start to finish, he embodied the belief in an "America without a racial divide." He identified health-care reform as the kind of leap forward that would change the country dramatically. Through measures like the Family Leave Act, the Brady Bill, welfare reform, and crime-containment policies, he addressed immediate concerns of average citizens. Shaping the economy to reflect both fiscal responsibility and entrepreneurial innovation, he created the longest sustained period of prosperity in the twentieth century. If there had been no Whitewater, if there had been no independent counsel, if there had been no sex scandals, if there had not been the debacle of health-care reform, Clinton would have realized his potential, and the Clintons, as spouses and partners, would have achieved approbation approaching that accorded to Franklin and Eleanor Roosevelt.

Yet there was something inside both Clintons that kept that from happening. In part, it was Hillary's obstinacy, her single-minded purposiveness, her reluctance to listen to others or be flexible at moments of potential compromise. Mostly, however, it was Bill Clinton's moral failings and his inability to find a personal core. David Gergen identified Clinton's "central problem" as "the lack of an inner compass": "He has 360-degree vision, but no true north . . . Clinton isn't exactly sure who he is yet, and tries to define himself by how well others like him." "This is a tale of two presidencies," said the White House aide Leon Panetta, "one obviously brilliant and extremely capable, with the ability to help produce the greatest economy in the history of this country and to focus on major domestic priorities, and the other . . . the darker side, the one that made a terrible human mistake that would forever shadow that other presidency." Todd Purdum noted: "His strengths and weaknesses not only sprang from the same source, but could also not exist without one another. In a real sense, his strengths are his weaknesses, his enthusiasms are his undoing, and most of the traits that make him appealing can make him appalling in the flash of an eye." Thus, in Purdum's words, Clinton was both "the bright sun and the bleak moon" of his administration, "embodying much of the best and the worst of his times." Above all, the tale of two presidencies was the tale of two lives, one secret, the other public, one egocentric and self-indulgent, the other devoted to reconciliation, unity, and reform. Precisely to the degree that Clinton's parallel lives were never integrated, the promise of a successful co-presidency foundered and sank.

It may be that Clinton succeeded in his career too quickly, too easily. He did not learn the hard way, internalize the lessons of his mistakes, confront the consequences of his failings, especially his inability to practice self-control in relation to women. All too often he used his facility with words, his charm, his expertise at dissembling, to escape trouble rather than face it head on. And because of his lack of an inner compass—of an integrated self—Clinton could never face up to his own amorality, or the need to be truthful with his wife. That, in turn, created an imbalance in their relationship which placed the president in a position of dependency and helplessness when he most needed to make clear and autonomous judgments. He had come too far and too fast, and notwithstanding his capacity for greatness, or his and his wife's potential for creating a new definition of marital and political partnership, by succumbing to his need for "an internal life where the secrets are hidden," he sabotaged his own chances of success.

CONCLUSION

From the Roosevelts to the Clintons, from Johnson to Nixon to Reagan, political life in modern America has produced surprising sagas. What political scientist could have foreseen the inveterate anticommunist Richard Nixon flying into Beijing and trading philosophical remarks with Mao Tse-tung? What pundit could have predicted that Lyndon Johnson would plummet from total political mastery in 1964 to such fragility four years later that he would decide to withdraw from the presidential race?

And who could have predicted the variety of the personal stories described here? If, before knowing about these particular leaders, we were asked to list characteristics likely to be found in people destined to become successful national leaders, our list might include, for example, a happy childhood, loving and nurturing parents, economic security, core moral values, a good marriage, mental stability, and concern for others, as well as intense ambition. But in fact, except for the ambition, the portraits presented in this book deviate strikingly from this upbeat formula. The majority of the leaders discussed here had unhappy childhoods. In most cases their parents' marriages were broken or deeply troubled. Three of the leaders grew up with an alcoholic parent. Nearly half came from families that were not economically secure. Although only one was divorced, marital unhappiness was the rule, not the exception, in these life stories, and at least five of the men engaged in blatant sexual infidelity. As for mental stability, in the cases of Lyndon Johnson and Richard Nixon, close friends and advisors worried that their president was on the verge of mental breakdown; Martin Luther King Jr. suffered bouts of profound depression; Ronald Reagan often seemed passive and ineffectual when not directed and protected by his aides; and Bill Clinton's compulsive philandering and dishonesty about it nearly led to his removal from office. What does the range of experience reflected in these lives teach us about the relationship between personality and political leadership?

Perhaps the first generalization that can be made is that overcoming adversity, having to fight daunting circumstances, often provided a critical incentive toward developing traits that later made it possible to overcome what otherwise might have been insuperable obstacles to success. Sometimes the adversity existed in the family itself: Eleanor Roosevelt, Johnson, Reagan, and Bill Clinton all grew up in situations that were potentially disabling. For Roosevelt, it was an alcoholic, reckless father; for Johnson, warring parents tugging in opposite directions; for Reagan, an alcoholic father who could not support the family; and for Clinton, a stepfather who was both alcoholic and abusive. In each instance, the only way to cope was to seek refuge beyond the family pain. By finding a higher goal outside the family dynamic and passionately pursuing that goal, these future leaders created new identities for themselves and also laid the groundwork for ever more ambitious future achievements.

For Eleanor Roosevelt, refuge outside the family meant a surrogate mother—her teacher Marie Souvestre—and a career of serving others. The dedication to a higher calling eventually permitted her to overcome even the pain of her husband's infidelity. For Lyndon Johnson, escaping from family tensions meant learning to achieve consensus and unanimity, thereby muting factionalism and becoming the single, indispensable force who could impose unity. For Ronald Reagan, it meant playing iconic roles—lifeguard, Hollywood leading man, cultural prophet for capitalist democratic values, and eventually visionary national hero. And for Bill Clinton, it meant becoming a popular and charismatic achiever, first in Boys Nation, then as a Rhodes Scholar, and then as a political wunderkind. Whatever the family circumstances or the individual trajectory, the journey for each of these people reflected an extraordinary determination to overcome the early roadblocks that might otherwise have halted their progress toward success.

Adversity could also come from outside the family, and in adulthood. One could argue that Franklin Roosevelt, Martin Luther King Jr., the two Kennedys, and Richard Nixon also came from families in which disputes between parents and pressure to conform to their goals amounted to a form of adversity. But these men faced clearer obstacles later in life. For Roosevelt it was polio and physical disability. For King it was the enmity of white supremacists and the FBI, each determined to destroy him. For Jack Kennedy it was the frantic effort to save himself and his crew when their ship went down. For Bobby Kennedy it was his brother's assassination. And for Richard Nixon it was the struggle to overcome the isolation of his Whittier childhood and a flawed early law career by determining to become an important political figure. In each instance, fighting back against seemingly insuperable odds was key. Tenacity, imagination, courage, vision—all these were involved. But the will to overcome adversity was critical.

A second theme of these leaders' lives is the existence of moments of crisis that shaped their future decisionmaking. Every life involves turns and choices. At times, these are of sufficient gravity and emotional impact that they become reference points on a personal compass, determining from that point forward a person's approach, attitude, or orientation to difficult decisions.

Four such moments stand out in these essays. The first is Franklin Roosevelt's experience with polio. Engaging with the horror of physical helplessness, he found the inner resources to transcend his disabling paralysis. There was in Roosevelt a profound calm, born of this crisis, that gave him the strength, the grace, the endurance, and the wisdom to handle any problem, whether it be the massive domestic wound of the Great Depression or the horrible international wound of Pearl Harbor. In fighting back against polio, Roosevelt learned how to fight back against other enemies. Moreover, the experience of trying countless treatments, *anything* that might work, made it easier for this president to practice "bold and persistent experimentation" in combating the Depression. And in reaching out to develop a coalition of allies to fight Nazism, he was applying in international politics a lesson he had learned from interactions with his fellow "polios" at Warm Springs: that when people provided support to one another they had a better chance of prevailing.

For Martin Luther King Jr., it was the night in the kitchen when a phone call threatening his wife, children, and future brought the shock of self-recognition. King had been fighting to find his own voice and direction for decades, faced with a father who tried to shape his son in his own image. But that night, horrified by what hatred might do to his family, King felt a divine intervention that from that point forward served as the wellspring of his faith and the inspiration for his continuing struggle. When King went back to Memphis in 1968, he recognized the risk of violence. But just as Jesus, leaving the Garden of Gethsemane, "set his face toward Jerusalem," committed to following the path he felt compelled to pursue, so King, in spite of his doubts and fears, "set his face toward Memphis." "I may not get there with you," he told the crowd the night before he fell to an assassin's bullet, "but we as a people will get to the Promised Land." It all went back to the connection with God he forged that night in the kitchen.

For much of his life, John F. Kennedy, like King, had to struggle to find his own voice and chart his own course in spite of a powerful and sometimes tyrannical father. Using intellectualism and detachment as defenses, he was reluctant to commit himself to people or causes. Then he went to the Pacific, taking command of a vulnerable navy vessel. When his craft was sunk by a Japanese destroyer, Kennedy, though he managed to save the lives of most of the men he commanded, suffered the anguish of watching others die. Those moments stayed with him, sparking reflection on the evils of war. They were part of his moral compass when he faced the imminent threat of nuclear war with the Soviet Union during the Cuban missile crisis. When virtually all his advisors were pressing for a preemptive attack (which we now know would have led to the launching of Russian nuclear missiles), Kennedy overruled them. Nearly twenty years earlier, he had learned the importance of being skeptical around generals, and he had come to a personal, profoundly existential understanding of the cost of war. After his success in the missile crisis, Kennedy moved his presidency in a very different direction—toward engagement, toward bold decisions on behalf of people he had previously ignored, such as the African Americans following Martin Luther King Jr. into the streets of Birmingham.

And then there was Bobby Kennedy. Like his brother, he spent part of his life trying to find his own identity in the face of conflicting parental demands to compete and to conform. But Bobby was much younger than Jack, and was more comfortable with the pietism of his mother and the patriotism and nationalism of his father. Then on November 22, 1963, all Robert Kennedy's certitudes and security were shattered. He suspected that his own crusade against organized crime might have provoked the attack on his brother. Although Kennedy had never before shared his innermost thoughts with the public, in speeches after his brother's assassination he ruminated on the meaning of good and evil, the awful power of the state to determine who was to live and die, and the brutal inhumanity shown toward so many people—Indians, Chicanos, black Americans, impoverished Peruvians and South Africans. No other politician raised such basic questions about morality and injustice, or proved as successful in reaching out and communicating those concerns to his audiences. Always remembering the political pragmatism he had practiced all his life, Kennedy nevertheless became a far more compassionate political presence after his brother's death.

Not all the leaders profiled in this book experienced such definitive moments. For some, future decisionmaking was shaped less by particular crises than by gradually developed patterns of behavior designed to suppress fear and failure. Very early in life, Lyndon Johnson determined to make himself indispensable to those in power, able to manipulate them so as to bring harmony out of discord, order out of chaos. Rather than leave himself vulnerable to the world, he would make the world revolve according to his wishes.

Bill Clinton, too, learned as a boy that the way to escape the conflicts at home was to build a public identity of undeniable achievement, seek to please those around him, keep secret his stepfather's unacceptable behavior, and live two "parallel lives" so that the tawdry, secret side of his inner self would never tarnish his public image of virtue and service. His failure to integrate those parallel lives, however, subverted his potential for greatness: he repeatedly engaged in liaisons with women which made him so guilty and defensive with his wife that he could not stand up to her when she took a position opposite to his. Ultimately, therefore, with Clinton as with Johnson, the pattern of impulsive behavior that created public success also led eventually to defeat.

Richard Nixon struggled throughout his life with the conflicts between his grand ambition to transform the world and his obsession with petty details of partisan politics, between the circumscribed world of his childhood and the larger stage of national and international achievement, between the Quaker vision of morality and the instinct for ruthless conquest. With his World War II military experience as a foundation, he used his mastery of the politics of anticommunism as a means of advancing himself rapidly from the House of Representatives, to the Senate, to the vice presidency. After suffering bitter defeat in 1960 and again in the governorship race in 1962, Nixon overcame his despair and charted a new course to win the presidency. Brilliant in his vision for transforming global politics, he nevertheless fell victim to his own penchant for using small-minded and destructive tactics to seek short-term political advantage. Nixon's tragedy is dramatically embodied in two contrasting images: the president alone in his sitting room doodling on a yellow pad about how to transform world politics through a new architecture of alliances; and the same president conspiring with his aides to bribe the Watergate burglars to keep their mouths shut.

For Ronald Reagan, politics was a world of grand visions on the one hand and dull policy details and difficult implementation on the other. Reagan preferred visionary leadership, grounded in using his consummate skills as an actor and performer to inspire others to share his dreams of a nuclear-free world and a regulation-free domestic economy. But in the end, there had to be a connection between such grandiose visions and the details of the policies necessary to implement them. It was here that Reagan withdrew, leaving the nitty-gritty to others. Success depended upon the effectiveness of his staff, and like Nixon, Reagan eventually fell victim to staff failures that jeopardized all his hopes. Inattentive to detail, Reagan may not have been aware that he was authorizing an arms-for-hostages deal with Iran or diverting secret funds to Nicaraguan Contras in direct violation of a congressional statute. With Reagan as with Nixon, the yawning gap between the worlds of grand vision and political implementation became an invitation to disaster.

Political leaders of the second half of the twentieth century had to cope with world politics of extraordinary complexity and overwhelming stakes. There was first of all the existence of nuclear arsenals, possessed initially by one nation, then two, then three, then five, then ten. At any moment the world could self-destruct. Ethnic rivalries erupted into murderous violence, as in the former Yugoslavia and in Rwanda. National economies became more closely interlinked in a global marketplace, with the strength of each one increasingly dependent on the strength of the others. And, though the devastating attacks of September 2001 were yet to come, terrorist violence became a threat to every society. The preparation and competence of leaders to deal with such crises were critical—and remain so in the twenty-first century.

In this context, two final lessons from the lives discussed in this book cry out for attention. The first is how close the United States came, on at least two occasions, to having mentally unbalanced leaders determining policies, including whether or not to launch nuclear weapons. Lyndon Johnson and Richard Nixon, two successive presidents dealing with the quagmire of the Vietnam war, verged on psychological breakdowns. In Johnson's case, White House staff believed the president was in the grip of paranoid fantasies, and worried that his lack of balance might lead to potentially disastrous decisions. If anything, the situation appears to have been even worse in the final months of Nixon's presidency. Tortured by the Watergate scandal and the seemingly inexorable move toward impeachment, and often consuming far too much alcohol, Nixon seemed to those around him close to the end of sanity and competence. When the secretary of defense issues orders that no presidential directives for military action should be carried out without the secretary's explicit authorization, the perils of leadership in the modern world are laid bare.

Equally remarkable, though, is the sustained quality of American political leadership over this period. Time after time, these leaders demonstrated courage, imagination, strength, and grace under pressure. Franklin Roosevelt showed the calm and the strength to lead a nation through both economic depression and war. Martin Luther King Jr. demonstrated the passion and courage to force a nation to face its own most grievous sin. John Kennedy displayed the grace and wisdom to resist pressure to go to war, saving the world from nuclear destruction. Robert Kennedy transformed his anguish over life's meaning into a dedication to the disenfranchised and powerless. Lyndon Johnson employed his obsession with consensus in the service of his other passion, advancing the cause of the poor and the dispossessed. Richard Nixon used his private, visionary side to launch initiatives that transformed geopolitics and led to a new era of cooperation with China. Ronald Reagan brought hope and optimism to the nation and created the preconditions for ending the Cold War. And Bill Clinton engineered a powerful economic recovery while simultaneously using his political skills to promote peace in Northern Ireland and in the Middle East. Clearly, while these life stories contain evidence of frailty, failure, and conflict, on balance, they suggest reason for hope.

These were not individuals predestined for leadership and success. Nor was there a formula for achievement that each followed. In the end, every human story stands on its own. But recognizing how these leaders-to-be acknowledged and overcame adversity, and how that experience shaped their political lives, may help us in assessing other political leaders, past and present. Certainly the personal experiences leaders bring to their mission are crucial determinants of what they can and will achieve.

BIBLIOGRAPHICAL ESSAY

ACKNOWLEDGMENTS

INDEX

BIBLIOGRAPHICAL ESSAY

The literature on the Roosevelts is voluminous. On FDR as an individual, a good place to start is with three books by Geoffrey C. Ward: *Before the Trumpet: Young Franklin Roosevelt, 1882–1905* (1985); *A First-Class Temperament: The Emergence of FDR* (1989), in which Ward uses his own experience as a "polio" to illuminate FDR's struggle with the disease; and the edited and annotated volume *Closest Companion: The Unknown Story of the Intimate Friendship between Franklin Roosevelt and Margaret Suckley* (1995), which includes letters from FDR and entries from Suckley's diary and discloses FDR's use of relationships with women to compensate for the absence of emotional intimacy in his marriage.

A long-established source for understanding Roosevelt's presidency is William E. Leuchtenburg's *FDR and the New Deal, 1921–1940* (1963). Leuchtenburg concludes that Roosevelt presided over a "halfway revolution" in America, one that left intact the fundamental structures of capitalism such as the banking system but nevertheless took unprecedented steps to create a safety net for millions of citizens through such programs as social security. The most comprehensive recent book on Roosevelt is David Kennedy's *Freedom from Fear: The American People in Depression and War, 1929–1945* (1999). Other classic books on the New Deal and its predecessors include Arthur Schlesinger Jr.'s three-volume *Age of Roosevelt* (1957); James MacGregor Burns's *Roosevelt: The Lion and the Fox* (1956) and *Roosevelt: The Soldier of Freedom* (1970); and multi-volume biographies by Kenneth Davis and by Frank Freidel. On civil rights see Harvard Sitkoff, *A New Deal for Blacks: The Emergence of Civil Rights as a National Issue* (1978), and Nancy Weiss, *Farewell to the Party of Lincoln: Black Politics in the Age of FDR* (1983). Two overall assessments of the New Deal are Alan Brinkley, *The End of Reform: New Deal Liberalism in Recession and War* (1995), and Steve Fraser and Gary Gerstle, *The Rise and Fall of the New Deal Order, 1930–1980* (1994).

The best book assessing the Roosevelts during the war years is Doris Kearns Goodwin's *No Ordinary Time: Franklin and Eleanor Roosevelt: The Home Front in World War II* (1994), which includes a comprehensive discussion of their inner circle of family, friends, and political advisors. Joseph Lash's *Eleanor and Franklin* (1971) is the best source on how the Roosevelts interacted, including discussion of FDR's affair with Lucy Mercer, ER's role in responding to FDR's polio, and her increasing political presence. Lash's *Eleanor: The Years Alone* (1972) is similarly comprehensive and insightful.

The best biography of ER is Blanche Wiesen Cooke's two-volume *Eleanor Roosevelt* (1992, 1999). Cooke discusses in depth ER's relationships with Lorena Hickok and the other women who constituted her network of social reformers. See also Joan Hoff-Wilson and Marjorie Lightman, eds., *Without Precedent* (Indiana University Press, 1984). Much of the chapter in this book is based on my biographical essay in *Without Precedent*. See also ER's three autobiographies—*This Is My Story* (1937); *This I Remember* (1949); and *On My Own* (1958)—brought together in one volume, *An Autobiography of Eleanor Roosevelt* (1961).

Other important books on ER include Tamara Hareven, *Eleanor Roosevelt: An American Conscience* (1968); James R. Kearney, *Anna Eleanor Roosevelt: The Evolution of a Reformer* (1968); Lois Scharf, *Eleanor Roosevelt: First Lady of Liberalism* (1978); Doris Faber, *The Life of Lorena*

Hickok: E.R.'s Friend (1980); and Allida M. Black, *Casting Her Own Shadow: Eleanor Roosevelt and the Shaping of Postwar Liberalism* (1996).

For discussions of ER's close relationships with young men, see Edna Gurewitsch, *Kindred Souls: The Friendship of Eleanor Roosevelt and David Gurewitsch* (2002); and William H. Chafe, *Never Stop Running: Allard K. Lowenstein and the Struggle to Save American Liberalism* (1993).

There are two magisterial biographies of Martin Luther King Jr., by Taylor Branch and David Garrow. Branch has thus far completed the first two-thirds of his assessment of King: *Parting the Waters: America and the King Years, 1954–63* (1988), in which he portrays King's emergence as a prophet and redeemer within the movement; and *Pillar of Fire: America in the King Years, 1963–65* (1998), which focuses on disruptions caused by the antecedents of Black Power and the hostility of the FBI. Garrow's volumes are *Bearing the Cross: Martin Luther King, Jr., and the Southern Christian Leadership Conference* (1986), which includes an account of King's religious encounter in his Montgomery kitchen in 1955; and *The FBI and Martin Luther King: From "Solo" to Memphis* (1981).

Other important books on King include David Levering Lewis, *King: A Critical Biography* (1970); Adam Fairclough, *To Redeem the Soul of America* (1987), a history of the SCLC; Adam Fairclough, *Martin Luther King, Jr.* (1990); Stephen B. Oates, *Let the Trumpet Sound: The Life of Martin Luther King, Jr.* (1982), which places King at the center of the civil rights movement; Stewart Burns, *To the Mountaintop: Martin Luther King Jr.'s Sacred Mission to Save America, 1955–1968* (2004); Michael Eric Dyson, *I May Not Get There with You: The True Martin Luther King, Jr.* (2000), a treatise on how to prevent the domestication of King's life by politicians and popularizers; and James R. Ralph Jr., *Northern Protest: Martin Luther King, Jr., Chicago and the Civil Rights Movement* (1993).

King's autobiographical writings include *Stride toward Freedom: The Montgomery Story* (1985); *Why We Can't Wait* (1964); and *Where Do We Go from Here? Chaos or Community* (1968). See also Clayborne Carson et al., eds., *The Papers of Martin Luther King, Jr.*, which are being published by the University of California Press (1992–).

For JFK, a good place to start is Doris Kearns Goodwin's comprehensive *The Fitzgeralds and the Kennedys: An American Saga* (1987). Nigel Hamilton's *JFK: Reckless Youth* (1992) offers a provocative take on Kennedy's earlier years. Theodore H. White's *The Making of the President, 1960* (1961) is the best account of the 1960 campaign. The best scholarly overview is Robert Dallek's *An Unfinished Life: John F. Kennedy 1917–1963* (2003). James N. Giglio's *The Presidency of John F. Kennedy* (1991) is a solid scholarly account. See also Herbert Parmet, *Jack: The Struggles of John F. Kennedy* (1980); and Parmet, *JFK: The Presidency of John F. Kennedy* (1984), which discusses the writing of *Profiles in Courage*.

The best-known memoir/biographies of the Kennedy years are Arthur Schlesinger Jr., *A Thousand Days* (1965), and Theodore C. Sorenson, *Kennedy* (1965). Others include Robert F. Kennedy, *Thirteen Days: A Memoir of the Cuban Missile Crisis* (1969); Robert S. McNamara, *In Retrospect: The Tragedy and Lessons of Vietnam* (1995); Evelyn Lincoln, *My Twelve Years with John F. Kennedy* (1965); Pierre Salinger, *With Kennedy* (1966); Richard Goodwin, *Remembering America* (1988); and Dean Rusk, *As I Saw It* (1990). On Kennedy's death see William Manchester, *The Death of a President* (1967); and Gerald Posner, *Case Closed: Lee Harvey Oswald and the Assassination of JFK* (1993).

Some of the most interesting commentary on JFK comes from journalist/historians. See, e.g., David Halberstam, *The Best and the Brightest* (1972); Richard Reeves, *President Kennedy: Profile of Power* (1993); and Garry Wills, *The Kennedy Imprisonment: A Meditation on Power* (1981).

On civil rights, see Carl M. Brauer, *John F. Kennedy and the Second Reconstruction* (1977); and Harris Wofford, *Of Kennedys and Kings* (1980). On Vietnam, see David Halberstam, *The Making of a Quagmire: America and Vietnam during the Kennedy Era* (1965); Fredrik Logevall, *Choosing War: The Lost Chance for Peace and the Escalation of War in Vietnam* (1999);

and David Kaiser, *American Tragedy: Kennedy, Johnson, and the Origins of the Vietnam War* (2000). On the Cuban missile crisis, see Michael R. Beschloss, *The Crisis Years: Kennedy and Khrushchev, 1960–1963* (1991); Ernest May and Philip Zekilow, eds., *The Presidential Recordings: John F. Kennedy: The Great Crises*, vol. 3: *October 22–28, 1962* (2001); Robert Wiesbrot, *Maximum Danger: Kennedy, the Missiles, and the Crisis of American Confidence* (2001); and the previously cited memoirs by RFK, and McNamara. On JFK's relationship to 1960s imagery, see W. J. Rorabaugh, *Kennedy and the Promise of the Sixties* (2002). On individual political styles, see Tom Wicker, *JFK and LBJ: The Influence of Personality upon Politics* (1968).

For RFK, the best place to start is Arthur Schlesinger Jr.'s *Robert F. Kennedy and His Times* (1978), which evocatively recounts Kennedy's growth through tragedy. Previously cited works on civil rights, Vietnam, and the Cuban missile crisis are also useful. A number of books have helped illuminate Kennedy's later years: see James W. Hilty, *Robert Kennedy: Brother Protector* (1997), which emphasizes the continuity in RFK's temperament and judgments; Joseph A. Palermo, *In His Own Right: The Political Odyssey of Senator Robert. F. Kennedy* (2001), which views sympathetically Kennedy's changes after he entered the Senate; Jeff Shesol, *Mutual Contempt: Lyndon Johnson, Robert Kennedy and the Feud That Defined a Decade* (1997), which sees Kennedy's shifts as driven more by political ambition; and Evan Thomas's comprehensive *Robert Kennedy: His Life* (2000).

Some of the best coverage of RFK is by journalists. See Jack Newfield, *RFK: A Memoir* (2003), a powerful testimony to Kennedy's personal impact; Jeremy Larner, *Nobody Knows: Reflections on the McCarthy Campaign of 1968* (1970); Jules Witcover, *85 Days: The Last Campaign of Robert Kennedy* (1969); and Witcover, *The Year the Dream Died: Revisiting 1968 in America* (1998).

There are multiple entry points for exploring the complex personality of LBJ. Doris Kearns Goodwin's *Lyndon Johnson and the American Dream* (1976) is an account of Johnson's personal history—focusing on the competing demands of his father and mother—as recounted by Johnson to Goodwin after he left the White House. Robert Caro's magisterial multi-volume biography, still in process, is entitled *The Years of Lyndon Johnson*. The first volume is *The Path to Power* (1982), followed to date by *Means of Ascent* (1990) and *Master of the Senate* (2002). My essay draws on all three, but especially *Master of the Senate*. The other indispensable work is Robert Dallek's two volumes: *Lone Star Rising: Lyndon Johnson and His Times, 1908–1960* (1991), which focuses on LBJ's Texas origins and rise to power; and *Flawed Giant: Lyndon Johnson and His Times, 1961–1973* (1998), which provides excellent accounts of the Great Society and of Johnson's entanglement with Vietnam.

Other assessments of the Great Society include Irwin Unger, *The Best of Intentions: The Triumphs and Failures of the Great Society under Kennedy, Johnson and Nixon* (1996); Irving Bernstein, *Guns and Butter: The Presidency of Lyndon Johnson* (1996); and John A. Andrew III, *Lyndon Johnson and the Great Society* (1998). On Vietnam, see the previously cited works by Logevall, Kaiser, Rusk, and McNamara, and also Lloyd C. Gardner, *Pay Any Price: Lyndon Johnson and the Wars for Vietnam* (1995); and H. W. Brands, *The Wages of Globalism: Lyndon Johnson and the Limits of American Power* (1995). An excellent memoir by an aide is Joseph A. Califano Jr., *The Triumph and Tragedy of Lyndon Johnson: The White House Years* (2000).

Nixon's *RN: The Memoirs of Richard Nixon* (1978) is a fine introduction to the major events of his career. The only multi-volume biography is by Stephen Ambrose: *Nixon: The Education of a Politician, 1913–1962* (1987); *Nixon: The Triumph of a Politician, 1962–1972* (1989); and *Nixon: Ruin and Recovery, 1973–1990* (1991). Roger Morris, *Richard Milhous Nixon: The Rise of an American Politician* (1990) is a shrewd study of Nixon's early career.

The classic telling of the Watergate story is Bob Woodward and Carl Bernstein's *All the President's Men* (1975). Other helpful accounts are J. Anthony Lukas, *Nightmare: The Underside of the Nixon Years* (1976); Stanley Kutler, *The Wars of Watergate: The Last Crisis of Richard Nixon* (1990); and Leonard Garment, *In Search of Deep Throat: The Greatest Po-

litical Mystery of Our Time (2000). The revelation that "Deep Throat" was Mark Felt of the FBI is written about in a forthcoming book by Bob Woodward.

On Vietnam, see the works by Gardner, Brands, Kaiser, and Logevall cited earlier, as well as Jeffrey Kimball's *Nixon's Vietnam War* (1998), which assesses Nixon's policies as part of an effort to trick North Vietnam into a peace agreement that would preserve the South Vietnamese government; Larry Berman's *No Peace, No Honor: Nixon, Kissinger and Betrayal in Vietnam* (2001), which views the peace accords of 1973 as a means by which America could retain a presence in Vietnam; and William Bundy, *A Tangled Web: The Making of Foreign Policy in the Nixon Presidency* (1998), which critiques Nixon's foreign policy as haphazard and chaotic.

On domestic policies, there are a number of intriguing books, including J. Brooks Flippen, *Nixon and the Environment* (2000); Joan Hoff, *Nixon Reconsidered* (1994); Leon Panetta and Peter Gall, *Bring Us Together: The Nixon Team and the Civil Rights Retreat* (1971); Alan Matusow, *Nixon's Economy: Boom, Busts, Dollars and Votes* (1998); and Kenneth O'Reilly, *Nixon's Piano: Presidents and Racial Politics from Washington to Clinton* (1995).

On the strangeness of Nixon's personality see, e.g., Richard Reeves, *President Nixon: Alone in the White House* (2001); and Garry Wills, *Nixon Agonistes: The Crisis of the Self-Made Man* (1970).

The best place to begin assessing Ronald Reagan is with Lou Cannon, a journalist who covered him both as governor of California and as president. Cannon's *Ronnie and Jesse: A Political Odyssey* (1969) is a biography of both Reagan and Jesse Unruh, the speaker of the California legislature. His *Reagan* (1982) covers Reagan's earlier life and his rise to the White House. His *President Reagan: The Role of a Lifetime* (1991) brings together all Cannon's insights into Reagan the performer, politician, and statesman. The other official biography is *Dutch: A Memoir of Ronald Reagan* (1999), by Edmund Morris, who tells his story through a quasi-fictional narrative voice.

Accounts by reporters and observers include Dinesh D'Sousa, *Ron-*

ald Reagan: How an Ordinary Man Became an Extraordinary Leader (1997); Ronnie Dugger, On Reagan: The Man and His Presidency (1983); and William Greider, The Education of David Stockman and Other Americans (1986). Memoirs include George P. Shultz, Turmoil and Triumph: My Years as Secretary of State (1993); Michael K. Deaver with Mickey Herskowitz, Behind the Scenes (1987); Michael Deaver, A Different Drummer: My Thirty Years with Ronald Reagan (2001); Terry Eastland, Energy in the Executive (1992); Alexander M. Haig Jr., Caveat: Realism, Reagan and Foreign Policy (1984); Michael A. Ledeen, Perilous Statecraft: An Insider's Account of the Iran-Contra Affair (1988); Peggy Noonan, What I Saw at the Revolution: A Political Life in the Reagan Era (1990); Donald T. Regan, For the Record: From Wall Street to Washington (1988); Larry Speakes with Robert Pack, Speaking Out: The Reagan Presidency from inside the White House (1988); William S. Cohen and George Mitchell, Men of Zeal: A Candid Inside Story of the Iran-Contra Hearings (1988); and David A. Stockman, The Triumph of Politics: How the Reagan Revolution Failed (1986).

Among the best essayists commenting on Reagan is Garry Wills, whose Reagan's America: Innocents at Home (1985) offers trenchant insights, particularly about Reagan's relationship to the movies. Also see Michael Paul Rogin, Ronald Reagan, the Movie and Other Episodes in Political Demonology (1987); Susan Jeffords, Hard Bodies: Hollywood Masculinity in the Reagan Era (1994); and Stephen Vaughn, Ronald Reagan in Hollywood: Movies and Politics (1994).

Matthew Dallek, The Right Moment: Ronald Reagan's First Victory and the Decisive Turning Point in American Politics (2000), argues that Reagan's 1966 victory over Edmund "Pat" Brown provided the turning point for Reagan to proceed with a "future-oriented" conservative politics, as opposed to earlier right-wing conservative anticommunism.

Michael Schaller, Reckoning with Reagan: America and Its President in the 1980s (1992) is an overview of the Reagan years focusing on his "feel good" style; and Frances FitzGerald, Way Out There in the Blue: Reagan,

Star Wars, and the End of the Cold War (2000), examines Soviet-American relations in the 1980s.

As with Nixon, a good place to start exploring the lives of Bill and Hillary Clinton is with their memoirs. See Bill Clinton, *My Life* (2004), and Hillary Rodham Clinton, *Living History* (2003). Both are most revealing in discussing their years prior to entering public life, and the stormy nature of their relationship with each other. For an opposite view of Hillary Clinton, see Richard Morris, *Rewriting History* (2004), a vehement polemic against the former first lady; and Joyce Milton, *The First Partner: Hillary Rodham Clinton* (1999). Morris has also written about Bill Clinton in *Behind the Oval Office: Getting Re-elected against All Odds* (1998). Also see Elizabeth Drew, *Showdown: The Struggle between the Gingrich Congress and the Clinton White House* (1996). Indispensable to understanding Bill Clinton's early life is David Maraniss, *First in His Class* (1995).

The best book on the Clintons and health care is Haynes Johnson and David Broder, *The System: The Death of Health Care Reform in 1993– 1994* (1997). See also Theda Skocpol, *Boomerang: Clinton's Health Security Effort and the Turn against Government in U.S. Politics* (1997); and Jacob S. Hacker, *The Road to Nowhere: The Genesis of President Clinton's Plan for Health Security* (1997).

Among the memoirs that are of interest, see George Stephan- opoulos, *All Too Human: A Political Education* (1999); Robert Reich, *Locked in the Cabinet* (1997), a series of witty diary entries concluding that Clinton's first term was, in essence, a failure; Sidney Blumenthal, *The Clinton Wars* (2003), which focuses on the impeachment process and is critical of the behavior of Kenneth Starr; Madeleine Albright with Bill Woodward, *Madam Secretary* (2003); Warren Christopher, *In the Stream of History: Shaping Foreign Policy for a New Era* (1998); Benjamin R. Barber, *The Truth of Power: Intellectual Affairs in the Clinton White House* (1998); Susan McDougal with Pat Harris, *The Woman Who Wouldn't Talk* (2002); and Mary Matalin and James Carville with Peter Knobler, *All's Fair: Love, War and Running for President* (1994).

One of the most valuable books on recent presidents generally, and particularly Clinton, is David Gergen, *Eyewitness to Power: The Essence of Leadership, Nixon to Clinton* (2000). And a brilliant journalistic account of the Clinton years, by the author of the anonymous novel *Primary Colors,* is Joe Klein, *The Natural: The Misunderstood Presidency of Bill Clinton* (2002).

ACKNOWLEDGMENTS

I am grateful to many people for helping to make this book possible. At the head of the list stand the superb historians and journalists who have produced the massive body of literature on which these essays are based. Although I have done some archival work on the individuals discussed here—most notably in the papers of John and Robert Kennedy and Franklin and Eleanor Roosevelt— these essays largely build on the work of others whose books are cited in the Bibliographical Essay. I have benefited enormously from the scholarship and ideas presented in their books.

For the period 1995–2004 I served as dean of the Faculty of Arts and Sciences at Duke University. It was not a position that provided extensive time for research and writing. But by virtue of the understanding and support of my colleagues in administration—particularly President Nannerl O. Keohane and Provosts John Strohbehn and Peter Lange—I was allowed to spend most of my summers reading and writing about history. I am indebted to these colleagues for that opportunity.

Equally important, I enjoyed the wonderful support of the staff in the dean's office. One of the happiest parts of my job was the constant interaction with people who shared my passion for politics and ideas. Discussions with them about leadership and personality helped inform these essays. My special thanks to Karla Holloway, Berndt Mueller, Robert Thompson, Thomas Mann, Lee Willard, Charles Byrd, Mary Jacobs, and Joan Shipman.

The person who has done most to nurture this project from its inception, and who has shown the patience of a saint, is Joyce Seltzer, my editor at Harvard University Press. Although there were times, I know, when she wondered whether the book would ever be completed, she never gave up on me. She has been a superb critic and editor, always raising the right questions and helping me refine my arguments.

I am similarly indebted to my dear friend and colleague Tim Tyson of the University of Wisconsin. A brilliant writer, historian, raconteur, and aficionado of politics (as well as a terrific chef), he has worked over each of these essays with stylistic precision, sharpening the ideas, asking for more pertinent illustrations, suggesting vivid quotations, and never being satisfied. To have such help from a former student is a tribute to almost two decades of colleagueship. I have also benefited greatly from the research assistance of Andrea Franzius.

Finally, I am indebted to my wonderful family—my wife, Lorna, my son and daughter, Christopher and Jennifer, my daughter-in-law, Katherine Kirsch, and the two people of the next generation who make everything else worthwhile, Lila and Jordan. May they have the chance to grow up in a society where leadership inspires confidence, not dismay.

INDEX